How to Fix Common (and Not So Common) Problems in a Hurry

Windows® XP HEADACHES

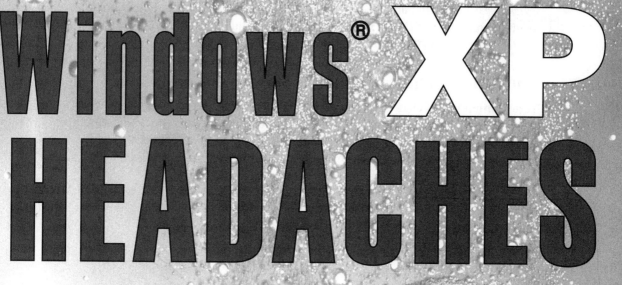

Second Edition

About the Author

Curt Simmons is a technology author and trainer who has suffered plenty of Windows XP headaches himself! A Microsoft product specialist and networking expert, Curt has been working with Windows XP since its early testing days. He is the author of over fifty high-level and consumer-level computing books, including *How to Do Everything with Windows XP* and *How to Do Everything with Your BlackBerry*, both also published by McGraw-Hill/Osborne. Curt lives in a small Texas town outside of Dallas with his wife, Dawn, and his daughters, Hannah and Mattie. Visit Curt on the Internet at www.curtsimmons.com.

About the Technical Editor

Tom Dunlap is a freelance editor and consultant specializing in technology. He is a former senior editor at CNET.com and his work has appeared on CNET.com, ZDNET.com, MSN.com, in the *San Francisco Chronicle,* and other publications. He penned 2004's *How to Do Everything with Your Sony VAIO*, published by McGraw-Hill/Osborne. Tom is based in Cupertino, CA

How to Fix Common (and Not So Common)
Problems in a Hurry

Windows® XP
HEADACHES

Second Edition

McGraw-Hill/Osborne

New York Chicago San Francisco Lisbon
London Madrid Mexico City Milan New Delhi
San Juan Seoul Singapore Sydney Toronto

Curt Simmons

McGraw-Hill/Osborne
2100 Powell Street, 10th Floor
Emeryville, California 94608
U.S.A.

To arrange bulk purchase discounts for sales promotions, premiums, or fund-raisers, please contact **McGraw-Hill**/Osborne at the above address. For information on translations or book distributors outside the U.S.A., please see the International Contact Information page immediately following the index of this book.

Windows® XP Headaches
How to Fix Common (and Not So Common) Problems in a Hurry, Second Edition

4567890 CUS CUS 019876

ISBN 0-07-225920-5

Vice President & Group Publisher	Philip Ruppel
Vice President & Publisher	Jeffrey Krames
Acquisitions Editor	Margie McAneny
Project Editor	Carolyn Welch
Acquisitions Coordinator	Agatha Kim
Technical Editor	Tom Dunlap
Copy Editor	Bob Campbell
Proofreader	Susie Elkind
Indexer	Claire Splan
Composition	Apollo Publishing Services
Illustrator	Michael Mueller, Lyssa Wald
Series Design	Mickey Galicia
Cover Series Design	Ted Holladay

This book was composed with Corel VENTURA™ Publisher.

This book is for my sister-in-law, Brenda Davis,
who graciously opened her home to me and gave me a place to stay
so I could attend graduate school.

Thanks Brenda—you're the best.

Contents

Acknowledgments   xxi

Introduction   xxiii

CHAPTER 1   **Windows XP Interface Headaches** **1**

Display Setting Headaches   2

Colors on my screen do not look good.   2

Everything on my desktop is too small or too big.   4

My display seems distorted at times.   5

My desktop fonts are too small.   6

I don't like my screen saver, or my screen saver
does not work the way I want it to.   7

Whenever I stop using my computer, it returns to
the logon screen.   8

The My Pictures screen saver does not work right.   9

My desktop wallpaper does not look right.   10

I don't want to use wallpaper on my desktop—
I want a color background only.   11

Icons do not appear on my desktop.   11

The Desktop Cleanup Wizard keeps running without
my permission.   12

Windows XP will not let me display a web page
on my desktop.   13

Windows Theme Headaches   14

Windows XP lists my XP theme as "Windows XP
(Modified)." What is wrong?   14

I can't get the Windows XP theme back after
making changes.   15

Start Menu Headaches   16

Windows XP keeps putting stuff on the Start menu
without my permission.   16

I want to control which items appear on the Start menu,
but Windows XP will not let me.   17

I use Netscape instead of Internet Explorer, but
Netscape does not appear on my Start menu.   19
The Start menu does not list all of the programs
I like to use.   20
I want to make a document appear permanently
on the Start menu.   20
I can't drag and drop items on the Start menu.   21
My Control Panel icons do not appear as menu
items on the Start menu.   22
Taskbar Headaches   23
I can't get the taskbar to do what I want.   23
How can I make the taskbar stay in one place?   25
Power Configuration Headaches   25
Windows XP keeps turning the monitor off.   25
My computer does not hibernate.   26
Notification Area Headaches   27
I don't like how the notification area behaves.   28
Old stuff I no longer use keeps appearing in the
notification area.   28
Balloon Tips are driving me crazy!   29

CHAPTER 2   **Windows XP File and Folder Headaches** **31**
Folder Headaches   32
I can't create a new folder.   33
Things in my folders are too big/small.   33
Files in a folder do not tell the size, type, and so forth. . . .   34
I can't see the items I need on my folder toolbars.   35
My folders do not look the way I want them to.   36
My folders are taking up too much room on my hard disk, or
I need to keep other users from looking in my folders. . . .   38
File Headaches   40
The wrong program opens a file.   40
I copied a picture file from the Internet, but Windows
cannot open it and does not seem to know that the
file is a picture file.   41
Offline Files Headaches   42
I can't get Offline Files to work.   42
Offline Files does not synchronize the way I want it to. . . .   43
Recycle Bin Headaches   44
I accidentally put stuff I need in the Recycle Bin.   44
I accidentally emptied the Recycle Bin, but I need the
items back.   44

My Recycle Bin keeps items for too long, taking up
  too much disk space.   45
Every time I put an item in the Recycle Bin, Windows
  gives me the Are You Sure box. How can I get rid of
  this confirmation box?   46
I don't want Windows to put items in the Recycle Bin—
  I want them automatically deleted.   46
Cleaning Up the Junk   46
How can I get rid of temporary files?   47
Does my PreFetch Folder slow me down?   48

CHAPTER 3   **Windows XP User Headaches** **49**
User Headaches   50
I can't create a new user account.   51
I can't delete an account.   53
I can't make a limited account become an administrator
  account.   54
My account does not work with .NET Passport.   55
I want a second person to be able to use the computer
  without the first person having to log out completely. . .   56
I don't want to use the Welcome screen.   57
Password Headaches   58
Users are able to log on without passwords.   58
I can't enforce password restrictions.   59
When I try to reset a password, a message appears
  telling me that data will be lost.   61
Account Feature Headaches   63
I don't like the account icon feature.   63
I can't stop a user from logging on without deleting
  the account.   65
I can't configure account lockout and other advanced
  account management features.   66

CHAPTER 4   **Windows XP Accessory and Software Headaches** **69**
Difficulties with Software   70
I can't install a program.   72
I can't remove a program.   74
I can't remove a program with Add / Remove Programs. .   75
When I uninstall a program, I receive warnings about
  shared files.   76
I need to use an older program that is not compatible with
  Windows XP.   76

I need to stop using compatibility settings on a
  certain program. 79
Windows XP keeps downloading stuff from Windows
  Update without my permission. 81
Removing Spyware and Adware 83
Controlling Startup Programs 84
Too many programs start when Windows XP starts. 84

CHAPTER 5   **Windows XP Hardware Headaches** **87**
Installing and Uninstalling Hardware 88
I can't connect my new device to my computer. 89
I don't know if a device I bought will work with
  Windows XP. 90
Windows XP does not detect my new device. 91
I can't use an older hardware device with Windows XP. ... 94
I can't uninstall a device. 95
Solving Problems with Drivers 96
I don't know how to install a new driver. 97
I installed a new driver, but now the device does not
  work, or does not work well. 100
I need to download a new driver, but Internet Explorer
  will not let me. 100
Managing Hardware 101
My device does not act the way I want it to. 101
I need to stop a device from working without
  uninstalling it. 102
My USB scanner does not work. 102
Devices and PC cards used on my laptop computer
  keep draining the battery when I am not connected
  to a power source. 103

CHAPTER 6   **Windows XP Disk Headaches** **107**
Problems with Hard Disks 108
My drive is not an NTFS drive. 109
My computer's hard disk is running out of space. 110
My hard disk seems to behave erratically, or I get
  error messages. 113
My hard disk makes strange noises. 115
My hard disk reads and writes data very slowly. 115
My computer is not able to boot, and I see "disk missing"
  messages. 117
One of my hard disks does not work. 117
I can't create a new partition. 119
All of my disks are listed as "basic." 122

Difficulties with Floppy Disks 123
   I can't open a floppy disk. 124
   When I try to open a floppy disk, an error
      message appears. 125
   I want to use NTFS on my hard disk, but I'm afraid
      that will prevent my system from being able to read
      floppy disks, which are formatted with FAT. 125
   A floppy disk will not hold a file I need to move
      to another computer. 126
Problems with CD and DVD-ROM Drives 127
   Windows Media Player keeps opening automatically
      when I insert a CD. 127
   I can't hear any sound when I play a DVD. 128
   When I try to play my DVD, the screen becomes black. . . . 129
   I receive a region error message when I try to use the
      DVD player. 129

CHAPTER 7   **Windows XP Peripheral Headaches** **131**
Windows XP Peripheral Problems 132
   My keyboard does not work. 132
   The keyboard works too slowly. 133
   My cursor blinks too fast/slow. 134
   My keyboard one-touch buttons do not work. 135
   Because of a disability, I can't use my keyboard correctly.
      How can I get help? 136
   My mouse keeps sticking. 137
   I am left-handed, and I find right-clicking difficult. 138
   Double-clicking does not work well. 139
   My mouse pointer is too small/large. 140
   My mouse pointer creates a trailing effect when
      I move it. 142
   My mouse pointer disappears when I am typing. 142
   My mouse wheel makes entire pages scroll by. 143
   I am having problems with a wireless mouse/keyboard. . . 143

CHAPTER 8   **Windows XP Printer, Scanner, and Camera Headaches** **145**
Printer Setup Problems 146
   Windows XP does not detect my printer. 147
   I cannot get an older printer to work with Windows XP. . . 149
   My USB printer does not work, even though other USB
      devices connected to the USB hub work. 150
   I can't connect to a network printer. 150

Solving Printing Problems 152
   My printer prints garbled text. 152
   A certain file will not print. 153
   No documents or files are printing, even though the
      printer was working fine previously. 153
   I can't stop a document from printing. 154
   My printer color or fonts do not look good. 154
   My printer works very slowly. 155
   My computer stops responding when I print something
      and begins to respond again only when the print job
      is finished. 155
   My printer keeps printing in landscape instead of portrait
      orientation. 156
   I can't share my printer so that other users on my network
      can use it. 157
   I want to make a shared printer available only at certain
      times, but I can't do it without also restricting myself. .. 157
Solving Problems with Scanners and Cameras 158
   I can't get my scanner or camera to install. 159
   My scanner/camera does not work correctly or works
      only intermittently. 160

CHAPTER 9   **Windows XP Internet Connection Headaches** **161**
Windows XP Internet Connection Headaches 162
   I don't know how to create an Internet connection. 163
   Which ISP Should I Use? 163
   I do not want other users accessing my Internet connection,
      but they can. 167
   I need to configure more than one dial-up number. 168
   I am having problems with dialing options or idle
      time hang-up. 170
   Dial-up to my corporate network requires additional
      security settings that I do not understand. 171
   I need a different connection to work as the default
      connection. 171
Solving Problems with Modems 172
   When my modem dials, the connection noise is too loud. ... 172
   My modem seems to be really slow when I am
      sending data. 173
   My modem keeps disconnecting after a certain period of
      idle time. My connection is not set to disconnect if idle. ... 174
   My connection requires different compression and flow
      control settings. How can I change these? 175

Downloading information from the Internet is slow. 176
My modem works sporadically or keeps disconnecting
randomly. 176
My modem keeps dialing a 1 in front of my ISP's
number, or it does/does not dial the area code. 177
Problems with Windows Firewall 177
I don't know how to turn on Windows Firewall. 178
I want to see what Windows Firewall is dropping from
the Internet. 179
I use firewall exceptions when I use my laptop at home,
but when I travel, I do not want to allow exceptions.
How can I easily configure this? 180

CHAPTER 10   **Windows XP Internet Explorer Headaches** **183**
IE Connection Problems 184
I get a Cannot Find Server message. 185
IE provides intermittent pages, but fails on many others. 186
I have two Internet connections, but IE automatically
dials the one I do not want to use. 187
IE does not automatically dial my Internet connection,
or I do not want IE to dial a connection. 187
IE dials a connection, even when I have a different connection
established or when using a broadband connection. 189
I cannot configure IE to connect through a proxy server
or broadband hardware. 189
Solving IE Configuration Problems 191
I don't like the setup of the IE toolbar. 191
I want IE to use a different default home page. 192
I want IE to keep more temporary Internet files, or I
want IE to not use temporary Internet files. 193
I want IE to keep History entries for a longer/shorter
period of time. 194
I want to stop pornographic or violent content from
being displayed in IE. 194
IE keeps trying to complete web addresses and forms
for me. 197
Whenever I click the Mail icon in IE, Outlook Express
opens, but I use another program. 198
When printing from IE, I don't want background colors
and images to print. 199
Managing Internet Explorer Security 200
IE keeps telling me that sites and/or actions are not
allowed. 200

I need to make sure a certain site is blocked.   202

Cookies are being blocked without my permission.   203

Pop-up windows are driving me crazy.   205

CHAPTER 11 **Outlook Express Headaches** **207**

Problems with Outlook Express Connections   208

I can't set up an account.   209

I can't change information about my account without

creating a new account.   211

I always have to type my password when I am trying

to download mail.   212

Solving Problems Using Outlook Express   213

When I try to download mail, I sometimes get a server

timeout message.   213

I can't get a new mail message I am creating to show

me a Blind Carbon Copy field.   214

I can't use stationery, fonts, or colors in my messages. . . .   214

I can't send an encrypted or digitally signed message.   215

I can't read or send a message in a different language. . . .   216

I can't remove the preview pane.   216

I don't like the appearance of e-mail that I read/ compose. . . .   218

I am afraid to open e-mail attachments because they

could contain viruses.   219

My news messages keep disappearing every few days. . . .   220

My Internet program keeps disconnecting after I send

or receive mail.   221

Solving Problems with Mail Management   222

I can't stop someone from sending me e-mail.   223

I accidentally put someone on the blocked senders list.   223

I can't create a mail/news rule.   225

CHAPTER 12 **Windows XP Networking Headaches** **229**

Problems with Network Setup and Access   230

I can't get my wired network set up.   233

I can't get my wireless network set up.   235

I can't install additional clients on my network.   236

I need to set up Windows network clients that are not

Windows XP clients.   238

I can't configure networking with a Linux or Macintosh

computer.   238

My computer does not connect to the network. All other

networked computers are functioning correctly.   239

I need to use a different IP address configuration
    on my network. 243
I get an "access denied" message when I try to access
    another computer on my network. 245
Difficulties with Network Shares 245
I want to see all of the shares available on a particular
    computer or on my network. 245
I am having problems sharing a folder (or a printer,
    a drive, or another device). 247
The options on the Sharing tab are grayed out. 248
I can't configure NTFS permissions. 249
I have configured specific permissions, but users still
    have full access to my share. 250
I have shared folders on my computer, but no one can
    access my computer. I can access other computers
    with no trouble. 251
Aggravations with Internet Connection Sharing 252
I did not set up ICS when I first configured my network,
    but I want to use it now. How can I configure it? 253
When I try to enable ICS, a message appears telling
    me that my user name and password are not saved
    for all users. 254
When I try to configure a computer for Internet Connection
    Sharing, I receive a message telling me there is an IP
    address conflict. 255
Users can disconnect the ICS Internet connection, and I
    don't want them to be able to control the connection. 256
The ICS computer does not dial a connection when
    a network user needs it. 256
ICS dial-up connections are slow. 257
My e-mail does not work with ICS. *................* **257**
No clients can use the ICS computer. 258
Pains with Remote Desktop and Remote Assistance 258
Remote Desktop 258
I can't use Remote Desktop. 259
Remote Desktop does not work with Windows Firewall. ... 260
I need to connect to a Remote Desktop computer from
    a Windows computer that does not use Windows XP
    Professional Edition. 261
Remote Desktop is slow. 261
Remote Assistance 262

I can't create a Remote Assistance invitation.   263
I want to use Remote Assistance, but I don't want
   the user to be able to control my computer.   264

CHAPTER 13   **Media Player Headaches** **265**
Configuring the Interface   266
   The menu bar keeps disappearing.   266
   Windows Media Player always opens in skin mode.   267
   I can't use the More Skins option.   268
   I don't know how to manage visualizations.   270
   I don't want to see the anchor window when I'm in
      skin mode.   271
Music and Movie Difficulties   272
   My CD player will not play CD music.   272
   My system's CD playback does not sound good.   274
   The quality of a video clip I'm playing is poor.   274
   I am having performance problems with streaming
      media.   276
   I can't play a DVD with Windows Media Player
      because of a decoder problem.   277
Media Library Aggravations   278
   I can't add CD music to Media Library.   278
   I can't figure out how to create a playlist.   280
   I can't import/export a playlist from another Windows
      Media Player.   281
Problems Ripping Music   282
   The defaults for the Rip feature do not work the way I
      want them to.   282
   The View Album Info feature of Copy Music does
      not work.   283
   The music ripping process takes too long or takes up
      too much disk space.   284
   Burning and Syncing Music   284

CHAPTER 14   **Movie Maker 2 Headaches** **285**
Difficulties with Video   286
   Movie Maker doesn't recognize my capture device.   287
   Movie Maker works very slowly.   288
   I don't know what capture device I need.   288
   I upgraded to Windows XP and now my capture device
      does not work.   289
   I can't copy or record a commercial movie.   289

When I record, I cannot hear the audio.   289
I'm having problems with my video capture device,
   or I receive a message telling me that the device is
   already in use.   289
Problems Editing Video   290
I can't create a trim point.   290
The Truth about Capture Devices   290
Trimming seems to throw away the pieces of the movie
   I want.   291
I can't split a clip.   291
I can't combine two clips.   292
I can't create a transition.   292
Annoyances with Audio   293
I can't import an audio file.   293
I can't record narration.   293
Audio levels on the movie track and my narration are
   not good.   294
Aggravations with File Types   294

CHAPTER 15   **Tools and Utility Headaches** **295**
I can't get my computer to play any sound.   296
My microphone does not work.   297
My computer plays sound, but works erratically or the
   computer locks up.   298
I use the Volume Control feature in my notification area,
   but the microphone volume does not appear.   298
My computer shows the wrong date/time.   299
My computer does not automatically adjust for daylight
   savings time.   300
I want my computer to automatically run Disk Cleanup, or
   automatically run another utility.   300
A scheduled task does not run.   301
Disk Defragmenter does not completely defragment my
   hard drive.   303
Disk Defragmenter stops working before it is finished. . . .   303
Error-checking stops working.   303
I need to easily move files and/or settings from one
   computer to my XP computer.   304
I think I may have unsigned digital files on my computer. . . .   308
I am having problems with DirectX.   309
System Restore does not work.   310
I can't back up data.   311

CHAPTER 16   **Performance Headaches** **315**
Windows XP Performance Problems 316
   My computer runs too slowly. 316
   My computer once worked great, but opening and closing
     files now takes a long time. 318
   My computer barely has enough RAM, but I cannot
     upgrade. 318
   Sometimes my computer works well and other times it
     seems very slow. 321
   The Truth About Virtual Memory 323
   My computer boots very slowly. 324
Application Performance Problems 325
   An application makes my computer run very slowly. 325
   My computer cannot run multiple applications at the
     same time. 326
   I have an application that locks up. 326
   I have an application that locks up repeatedly. 327
Aggravations with Printing Performance 328
   Printing slows my computer's responsiveness down. 328
   I lose control of my computer until printing is finished. 328
   Windows XP and Lockups 328
   My printer's output does not look good. 329
Performance Issues with Laptops 330
   Battery power runs down quickly. 330
   Colors are difficult to see on the LCD screen. 330

CHAPTER 17   **Windows XP *Migraine* Headaches** **331**
Problems with Installation 332
   My computer stops responding during installation. 332
   My computer gives me a file copy error message during
     installation. 333
   I receive a Stop message or an Error message during
     installation. 334
   I want to perform a clean installation. 334
   I upgraded to Windows XP from Windows 98/Windows Me,
     but now my computer runs slowly. 334
Problems with System Crashes and Boot Failures 335
   Don't Dig Your Own Installation Grave 335
   My computer has stopped responding. 336
   My system has crashed; and upon reboot, it gives me an
     error message. 336
   I have tried to use System Restore, but now the system
     does not work well or I receive error messages. 338

I have tried to use System Restore, but now my computer
will not boot. 339

I installed a new device driver, and now the computer
will not boot. 340

My computer fails during bootup. 340

When I try to boot my computer, a message appears that
says "Invalid System Disk." 341

One of my applications keeps crashing. 341

Problems with Activation 341

I am having trouble connecting to the Internet for activation.
342

APPENDIX A   **Curt's Top 20 Windows XP Headaches** **343**

20: My printer/scanner used to work fine, but now that
I've upgraded to Windows XP, it does not work or
does not work well. 344

19: I want to use the New Technology File System
(NTFS) because Windows XP is optimized for it,
but my hard disk is a FAT32 drive. 344

18: Windows Update keeps trying to connect to the Web
and download stuff without my permission. 345

17: Windows XP keeps turning itself off when I leave
it idle. 346

16: I don't like the appearance of Windows XP, or I am
having difficulty managing the Start menu. 347

15: Folder views use large icons that require me to scroll
around a lot. 348

14: I can't find the encryption or Remote Desktop features
in Windows XP Home Edition. 348

13: My network does not work. 348

12: On my ICS network, network users can control the
Internet connection. 349

11: On my network, I can access all other computers,
but none can access mine. 349

10: Internet Explorer will not let me view certain sites due
to "security settings." 350

9: My modem keeps hanging up when there is idle time. . . . 350

8: The Internet is too slow. 351

7: On a Windows XP Professional computer, I cannot
configure individual NTFS permissions for a share. 352

6: My wireless network does not work. 353

5: Certain applications do not work on Windows XP. 353

4: Windows XP performs tasks slowly. 354

3: Windows XP will not boot, or a new configuration
causes the system to crash. 355

2: A hardware device will not work with Windows XP. ... 355

1: Windows XP keeps giving me a permissions message
instead of letting me perform certain actions. 356

APPENDIX B   **Four Signs You Need Help from Technical Support** **357**

Your Computer Often Locks Up/Acts Strangely 358

You Get the Blue Screen of Death 358

Windows XP Makes No Attempt to Boot/Fails to Boot ... 358

A Hardware Device Will Not Work 358

APPENDIX C   **Five Things Computer Users Do That Cause Headaches!** **359**

Use the Internet Without Antivirus Software 360

Change Settings Randomly 360

Fail to Read Device Instructions 360

Use Incompatible Software 360

Upgrade to Windows XP Without Doing Your
Homework 361

APPENDIX D   **Service Pack 2 Headaches** **363**

Some of my programs do not work now that SP2 is
installed. 364

Windows Firewall does not allow some programs
to work. 364

The Windows Security Center doesn't appear in my
Notification Area. 367

I don't want the Security Center in my
Notification Area. 367

My wireless network is giving me difficulties. 368

I'm having problems with some hardware. 369

Index **371**

Acknowledgments

Many thanks to all the great folks at Osborne for giving me the chance to write the second edition of this book. A special thanks to Margie McAneny for sharing the idea and to Agatha Kim for keeping things moving the right direction. Thanks to Carolyn Welch for keeping everything moving and attending to the details. Thanks to Tom Dunlap for a fine technical review. Finally, and as always, thanks to my agent, Margot, and my family for their support.

Introduction

You know the feeling, sure you do. You sit with your elbows propped against your desk, staring intently at your computer screen. You've been doing this for some time now, and soon enough, you feel it: that tense, grinding feeling beginning to build in your temples. You rub them with your fingers and you let out a long, tired sigh…. Windows XP has got you again.

As a technology author and trainer, I've been suffering from Windows XP headaches for quite some time now—in fact, even way back before Windows XP was released to the public when I was testing the *beta* version of XP. Since then, I've also felt the tension of headaches caused by Service Pack 2. I've learned a lot and have spent a lot of time undoing or repairing problems I have encountered. Simply put, I know all too well that grinding feeling in my temples, and it is no fun.

Windows XP Headaches: How to Fix Common (and Not So Common) Problems in a Hurry, Second Edition is just for you. In this book, you will find hundreds of commonly occurring problems as well as the uncommon ones that you just might experience with Windows XP along with ways to cure them quickly and easily. I'll bet that if you are buying this book, you've had enough XP headaches of your own that you want some help with, and you are hoping this book will come to your rescue.

That is what this book is all about—getting you the information you need for your Windows XP problems. This book is divided into logical sections that give you a bunch of different headaches. Each headache tells you which operating system is affected (Windows XP Professional or Home Editions), why the headache occurs, and how to resolve it, often in a simple step-by-step format. In fact, my goal is for you to be able to pull this book off your shelf, find the problem you are experiencing, and then find a quick remedy for that problem.

You don't have to read this book in any particular order. You can read it from cover to cover if you like, or you can jump around and find the answers to headaches when you need them—the choice is yours. Just use the table of contents or the book's index to find help on the most all-important Windows XP topics with ease.

This book is for the beginning to intermediate computer audience—you don't need a Ph.D. in computer science to use it; in fact, you don't need to know anything at all except how to turn Windows XP on and how to use your keyboard and mouse. To help you along the way, I've also included a few other elements:

- ■ **Tip**   Tips are friendly suggestions I have thrown in from time to time that can make your work and play with Windows XP easier.

- ■ **Note**   Notes are little bursts of information that give you some additional headache cure information. You don't have to read these, but they can help you.

- ■ **Sidebars**   I have added a few sidebars here and there. Sidebars contain extra information about some subject that will help you understand Windows XP components. These can help you understand what is going on and why the headache occurred in the first place. Again, you don't have to read these, but they can give you quick information in a nontechnical way.

- ■ **Appendixes**   See the appendixes at the back of this book for some additional help and goodies!

Finally, what should you do if you are experiencing a Windows XP headache that this book does not mention? It is impossible for me to list every possible headache that can occur (unless you want this book to be the size of subcompact car), so if you don't find it here, do this:

- ■ Check the book's index and look for topics similar to what you are experiencing. Although your specific headache may not be listed, another headache could help you solve the problem!

- ■ Check www.microsoft.com and search for your problem on Microsoft's site. If you have technical support available with your computer, don't be afraid to use it!

- ■ There are lots of newsgroups for Windows XP users on all different kinds of subjects. You may find the answer to your headache, or you can ask others to help you solve the headache. Search on any search engine, such as Yahoo.com or MSN.com for Windows XP Newsgroups, and you'll find plenty.

- ■ Finally, if you are stuck in headache-land, feel free to send me an e-mail and I'll try to help you out. You will always be able to reach me at curt_simmons@hotmail.com.

Okay, are you ready? Then let's get started! Your headache cure is only pages away...

Thanks! Enjoy the book!

Chapter 1

Windows XP Interface Headaches

In this chapter, you'll cure...

■ Difficulties with display settings and themes

■ Start menu and taskbar aggravations

■ Power management and notification area pains

Ah, the Windows XP interface—the desktop area that makes Windows easy to use and problem free. Okay, right. While the XP interface does offer a lot of really cool and helpful features, it can also give you a lot of grief. Don't worry, though, because most of the Headaches you'll learn about in this chapter are easy to kill and you'll have Windows XP following you and doing what you want in no time. So then, let's get busy and take care of those interface problems!

Display Setting Headaches

Display settings refer to a collection of Windows XP settings that govern how your display looks and how icons and fonts appear on your screen. When you get everything looking the way you want, it's great. When it's not, it is a real drag. The good news is that most display settings are easy to fix, once you know where to go. The following sections explore the most common Headaches you are likely to encounter.

 ## Colors on my screen do not look good.

Operating Systems Affected Windows XP Professional and Home Editions are affected.

Cause If your display color simply does not look good, you probably have a problem with your display driver, or the driver is not compatible with Windows XP. A driver is a piece of software that allows a hardware device, such as your video card, to work with Windows XP. If the driver is messed up or isn't compatible, Windows XP tries to use one of its own drivers to make everything work for you. Sometimes that works out and sometimes not. Fixing the problem, however, requires a little investigative work on your part. It is important to keep in mind that every display adapter—every piece of hardware for that matter—has a driver that enables Windows XP to control and manage it. If the driver doesn't work, the device will not work. If the driver isn't the right driver, the device might work okay, but not the way it should. The basic rule is simply this: You have to have the right driver or you will have problems for which there are no workarounds.

Always make sure any new hardware that is installed on your computer is compatible with Windows XP before you install it. Simply getting the right hardware can stop multiple headaches before they occur.

The Pain Killer   To fix the color problem, follow these steps:

1. Click Start | Control Panel.

2. Open the Display icon by double-clicking it.

If you don't see Display, you need to click the Switch to Classic View option in the left Control Panel pane. Then, you'll see the Display icon.

3. Click the Settings tab. The Color Quality drop-down menu should be able to display several different settings, such as 16 bit, 32 bit, and so forth. If you are stuck with only one color quality setting—and it is low—then the problem is the driver.

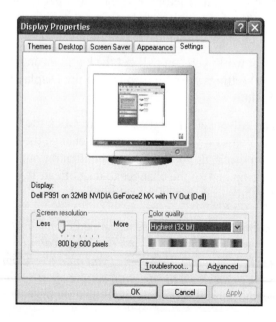

4. In order to resolve the driver problem, you will need to visit the video card manufacturer's web site and see about downloading a new driver. Microsoft does not provide drivers for hardware vendors, so you'll have to get the driver from the manufacturer's web site.

Everything on my desktop is too small or too big.

Operating Systems Affected   Windows XP Professional and Home Editions are affected.

Cause   The size of the icons on your desktop is determined by the resolution settings of your video card. If everything seems too big or too small, all you probably need to do is choose a different resolution so that items appear the size you want. This is an easy fix, fortunately!

The Pain Killer   To fix the size problem, follow these steps:

1. Click Start | Control Panel.

2. Open the Display icon by double-clicking it. Click the Settings tab.

3. On the Screen Resolution setting, use the slider bar to choose a different resolution—800 × 600 pixels is right for most people. If you have a larger monitor (19" +), consider using a higher resolution.

4. If that does not work, you can pull out the big guns and change the Dots Per Inch (DPI) settings for your display. On the Display tab, click the Advanced button.

5. This opens an Advanced Properties window. Click the General tab. If you want to make items on your desktop larger, change the DPI Setting using the drop-down menu, as you can see in the illustration. You'll need to restart your computer for the changes to take effect. If you don't like the results, return here and change the setting back.

NOTE   *DPI settings can cause some problems, however, such as dialog boxes getting cut off and even some distortion. You can play around with these settings to see if they help you any. However, if you plan to change settings, you would be wise to jot down the original settings first so that you are able to change them back in the event that your new settings do not work well.*

Dell P991 and 32MB NVIDIA GeForce2 MX with TV Ou... [?] [X]

GeForce2 MX/MX 400

| | Device Selection | | | Color Correction |

| General | Adapter | Monitor | Troubleshoot | Color Management |

Display

If your screen resolution makes screen items too small to view
comfortably, you can increase the DPI to compensate. To change
font sizes only, click Cancel and go to the Appearance tab.

DPI setting:

| Normal size (96 DPI) | ⌄ |

Normal size (96 DPI)
Large size (120 DPI)
Custom setting...

Compatibility

Some programs might not operate properly unless you restart the
computer after changing display settings.

After I change display settings:

○ Restart the computer before applying the new display settings

⦿ Apply the new display settings without restarting

○ Ask me before applying the new display settings

Some games and other programs must be run in 256-color mode.
Learn more about running programs in 256-color mode.

[OK]   [Cancel]   [Apply]

My display seems distorted at times.

Operating Systems Affected   Windows XP Professional and Home Editions are
affected.

Cause   More than likely, you really need a new video card. However, if you can't
change the card just yet, you might resolve the problem by adjusting the hardware
features of the card. This is easy to try, so if the headache doesn't go away, there is
no harm done.

The Pain Killer   To fix the distortion problem, follow these steps:

1. Click Start | Control Panel.

2. Open the Display icon by double-clicking it. Click the Settings tab.

3. Click the Advanced button, and then click the Troubleshoot tab.

4. You can try to resolve the problem by lowering the Hardware Acceleration slider bar. When you move the bar a notch, you'll see what display features are being removed. You can try different settings and see if the problem is resolved.

5. Also, try clearing the Enable Write Combining check box. This may also resolve distortion problems. You'll need to experiment here to see if the settings will help you, but they may just do the trick.

6. Finally, check the controls on the monitor itself. Something in the controls might be off as well.

My desktop fonts are too small.

Operating Systems Affected　Windows XP Professional and Home Editions are affected.

Cause　If the fonts under your icons and on window menus are too small, you can easily change the size of the font without screwing up everything else. Windows XP automatically assigns a standard font size, but that size may not be right for you. No problem though—this headache is easy to kill.

The Pain Killer　To fix the font size problem, follow these steps:

1. Click Start | Control Panel.

2. Open the Display icon by double-clicking it.

3. Click the Appearance tab. As you can see in the illustration, you have a drop-down menu for Font Size. Click the menu and choose a larger size. Then click OK.

I don't like my screen saver, or my screen saver does not work the way I want it to.

Operating Systems Affected   Windows XP Professional and Home Editions are affected.

Cause   Screen savers are great ways to give your computer something interactive to do when you step away from the screen. In the past, screen savers protected a computer screen from "burn," which happened when not enough activity was going on. Today's monitors are not really susceptible to this problem, but screen savers remain for entertainment purposes. The good news is that you can easily change or reconfigure the screen saver—you can even make a screen saver of your favorite pictures! You can do all of this on the Screen Saver tab of Display Properties.

The Pain Killer   To make screen saver changes, follow these steps:

1. Click Start | Control Panel.

2. Double-click Display, and then click the Screen Saver tab.

3. On the Screen Saver tab, you can make changes to the current screen saver by clicking the Settings button and making any changes that appear. You can adjust the timeout value for the screen saver using the Wait selection box (the default is about ten minutes). Finally, if you do not want to use the screen saver, use the drop-down menu and pick a new one. If you do not want to use a screen saver at all, choose the (None) option in the drop-down list, as you can see in the illustration.

Whenever I stop using my computer, it returns to the logon screen.

Operating Systems Affected   Windows XP Professional and Home Editions are affected.

Cause   As a safety feature, Windows XP sends you back to the logon screen if the computer is idle for a certain period of time. This can be a real pain, but the problem is easily fixed. This XP security feature works with screen saver functions, and you can easily stop it from happening.

The Pain Killer   To stop XP from taking you back to the logon screen after an idle period, follow these steps:

1. Click Start | Control Panel.

2. Double-click Display, and then click the Screen Saver tab.

3. On the Screen Saver tab, clear the check box that says On Resume, Password Protect.

The My Pictures screen saver does not work right.

Operating Systems Affected   Windows XP Professional and Home Editions are affected.

Cause   Windows XP has a cool feature that allows you to easily create a screen saver from your digital pictures. This is a great way to have your family members, cat, dog, or whatever on your screen saver. My Pictures is easy to use—just access the Screen Saver tab of Display Properties and choose the My Pictures Slideshow from the drop-down menu. Windows XP will look in your My Pictures folder (found in the My Documents folder) for pictures to use, so you should put any pictures you want displayed there. After that, you can use the Settings button to configure how the pictures should be displayed.

The Pain Killer   To make the My Pictures Slideshow work the way you want, follow these steps:

1. Click Start | Control Panel.

2. Double-click Display, and then click the Screen Saver tab.

3. On the Screen Saver tab, make sure the My Pictures Slideshow is selected in the drop-down menu and make sure you have the pictures you want to use in the My Pictures folder.

4. Click the Settings button on the Screen Saver tab. This opens the My Pictures Screen Saver Options window, shown in the illustration. Make any adjustments in this window as needed. You can change how often pictures should be displayed and how they should appear in the screen. You can also choose to use different transitions between pictures, which is sort of cool. When you select a transition, the effect is used to change pictures. Common examples are blend, slide left/right, cover, and so forth. Once you are done, click OK and test your screen saver again.

Did you notice the Use Pictures in This Folder option in the illustration? While it is true that the My Pictures screen saver looks for pics in the My Pictures folder, you can change that behavior here and choose a different folder. This allows you to tell the screen saver to get pictures from any folder on your hard drive, which might be a lot easier if you have pictures stored in another location or even in several different folders.

My desktop wallpaper does not look right.

Operating Systems Affected   Windows XP Professional and Home Editions are affected.

Cause   Windows XP can display just about any kind of picture file as desktop wallpaper (which is what you see as the background on your desktop). However, some pictures may not display correctly if you try to make them take up the entire screen. There is no direct fix for this problem, but you can adjust how the picture is displayed so that distortion is removed.

The Pain Killer   To make the picture look good, follow these steps:

1. Click Start | Control Panel.

2. Double-click Display. Click the Desktop tab.

3. Your current wallpaper is selected in the list and appears in the test monitor window, as you can see in the illustration. If you want to use a different wallpaper, select a new one from the list or use the Browse button to select something different on your operating system (such as your own pictures). To try to fix the distortion problem, change the Position setting from Tile or Stretch to Center. Then, you use the Color drop-down menu to choose a background color to fill the rest of the leftover space.

4. Click OK when you are done.

TIP   *Desktop wallpaper settings are very forgiving. If you configure something you don't like or want to change later, you can always return to the Desktop tab and make changes at any time. Some people even change their wallpaper every week!*

I don't want to use wallpaper on my desktop—I want a color background only.

Operating Systems Affected   Windows XP Professional and Home Editions are affected.

Cause   Depending on your computer, wallpaper may already be set up for you. No problem, you can change it to different wallpaper or none at all. If you do not want to use wallpaper, but a simple background color, you can do that too.

The Pain Killer   To use no wallpaper, follow these steps:

1. Click Start | Control Panel.

2. Double-click Display. Click the Desktop tab.

3. On the Desktop tab, change the Background setting to (None) in the list. Then, use the Color drop-down menu and select a background color that you want to use. Remember that you can experiment and use different colors until you find the one that is right for you.

Icons do not appear on my desktop.

Operating Systems Affected   Windows XP Professional and Home Editions are affected.

Cause   Windows XP attempts to make your life easier by removing all of the icons, except Recycle Bin, from the desktop. This may annoy you, however, so you can easily get back standard desktop icons if you want. You can do this in a couple of different ways, but the easiest is to use the Customize Desktop feature.

The Pain Killer   To put icons back on the desktop, follow these steps:

1. Click Start | Control Panel.

2. Double-click Display. Click the Desktop tab.

3. Click the Customize Desktop button.

4. On the Desktop Items window, General tab, click the check boxes next to the desktop icons you want to show, such as My Documents, My Computer, and so forth. When you are done, click OK.

Desktop Items ? X

General | Web

Desktop icons

☑ My Documents   ☐ My Network Places
☐ My Computer   ☐ Internet Explorer

My Computer   My Documents   My Network   Recycle Bin   Re
                              Places   (full)   (

[Change Icon...] [Restore Default]

Desktop cleanup

Desktop cleanup moves unused desktop items to a folder.

☑ Run Desktop Cleanup Wizard every 60 days

[Clean Desktop Now]

[OK]   [Cancel]

The Desktop Cleanup Wizard keeps running without my permission.

Operating Systems Affected   Windows XP Professional and Home Editions are affected.

Cause   The good news about Windows XP is that it tries to help you. The bad news about Windows XP is that...well...it tries to help you. Case in point—the Desktop Cleanup Wizard. This handy wizard is designed to help you get rid of junk that might have collected on your desktop over a period of time. Its default setting is to run every 60 days. However, you may be like me and find the wizard annoying, in which case, you don't want it to run at all. No worries, though—you can stop this headache easily.

The Pain Killer   To stop the Desktop Cleanup Wizard from automatically running, follow these steps:

1. Click Start | Control Panel.

2. Double-click Display. Click the Desktop tab.

3. Click the Customize Desktop button.

4. On the Desktop Items, General tab, locate the Run Desktop Cleanup Wizard every 60 days check box. Clear the check box and click OK.

Windows XP will not let me display a web page on my desktop.

Operating Systems Affected   Windows XP Professional and Home Editions are affected.

Cause   Don't worry. If you loved the web-based desktop you used in Windows 98, it still exists in Windows XP. In Windows 98, you had to turn on the Active Desktop to use web content, but this feature is integrated into Windows XP. In other words, the feature is here all the time, but the configuration place is a little more hidden.

The Pain Killer   To display a web page on your desktop, follow these steps:

1. Click Start | Control Panel.

2. Double-click Display. Click the Desktop tab.

3. Click the Customize Desktop button.

4. Click the web tab. To choose a web page to download and display on your desktop, click the New button.

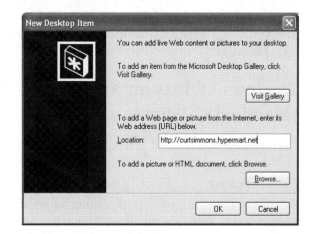

5. In the New Desktop Item window, enter the URL for the web page you want to display, as you can see in the illustration, and click OK. Windows XP will connect to the web site and download the page to your desktop.

TIP *If you want to stop using a web page at any time, simply return to the web tab and clear the check box next to the web site so that it will not be used. If you never want to use it again, you can click the Delete button to permanently remove it.*

Windows Theme Headaches

If you have been around computers since the days of Windows 98, you remember that Windows 98 came with a number of "themes," and you could get more with the Windows 98 Plus CD. This started the theme craze among Windows users, which is still going strong today.

First things first—what is a theme? A theme is a collection of settings that make your interface appear a certain way. This usually includes wallpaper, mouse pointers, sounds, icons, and screen savers. For example, a popular theme under Windows 98 was Flower Power. Desktop colors, mouse pointers, and sounds all looked like stuff from the sixties—groovy baby!

In Windows XP, the XP interface is, in fact, a theme. This means that the default interface you see when you install Windows XP is the XP theme—a collection of settings that make Windows XP look the way it does. You can use the Windows XP theme the way it is, change it, use the Windows Classic theme, or even download additional themes from the Internet. For the most part, themes are easy to use, but there are two Headaches associated with them that you should know about.

Windows XP lists my XP theme as "Windows XP (Modified)." What is wrong?

Operating Systems Affected   Windows XP Professional and Home Editions are affected.

Cause   The (Modified) note appears when you change anything on the current XP theme. For example, if you change your wallpaper to something you want to see, the theme will appear as modified. This is because the theme has a specific list of settings but also allows you to edit and change those settings as you like so that XP looks the way you want.

The Pain Killer   In this case, you don't need to do anything. The Modified listing is a normal occurrence when you change interface settings—nothing is wrong.

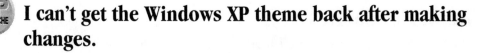

I can't get the Windows XP theme back after making changes.

Operating Systems Affected   Windows XP Professional and Home Editions are affected.

Cause   When you make a change to the Windows XP theme, Windows XP renames the theme as Windows XP (Modified). You can easily return the default Windows XP theme at any time by choosing it from the provided list.

The Pain Killer   To use the default theme, follow these steps:

1. Click Start | Control Panel.

2. Double-click Display. Click the Themes tab.

3. In the Theme drop-down list shown here, select Windows XP and click OK to apply the default theme.

> You can access themes on the Internet that are specifically designed for Windows XP. These are a part of the Windows XP Plus Pack CD that you can purchase. There are also additional screen savers and games. You can learn more at http://www.microsoft.com/windows/plus/PlusHome.asp.

Start Menu Headaches

The Windows XP Start menu is different than in previous versions of Windows. It does more, holds more, is more flexible, and often does things to try to help you. All of that is great, but the Start menu configuration can definitely cause you some headaches.

Windows XP's approach to the Start menu is to provide an all-in-one place to get to items. For the most part, it does a good job of this, since the default Windows XP desktop has no icons. You access items from the Start menu, and you can customize what items appear there. The good news is that most Start menu Headaches are easily fixed, and in the following sections, I'll show you how!

Windows XP keeps putting stuff on the Start menu without my permission.

Operating Systems Affected   Windows XP Professional and Home Editions are affected.

Cause   Windows XP remembers documents and programs that you open and puts icons for them on the Start menu. This way, you can get to those items by simply clicking Start the next time you want to use them. In other words, the Start menu tries to learn what you use and keep it available to you. However, this behavior may get on your nerves or cause too much stuff to be listed on the Start menu.

The Pain Killer   To stop or control Windows XP putting popular items on the Start menu, follow these steps:

1. Click the Start menu.

2. Any item that has been added can be easily removed by simply right-clicking the icon and clicking Remove from This List.

3. There is no way to keep the XP Start menu from putting popular items on the Start menu, unless you change the Start menu to the Classic style. This makes the Start menu look and act as it did in older versions of Windows. To use the Classic Start menu, right-click the Start button in the lower-left corner of your screen and click Properties. On the Start Menu tab, click the Classic Start Menu radio button.

What, Exactly, Are the Items on the Start Menu?

Start menu items are shortcuts. They are simply icons that provide the operating system with a "link" to the real item. For example, let's say that a program called "My Program" is on your Start menu. The My Program on the Start menu is not the actual program—it is a link to the program, which is in your folder structure on the operating system. No item on the Start menu is a real item—they are all links to items stored in other places. Because of this, you can add and delete items from the Start menu in any way you want without actually deleting the real item on your system or moving it. As you are working, remember this important tip—there is never any danger of harming programs, documents, files, or anything else by adding or removing them from the Start menu.

I want to control which items appear on the Start menu, but Windows XP will not let me.

Operating Systems Affected   Windows XP Professional and Home Editions are affected.

Cause   Windows XP has a default configuration that puts certain items on the Start menu. You can change this configuration and even how the items are displayed by customizing the Start menu options.

The Pain Killer   To customize the Start menu, follow these steps:

1. Right-click the Start button at the lower-left corner of your screen and click Properties.

2. Click the Customize button that appears.

3. On the General tab, you can choose to use large or small icons, the number of programs Windows XP can put on your Start menu, and whether or not you want to show your web browser or e-mail client on the Start menu, shown here.

4. Click the Advanced tab. Here, you can determine what items appear on the Start menu, and if they appear as a link or a menu. Make any changes you want and click the OK button.

If you make a change here that you do not like, don't worry. You can return to these configuration tabs at any time and make new changes or change items back to the way they were.

I use Netscape instead of Internet Explorer, but Netscape does not appear on my Start menu.

Operating Systems Affected   Windows XP Professional and Home Editions are affected.

Cause   Windows XP displays a default browser on the Start menu, which is Internet Explorer (of course). However, you can easily change this behavior so that Netscape (or any other browser set up on your computer) will appear there instead.

The Pain Killer   To make Netscape appear on the Start menu, follow these steps:

1. Right-click the Start button at the lower-left corner of your screen and click Properties.

2. Click the Customize button that appears.

3. On the General tab, make sure the Internet check box is selected. Use the drop-down menu and select Netscape instead of Internet Explorer. Click OK. Netscape should now appear on your Start menu.

The Start menu does not list all of the programs I like to use.

Operating Systems Affected   Windows XP Professional and Home Editions are affected.

Cause   Windows XP displays popular programs that you access; however, it is limited as to the number of programs that can be displayed. The default setting is six programs. If you access a seventh program, the most unpopular of the original six is removed to make way for the new program. You can change this behavior so that the Start menu will display more programs (up to 30). This way, you can see all of your popular programs at one time.

The Pain Killer   To make more programs appear on the Start menu, follow these steps:

1. Right-click the Start button at the lower-left corner of your screen and click Properties.

2. Click the Customize button that appears.

3. On the General tab, change the number of programs that can be displayed from 6 to a higher number. You can move the number allowed up to 30. Click OK.

I want to make a document appear permanently on the Start menu.

Operating Systems Affected   Windows XP Professional and Home Editions are affected.

Cause   You can make a document, file, application, or just about anything appear on the Start menu permanently instead of as a temporary item. This action, called "pinning," makes the item always appear on the Start menu until you remove it at a later time.

The Pain Killer   To pin an item to the Start menu, follow these steps:

1. Click Start.

2. Look on the Start menu for the item you want to pin. If it is there, right-click the item that you want to appear permanently on the Start menu and

click Pin to Start Menu. The item moves up to the permanent "pinned" item section of the Start menu and will remain there until you remove it. Items on the left side of the Start menu are pinned and unpinned items. Items above the divider bar are already pinned, while items underneath it are recently used items that can be pinned to the Start menu, if you so choose. The right side of the Start menu contains commonly accessed items, such as My Computer, My Documents, and so on. These items appear by default on the Start menu, so they do not need to be pinned.

3. If the item you want to pin is not on the Start menu, such as a document or a file, you can simply drag the document or file to the Start button. This will create a shortcut to the item on the Start menu (but will not move or change your original document or file.)

4. Now, click the Start menu again. You can see that the item is listed in the pinned section of the Start menu. Documents or files that you drag to the Start menu are automatically pinned there until you decide to remove them, which you can do by right-clicking them and clicking Remove from This List.

I can't drag and drop items on the Start menu.

Operating Systems Affected   Windows XP Professional and Home Editions are affected.

Cause   Windows XP allows you to drag and drop items on the Start menu. For example, let's say you are working on a document. You want that document to appear on the Start menu so that you can easily access it while you are working on it. No problem, just drag and drop the document on the Start button. This creates a "shortcut" to your document—it does not actually move the document to the Start menu but just creates a shortcut to it. If you can't drag and drop items, then you simply need to turn on the drag and drop feature.

The Pain Killer   To turn on dragging and dropping on the Start menu, follow these steps:

1. Right-click the Start button at the lower-left corner of your screen and click Properties.

2. Click the Customize button.

3. On the Customize Start Menu window, click the Advanced tab.

4. In the Start menu items portion of the window, locate the check box called Enable Dragging and Dropping. Click the check box so that a check appears. Click OK and OK again. You can now drag and drop items on your Start menu.

 ## My Control Panel icons do not appear as menu items on the Start menu.

Operating Systems Affected   Windows XP Professional and Home Editions are affected.

Cause   By default, Windows XP will show the Control Panel on the Start menu as a "link." This means that you have to click the Control Panel to open it from the Start menu. However, you can change this link behavior to a menu so that you can access Control Panel icons directly from the Start menu. When you point to Control Panel on the Start menu, a submenu will pop out showing the icons.

The Pain Killer   To change the link behavior so that you see a Control Panel menu, just follow these steps:

1. With your mouse, right-click the Start menu and click Properties.

2. In the Properties menu that appears, click the Start Menu tab, and then click the Customize button.

3. In the Customize Start Menu window, click the Advanced tab.

4. In the Start Menu Items box, click the Display as a Menu radio button and click the OK button.

5. Click OK again on the Start menu and the taskbar properties window.

6. Now, click Start and point to Control Panel. A pop-out menu now appears so that you can directly access Control Panel icons.

TIP   *If there are other items that do not work the way you think they should, always check the Advanced tab. There are a number of setting options here that you can use by simply clicking to enable them.*

Taskbar Headaches

The taskbar runs along the bottom of your screen and provides three different items—the Start menu, the taskbar area, and the notification area, as you can see in the following illustration. You already know about the Start menu, so I'll quickly define the other two:

![Taskbar illustration showing start button, XP Headaches CH 1..., untitled - Paint, Calculator, and notification area with 11:00 AM Tuesday]

- **Taskbar area**   The taskbar area takes up most of the taskbar and shows you what programs are currently open, as you can see in the preceding illustration. You can click an item on the taskbar and bring it to the foreground to use. For example, if I am working with a Word document, I can easily switch to the calculator by just clicking it on the taskbar. Once I close a program, the program disappears from the taskbar.

- **Notification area**   The notification area, which used to be called the System Tray, appears in the right-hand corner of the screen. It contains your clock and possibly several other icons of items that are currently in use. For example, if you print an item, your Printer icon will appear here. The notification area keeps you informed about processes that are running on your system.

The good news is that the taskbar is usually easy and problem free, but there are a couple of XP Headaches you might want to know about. Check out the following sections!

I can't get the taskbar to do what I want.

Operating Systems Affected   Windows XP Professional and Home Editions are affected.

Cause   The taskbar is governed by settings, just like any component of Windows XP. You can make some changes to those settings so that the taskbar will operate in a way that is right for you.

The Pain Killer   To change the taskbar's settings, just follow these steps:

1. Right-click an empty area of the taskbar and click Properties. If you have trouble, open the Control Panel and double-click Taskbar and Start menu.

2. On the Taskbar tab, as you can see in the illustration, you have several different settings that you can change by clicking the check boxes. A few important ones to note are

   ■ **Auto-hide the Taskbar** This option makes the taskbar disappear when you are not using it. To see it, just move your mouse to the bottom of the screen and it will appear.

   ■ **Show Quick Launch** Quick Launch is a small section of the taskbar that holds Internet Explorer and other popular programs. It was available on other Windows operating systems but does not appear by default in XP. You can make it appear by clicking the check box.

   ■ **Hide Inactive Icons** The notification area holds a number of icons, which can get in the way and make the taskbar kind of junky. The Hide Inactive Icons option, which is selected by default, hides the icons until you click the arrow on the taskbar to make them appear.

3. Make any selections that you want and click OK. Remember that you can return to this page at any time and make additional changes.

How can I make the taskbar stay in one place?

Operating Systems Affected   Windows XP Professional and Home Editions are affected.

Cause   The taskbar can be moved to the side or top of your screen by simply dragging it there. If you do not want a user on your computer to be able to move the taskbar, you can lock it into place.

The Pain Killer   To lock the taskbar, just follow these steps:

- ■ Right-click an empty area of the taskbar and click the Lock the Taskbar option.

- ■ You can also lock the taskbar by accessing the taskbar and Start menu properties and clicking the Lock the Taskbar option on the Taskbar tab.

Power Configuration Headaches

Windows XP is designed to conserve power when it is running. Using a number of advanced power management features, Windows XP can automatically power down portions of your system when they are not in use, and it can even put itself into a hibernation state. All of these features are very important, but they can cause you some Headaches. The following sections explore these.

 ## Windows XP keeps turning the monitor off.

Operating Systems Affected   Windows XP Professional and Home Editions are affected.

Cause   Windows XP uses a default power scheme that helps conserve energy. A typical default setting is for XP to turn off your monitor after 20 minutes of inactivity. You can turn the monitor on again by simply moving your mouse. If you want to stop this behavior or adjust it, you can easily do so.

The Pain Killer   To adjust power options, just follow these steps:

1. Click Start | Control Panel.

2. Double-click Power Options.

TIP *If you don't see Power Options, you need to click the Switch to Classic View option in the left Control Panel pane. Then, you'll see the Power Options.*

3. On the Power Schemes tab, shown in the illustration, you can change the monitor and hard disks turn-off value. You can also use the Power Schemes drop-down menu and choose a different scheme that might work well for you. The schemes simply preconfigure the monitor and hard disks turn-off features, but you can manually change them to whatever you want.

4. Click OK to save your changes.

Power Options Properties

Power Schemes | Advanced | Hibernate | UPS

Select the power scheme with the most appropriate settings for this computer. Note that changing the settings below will modify the selected scheme.

Power schemes

Home/Office Desk

Save As... | Delete

Settings for Home/Office Desk power scheme

Turn off monitor: After 20 mins

Turn off hard disks: Never

System standby: After 1 hour

System hibernates: Never

OK | Cancel | Apply

TIP *Some computer manufacturers make changes to the power options so that the features are specific to the hardware they use. Don't let this confuse you—you should still see the same power options and features.*

My computer does not hibernate.

Operating Systems Affected Windows XP Professional and Home Editions are affected.

Cause Windows XP supports a hibernate feature. This feature enables Windows XP to write data that is currently in memory to the hard disk and power itself down when not in use. When you bring the computer out of hibernation, the applications and documents are the same as when you left them—even though the computer has been shut down. In order to support hibernation, your computer must support the Advanced Configuration Power Interface (ACPI), which must be supported on your computer's hardware. If it is supported, then a Hibernate tab appears in Power Options. If not, you have to have your computer's BIOS upgraded, if possible. If the Hibernate tab does appear, then you simply have to turn on the feature.

The Pain Killer   To turn on the hibernation feature, just follow these steps:

1. Click Start | Control Panel.

2. Double-click Power Options.

3. Click the Hibernate tab.

4. Click the Enable Hibernation button, shown here.

5. Click the Power Schemes tab. Use the drop-down menu under System Hibernates to determine how much time should pass before hibernation occurs.

Notification Area Headaches

The notification area is the little portion of your taskbar that appears on the lower-right side of your screen. It is designed to show you the clock and a number of other startup programs and processes that occur as you use Windows XP. That's both good and bad, because you can get too many items appearing in the notification area, which makes it look like a junk store. The following Headaches and solutions show you how to fix some common aggravations.

I don't like how the notification area behaves.

Operating Systems Affected   Windows XP Professional and Home Editions are affected.

Cause   The notification area is configured by default to hide icons when they are not in use, along with some other basic settings. You can easily change these, however.

The Pain Killer   To change the notification area behavior, follow these steps:

1. Right-click the clock in the notification area and click Customize Notifications.

2. In the dialog box that appears, you see the items that appear in the notification area. Click an item and you'll see a menu option where you can determine how the item behaves, such as auto-hiding, always appearing, and so forth.

3. Click OK when you're done.

Old stuff I no longer use keeps appearing in the notification area.

Operating Systems Affected   Windows XP Professional and Home Editions are affected.

Cause   The notification area keeps a history of past used items, and those items may appear in the notification area, even though you don't use them any longer. In order to stop this behavior, you have to edit the Registry.

CAUTION   *Editing the Registry is a serious action that can cause many problems in Windows XP if you do not carry it out correctly. If you have no experience editing the registry, you should visit http://support.microsoft.com/kb/322756 and explore the process before attempting these steps.*

The Pain Killer   To remove old notification area items, follow these steps:

1. Click Start | Run. Type **regedit** and click OK.

2. In the Registry editor, navigate to HKEY_CURRENT_USER\Software\ Microsoft\Windows\CurrentVersion\Explorer\TrayNotify. In the right-hand pane, examine the data values.

3. Right-click IconStreams in the right-hand pane and click Delete.

4. Right-click PastIconStreams in the right-hand pane and click Delete.

5. Close the Registry Editor and restart your computer.

Balloon Tips are driving me crazy!

Operating Systems Affected   Windows XP Professional and Home Editions are affected.

Cause   Balloon Tips are a Windows XP feature designed to help you. They pop up when you point to things and tell you about them. However, this help quickly becomes a big frustration. You can stop Balloon Tips from working by editing the Registry.

> **CAUTION**   *Editing the Registry is a serious action that can cause many problems in Windows XP if you do not carry it out correctly. If you have no experience editing the registry, you should visit http://support.microsoft.com/kb/ 322756 and explore the process before attempting these steps.*

The Pain Killer   To remove Balloon Tips, follow these steps:

1. Click Start | Run. Type **regedit** and click OK.

2. In the Registry editor, navigate to HKEY_CURRENT_USER\Software\ Microsoft\Windows\CurrentVersion\Explorer\TrayNotify.

3. Right-click the BallonTip value and click Modify.

4. In the modification dialog box that appears, enter a value of **0**.

5. Close the Registry editor, then log off Windows and log back on again.

Chapter 2

Windows XP File and Folder Headaches

In this chapter, you'll cure...

- ■ Problems with Windows XP folders

- ■ Trouble with Windows XP files

- ■ Offline files and folder pains

- ■ Recycle Bin blues

- ■ Cluttered operating system and hard disk

Whenever information is created and saved—whether that is a document, a picture, a spreadsheet, or just about anything else—that item is saved as a file. A file can then be opened by certain applications that were written to open that kind of file. A folder is an electronic storage place in which you can organize and keep files. Sounds simple enough, huh? No, not really. Although file and folder usage is quite simple on the surface, there are a number of underlying configuration problems and issues that, quite frankly, can be real sources of headaches. In this chapter, you'll find out all about common file and folder Headaches and how to solve those painful problems. Keep in mind that if the problem you are experiencing is not explicitly listed in this chapter, make sure you read about Headaches that are most similar to yours—you still may be able to solve the problem.

Folder Headaches

As I mentioned in the introduction, folders are Windows XP containers that are designed to hold files and other folders. The purpose of folders, as you might guess, is to organize information. Just as a filing cabinet needs folders in order to structure information in a logical, useful way, Windows XP uses folders to help you store and locate information. In fact, Windows XP even uses its own internal folders to keep operating system files organized and accessible to system files and applications. Windows XP tries to help you manage information by giving you a basic folder, My Documents, which also contains My Music and My Pictures. Windows XP is smart enough to understand different types of files, and it will try to help you organize your information. For example, Windows XP can recognize a picture file and will prompt you to save the file in the My Pictures folder. You don't have to do that, of course, but this is another example of Windows XP trying to help you.

Basically, folders are a mainstay of information management, and your use of them can make your work with Windows XP much, much easier. The following

Headaches are common problems and solutions you are likely to experience when using folders and creating your own folders.

I can't create a new folder.

Operating Systems Affected   Windows XP Professional and Home Editions are affected.

Cause   Folders can be created directly on your desktop by right-clicking an empty area of the desktop and clicking New | Folder. They can also be created within any folder by clicking File | New | Folder. However, in order to create a new folder, you must actually be in a current folder, or else the option does not appear on the File menu. For example, you cannot create a new folder while you are working in an application, such as Microsoft Word. Also, some folders do not allow you to create subfolders. An example is My Computer. My Computer, which you can find on your Start menu, is a special folder that contains drives on your computer. If you click the File menu in My Computer, there is no option to create a new folder.

> **TIP**   *Now, I just said that you cannot create a new folder from within an application—technically, that may not be true. For example, if you are using Word, you can click File | Open or File | Save As, which opens a mini-explorer window. You'll see a button option there to create a new folder. When you perform this action, you are actually getting back out of the Word application and you are working with Windows again.*

The Pain Killer   To fix the problem, make sure you are trying to create a new folder on your desktop, or you are trying to create a new folder using the File menu in a folder that supports subfolders.

Things in my folders are too big/small.

Operating Systems Affected   Windows XP Professional and Home Editions are affected.

Cause   In order to be all things to all people, Windows XP supports a number of different folder features. For example, you can see the icons in a simple list, by small icons, by thumbnails, and a number of other options. If the icons are too big, you have to scroll all over the place to see what is in the folder—if things are too small, you may have difficulty seeing them. No problem, though. You can easily change how things look in your folders.

The Pain Killer   On the folder that you want to change, just click the View menu on the top toolbar. You see a section containing different file view options, as you can see in Figure 2-1. Just choose the option you want by clicking it. You can return to this menu at any time and try a different setting.

If you would rather not use the View menu, there is also a View icon on the toolbar. Just click it and select the view you want!

Files in a folder do not tell the size, type, and so forth.

Operating Systems Affected   Windows XP Professional and Home Editions are affected.

Cause   Windows XP gives you a number of options that can be displayed with a file. For example, let's say you are looking at a bunch of files in a folder. With the right configuration, you can see not only the names of the files, but also their size, their type, who created them, and other details. You can easily determine what details you want to display for files in a folder.

The Pain Killer   To make changes to the details settings of files, open the folder and click the View menu. Click the Choose Details option. A Choose Details

 FIGURE 2-1   Use the View menu to change icon size and appearance.

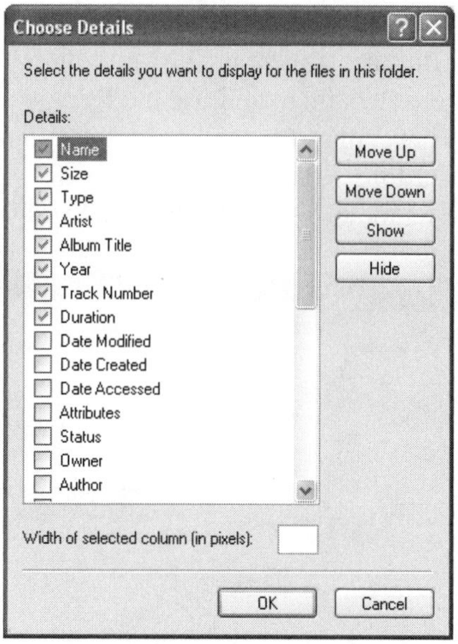

Choose Details

Select the details you want to display for the files in this folder.

Details:

- ☑ Name
- ☑ Size
- ☑ Type
- ☑ Artist
- ☑ Album Title
- ☑ Year
- ☑ Track Number
- ☑ Duration
- ☐ Date Modified
- ☐ Date Created
- ☐ Date Accessed
- ☐ Attributes
- ☐ Status
- ☐ Owner
- ☐ Author

Move Up
Move Down
Show
Hide

Width of selected column (in pixels):

OK   Cancel

FIGURE 2-2   Choose Details options

window appears, as you can see in Figure 2-2. Click the details you want presented with the file and click OK. You can come back to this window and change the detail items you want to see at any time.

I can't see the items I need on my folder toolbars.

Operating Systems Affected   Windows XP Professional and Home Editions are affected.

Cause   Folder toolbars contain a number of management buttons, such as Back, Forward, Address, Search, and others. If you need certain items to appear on the toolbar that do not appear there, you have two different painkillers you can use.

The Pain Killer   First, click the View menu in the folder and check out the Toolbar menu, status bar, and Explorer bar menu. The Toolbar menu and Explorer bar menu give you additional menu features you can click in order to display. If you do not find the item that you need there, or if you want to create a customized toolbar for the folder, follow these steps:

1. In the desired folder, click View | Toolbars | Customize.

2. You see the Customize Toolbar window. Scroll through the Available Toolbar Buttons and use the Add button to add the ones you want to the Current Toolbar Buttons. If there are any current toolbar buttons that you do not want to use, select them and use the Remove button. Continue this process until you have all of the toolbar buttons you want to use in the Current Toolbar Buttons window. Notice also the two check box options at the bottom of the window. You can use these to adjust button text and size.

Customize Toolbar		? X
Available toolbar buttons:	Current toolbar buttons:	Close
Separator	Search	Reset
Stop	Folders	
Refresh	Separator	
Home	Add ->	Views	
Map Drive	<- Remove	Separator	Move Up
Disconnect		Move Down
Text options:	Selective text on right	
Icon options:	Large icons	

3. When you are done, simply click Close. The options you selected now appear on the toolbar.

> **NOTE**
> *As you have probably noticed in this section, most every important folder configuration option is found on the View menu. If you are having problems with a folder's appearance for functionality, the View menu is always your starting point to solve the problem.*

My folders do not look the way I want them to.

Operating Systems Affected   Windows XP Professional and Home Editions are affected.

Cause   Windows XP folders have a number of different appearance features—some of which you may like and some of which you may not. No matter, you can change most anything about the way your folders look, and you can solve this problem in a few different places.

The Pain Killer   To make the folder look the way you want, follow these steps:

1. In the desired folder, click View | Customize This Folder. This action opens the Customize tab of the folder's properties pages, shown in the

illustration. You can choose a folder template if one is needed (such as
pictures, music, and so forth). If the
folder is just for a mix of files or
documents, choose the Documents
option. Notice that you can have all
subfolders also use the template by
clicking the check box.

2. Next, notice that you can put a
picture on the folder in order to
remind you of what is held in the
folder. Click Choose Picture if you
want to change this option. Finally,
you can have the folder displayed
with a different icon by clicking the
Change Icon button. When you are
done, just click OK.

NOTE *The following steps assume you are using the Classic view of Control Panel.
If you are not sure if you are using the Classic view of Control Panel, click
Start | Control Panel. In the left window pane, click the Switch to Classic
View option.*

3. You can also change the way folders provide you with information. Open
Control Panel and open Folder Options (which is also available in any folder
by clicking Tools | Folder Options).
This opens the Folder Options
window. Take a look at the General
tab. Notice that you can use the
Common Tasks feature (which
displays the Tasks features along the
left side of the window). You can get
rid of this by clicking the Use
Windows Classic Folders option. In
the Browse section, you can have
each folder open in the same window
or have each folder open in its own
window. Finally, you can use the
single-click or double-click feature.
Make any selections you want to try.

4. Click the View menu. You'll see check boxes for a number of Advanced Settings. For example, you can choose to show hidden files and folders, show file extensions, show Control Panel in My Computer, show encrypted or compressed NTFS files in color, and make a number of other settings. You can read through this list and enable or disable any folder features that you want by clicking the check box. If you don't know what a setting means, right-click the setting and click What's This. If you are still not sure if you should change the setting, then don't. The default settings are usually right for most people. When you're done, click OK.

TIP   *One setting you might consider changing is the Show File Extensions setting. This feature puts the extension on the end of a file. For example, let's say you have a JPEG file called "dog." Under the default setting, you only see the filename, but if you choose to show file extensions, the file appears as dog.jpeg. Since you can see all file extensions, you can often head off file type confusion.*

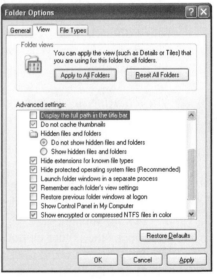

TIP   *Have you tried some of these settings and now you are having a lot of problems? Don't despair. You can put everything back like it was before you made the changes by clicking the Restore Defaults button on the View tab of Folder Options.*

My folders are taking up too much room on my hard disk, or I need to keep other users from looking in my folders.

Operating Systems Affected   Windows XP Professional and Home Editions are affected.

Cause   The more data you have stored in folders, the more hard disk space is consumed. This is particularly true for multimedia files, such as pictures, music, and video, which consume a lot of megabytes on the hard disk. The good news is that Windows XP supports a compression feature that reduces overall folder size, which helps conserve hard disk space. Once you compress the folder, you can still use it just as you normally would.

If multiple people use your computer, or if your computer is on a network and you are worried about someone looking at files in your folders, you can also encrypt folders so that no one can view what is inside except you. To you, the folders and files appear the same, but if anyone else tries to access them, he or she gets an Access Denied message.

> **TIP** *Compression and encryption are not compatible with each other. You can compress a folder or you can encrypt a folder, but you cannot do both. Also, compression and encryption only work on NTFS-formatted drives— not FAT32. If your hard drive is not formatted with NTFS, you can't use compression or encryption. If you want to learn how to convert a FAT32 drive to NTFS, see Chapter 6. It should also be noted here that compressed folders are not the same as zipped folders, which can be compressed with the popular WinZip utility. WinZip works on either FAT or NTFS folders. You can learn more about WinZip and even download a trial version at http://www.winzip.com.*

The Pain Killer To use compression or encryption on a folder, follow these steps:

1. In the folder that you want to compress or encrypt, click File | Properties.

> **NOTE** *Encryption is not available on the Home Edition of XP. You'll see the option listed, but it is grayed out.*

2. The properties pages appear. On the General tab, click the Advanced button. (If the Advanced button is not there, the folder is on a FAT32 drive. Compression and encryption are not available on FAT32 drives.)

3. Click the Compress Contents check box to compress the folder. If you want to encrypt the folder, click the Encrypt Contents check box. Click OK and OK on the General tab. You can remove the compression or encryption at any time by returning to this window and removing the check from the box.

File Headaches

For the most part, dealing with files is rather easy. You either open and use them or you close and store them in a folder. It doesn't get more complicated beyond that, but there are a few Headaches you may encounter when dealing with files. The fix for them, however, is easy!

The wrong program opens a file.

Operating Systems Affected   Windows XP Professional and Home Editions are affected.

Cause   Windows XP is able to understand file extensions and therefore take a guess at the program you might want to use in order to work with the file. For example, Windows XP knows that mypic.jpeg is a picture file, and Windows XP uses Windows Picture and Fax Viewer to open the file. The problem is that Windows XP's guesses may be wrong and you may want a different program to open a particular file.

The Pain Killer   To solve the file/program problem, follow these steps:

1. Right-click the file that is giving you problems and click Open With | Choose Program. If the Open With option does not appear, click Open.

2. In the Open With window, choose the program to use. If you always want Windows to open the same kind of file with the same program, select the Always Use the Selected Program to Open This Kind of File check box. If the program you want to use is not listed, click the Browse button to locate it. Click OK when you are done.

3. You can also configure the same option using the Folder Options icon in Control Panel. Open the icon and click the File Types tab.

4. In the File Types window, shown in the illustration, locate the file type. For example, if I want to make certain that all JPEG files are opened with Internet Explorer, I would locate JPEG in the list, select it, and click the Change button to select Internet Explorer. From now on, all JPEG files will be automatically opened by Internet Explorer. Click OK when you are done.

 NOTE   *If you want to change a file/ program association, you can make the change in either of the two ways previously described—you don't have to do both in order to make the change.*

I copied a picture file from the Internet, but Windows cannot open it and does not seem to know that the file is a picture file.

Operating Systems Affected   Windows XP Professional and Home Editions are affected.

Cause   Sometimes, a file arrives from the Internet when you choose to download it without the right kind of file extension. Windows XP does not know what kind of file the file is or what to do with the file without an extension.

The Pain Killer   In most cases, all you need to do is right-click the file and rename it with a valid extension. For example, let's say you download a picture file named Picture. Simply right-click the File icon, click Rename, and give the photo the name of picture.jpg (or you can try picture.bmp). This will help Windows XP identify the file as a picture file so that programs can open the file. If this does not work, try downloading the file again in case there were transmission problems or errors.

> TIP
>
> *Like folders, you can also compress or encrypt individual files. Simply right-click the file and click Properties. On the General tab of the properties pages, click the Advanced button. The file must be located on an NTFS drive in order for compression or encryption to work.*

Offline Files Headaches

Windows XP supports offline files. The Offline Files feature enables you to connect to resources on a network and make the file available locally on your computer. Should you become disconnected from the network, you can continue to use the file because it is located on your hard drive. If you have made changes to the file, such as in the case of a shared network file that several people are using, then the Offline Files feature runs a synchronization process when you are connected to the network again so that the file located on your computer is the same as the network file. Overall, offline files can be very helpful, but they can cause you some headaches. It is important to note here that Windows XP Home Edition does not technically support Offline Files, although the Synchronization tool enables you to connect to and synchronize a web site with your desktop PC. The following sections primarily apply to Windows XP Professional, and point those Headaches out and solve them for you!

 ## I can't get Offline Files to work.

Operating Systems Affected   Windows XP Professional is affected.

Cause   Offline Files has to be turned on and configured before you can use it on your computer.

The Pain Killer   To turn on and configure Offline Files, follow these steps:

1. To set up Offline Files, open Folder Options in Control Panel and click the Offline Files tab.

2. On the Offline Files tab, click the Enable Offline Files check box. You can then make some additional configurations as desired. For example, you can choose to have Windows synchronize offline files when you log on/log off, and even the amount of disk space that offline files can use.

3. When you are done, click OK.

4. You can now access the desired network resource, right-click it, and click Make Available Offline.

TIP *Offline Files is not compatible with Fast User Switching. In order to set up Offline Files, you must first disable Fast User Switching with the Users icon in Control Panel. See Chapter 3 to learn more about User Headaches.*

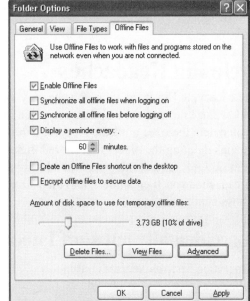

XP HEADACHE Offline Files does not synchronize the way I want it to.

Operating Systems Affected   Windows XP Professional is affected.

Cause   Offline Files follow a basic synchronization routine, depending on what items you have selected on the Offline Files tab of Folder Options. You can make adjustments on this tab, but you can also use the Synchronization tool to manage synchronization.

The Pain Killer   To make changes to the way Offline Files synchronize, follow these steps:

1. Click Start | All Programs | Accessories | Synchronize.

2. In the Synchronization window, you see your offline files. If you want to stop synchronizing an offline file, simply clear its check box and the file will no longer be synchronized, as shown in the illustration.

3. If you want to change the way items are synchronized, click the Setup button. You'll see some tabs that enable you to

determine when synchronization should occur, and you can even create a schedule if you like.

Recycle Bin Headaches

The Recycle Bin is the icon you see on your desktop where you put junk you do not want. Files and folders that you place in the Recycle Bin are held there until you delete them, or until the Recycle Bin gets too full, in which case Windows XP begins deleting the oldest files stored there to make room for new ones being added. As a general rule, the Recycle Bin is trouble free, but there may be a few Headaches you'll encounter, and the following sections tell you about the cures for those headaches.

I accidentally put stuff I need in the Recycle Bin.

Operating Systems Affected   Windows XP Professional and Home Editions are affected.

Cause   People often accidentally put items in the Recycle Bin that do not belong there when dragging and dropping. The good news is that the Recycle Bin is just a folder, and is mostly like other folders on your computer. Since the Recycle Bin does not automatically delete items when they are put in the folder, you can get the files back.

The Pain Killer   Open Recycle Bin and drag the file(s) you want to keep out of the Recycle Bin and to another place on your computer, such as My Documents. The file(s) has not been harmed in any way.

I accidentally emptied the Recycle Bin, but I need the items back.

Operating Systems Affected   Windows XP Professional and Home Editions are affected.

Cause   If you accidentally empty the Recycle Bin, the items in the Recycle Bin are erased from your hard drive.

The Pain Killer   I'm afraid this is one headache that Windows cannot solve. Once you empty the Recycle Bin, the items are gone. However, there may be a workaround. Some third-party utilities are available that can recover items, even after you empty them from the Recycle Bin. There are a number of tools available, some

even for free, such as the Restorer 2000, which you can download from http://
www.bitmart.net/r2k.htm. You can also purchase other Undelete utilities from your
favorite computer store.

My Recycle Bin keeps items for too long, taking up too much disk space.

Operating Systems Affected   Windows XP Professional and Home Editions are
affected.

Cause   By default, Windows XP uses 10 percent of your computer's hard drive(s)
for Recycle Bin storage. When the Recycle Bin reaches near capacity, it begins
deleting items to stay under the 10-percent mark. If you think 10 percent is too
much, you can do one of two things.

The Pain Killer   First, simply right-click the Recycle Bin and click Empty Recycle
Bin to remove items. If you do not want to manually remove items, you can lower
the amount of storage space that is used for the Recycle Bin. Simply right-click
Recycle Bin and click Properties. On the Global tab, change the amount of disk
space that is used from 10 percent to a lower value by moving the slider bar, as
shown in Figure 2-3. Click OK when you are done.

FIGURE 2-3   Adjust the settings on the Global tab.

Every time I put an item in the Recycle Bin, Windows gives me the Are You Sure box. How can I get rid of this confirmation box?

Operating Systems Affected   Windows XP Professional and Home Editions are affected.

Cause   Windows XP tries to make sure that you want an item in the Recycle Bin before you put it there. However, these confirmation messages can get to be a real pain. Fortunately, you can stop the message behavior.

The Pain Killer   To stop the confirmation message from appearing, right-click Recycle Bin and click Properties. On the Global tab, clear the check box at the bottom of the screen, as shown in Figure 2-3, that says Display Delete Confirmation Dialog. You will not see the message again when dragging items to the Recycle Bin.

I don't want Windows to put items in the Recycle Bin—I want them automatically deleted.

Operating Systems Affected   Windows XP Professional and Home Editions are affected.

Cause   Windows XP's default behavior is to put items in the Recycle Bin. This gives you a fail-safe so that you can get files back in the event that you make a mistake. However, if you do not want the Recycle Bin to be used, you can have files immediately deleted when you put them in the Recycle Bin. Again, let me warn you that you'll have no protection under this configuration.

The Pain Killer   To have files immediately deleted without using Recycle Bin storage, right-click Recycle Bin and click Properties. On the Global tab, click the Do Not Move Files to the Recycle Bin check box. Click OK. At this point, files are automatically deleted when you put them in the Recycle Bin.

Cleaning Up the Junk

Files are used by essentially everything on Windows XP. In fact, Windows XP itself is made up of files. However, the more files you use, the more cluttered your operating system and hard disk can become. As such, it is a good idea to clean up some of the file junk from time to time in order to keep Windows XP running more quickly and cleanly. Here are a few cleanup problems and solutions you should put to work.

How can I get rid of temporary files?

Operating Systems Affected   Windows XP Professional and Home Editions are affected.

Cause   Windows XP maintains a folder of temporary files. These are files used by programs as well as the operating system and other processes. However, over time, the temporary files tend to stack up and junk up Windows XP. Temporary files are held in the Temp folder, and you should get in the habit of cleaning it out from time to time, such as once a month.

The Pain Killer   To clean out the Temp folder, follow these steps:

1. Click Start | My Computer.

2. Right-click the desired hard drive and click Properties.

3. On the General tab, click the Disk Cleanup button.

4. The utility will perform a check on your system and eventually display a dialog box showing the different categories of temporary files that can be deleted and the amount of disk space you can gain by deleting the files in each category. Review the dialog box and select the check box next to each category you want to clean up, such as the Temporary files.

5. Complete the wizard and the Temp folder will be cleaned.

Aside from using Disk Cleanup to clean the Temp folder, you can also clean it manually be simply opening the Temp folder and deleting everything inside. This is a safe procedure, since Windows XP will automatically re-create temp files that it needs as you use Windows XP. Do this:

1. Click Start | Run. In the dialog box that appears, type **C:\Windows\Temp** and click OK.

2. This opens the Temp folder. You can delete everything in the Temp folder, including all subfolders. Click Edit | Select All, then just press DELETE on your keyboard.

TIP *You can also use a number of third-party utilities that will automatically clean the Temp folder on a periodic basis. You can find one of these free utilities at http://www.snapfiles.com/get/tempcleaner.html.*

Does my PreFetch Folder slow me down?

Operating Systems Affected   Windows XP Professional and Home Editions are affected.

Cause   In an attempt to make programs start faster, Windows XP keeps certain portions of a program's startup files in a folder called Prefetch. There has been a lot of controversy about the Prefetch folder. While the process can help Windows XP start programs faster, does the Prefetch folder also junk up your system? Possibly so, and there doesn't seem to be a definitive answer on the subject. However, you can easily clean your Prefetch folder and see if it makes a performance difference on your system. Note that when you clean the prefetch folder, some programs will start more slowly the first time they are opened because Windows XP will rebuild the needed files in the Prefetch folder for that program. This fix may be useful if you have used a lot of programs in the past that you no longer use, but if you tend to use the same programs over and over, cleaning the Prefetch folder will probably not help you.

The Pain Killer   To clean the Prefetch folder, follow these steps:

1.   Click Start | Run. In the dialog box that appears, type **C:\Windows\ Prefetch**.

2.   In the Prefetch folder, click Edit | Select All. Then, right-click the selected files and click Delete, or just press the DELETE key on your keyboard.

Chapter 3

Windows XP User Headaches

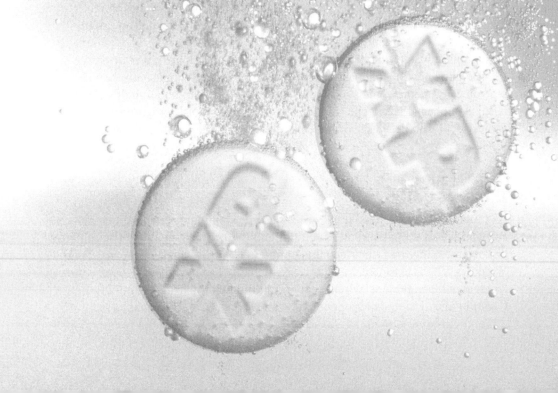

In this chapter, you'll cure...

- User problems
- Password difficulties
- Account feature pains

Windows XP provides people access to the computer through a user account. A user account is simply a way for Windows XP to know who you are, if you have the correct permission to access the computer, and what permission you have to make changes to the computer. When Windows XP is installed, a default "administrator" account is created. This account gives you full access to the computer so you can do anything and make any changes you want. If you are a home user and you are the only one accessing your computer, then you do not need to do anything else. However, what if you want your children to use the computer, but not make any configuration changes? What if you are in a small office and seven people need to use the computer?

You can easily solve these questions using different accounts. When you create different accounts, each user has his or her own folder. Documents, computer settings, e-mail, and Internet Explorer settings all remain in your private folder structure and cannot be accessed by anyone else. Changes you make to the computer are not given to anyone else either. For example, this feature let's one person use the Windows XP background while another uses a neon pink background; no matter, all settings are kept separate, and the other user's settings are not interfered with.

The good news is that user configuration and settings are usually trouble free, but you can run into some sticky spots, which you'll learn about in this chapter. Also, a number of Headache solutions in this chapter only apply to Windows XP Professional, since the user management features in the Home Edition are more limited.

User Headaches

As I mentioned, each person who accesses your computer can be given a user account, which keeps everyone's settings and information separate. You can create an account using the User Accounts option in Control Panel. If you are using Windows XP Professional, you can also use the Local Users and Groups option in Computer Management, which is found in the Administrative Tools folder in Control Panel. Using either option, you can solve user problems and issues.

I can't create a new user account.

Operating Systems Affected   Windows XP Professional and Home Editions are affected.

Cause   If you cannot create a new account on a Windows XP computer, the problem involves permissions. More than likely, you are not logged onto the computer with an administrator account. The administrator account is the initial account that was created when you installed Windows XP. You can also use a different user account that you might have created later.

If you do not have proper permissions, you will see options to change your account only when you open User Accounts in Control Panel, as shown in Figure 3-1.

> **NOTE**   *I will assume you are using the Classic view of Control Panel (which enables you to see all icons). If you are not sure if you are using the Classic view of Control Panel, click Start | Control Panel. In the left window pane, click the Switch to Classic View option.*

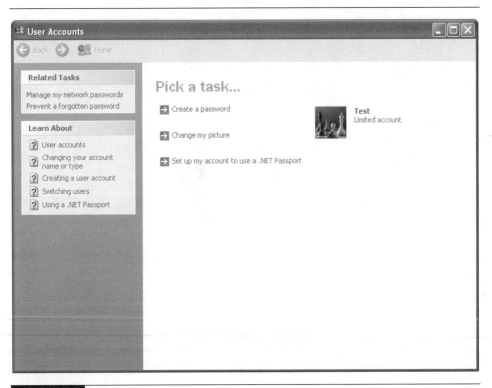

FIGURE 3-1   User management

As you can see in the figure, I can only create a password, change my picture, or set up my account to use a .NET Passport. I cannot create a new user or change any other user's account. So, you'll have to log off the computer and log back on with an administrator account.

The Pain Killer Once you have logged off the computer and logged back on with an administrator account, follow these steps to create a new user:

1. Click Start | Control Panel | User Accounts.

2. In the User Accounts window, click the Create a New Account option.

3. In the Name the New Account screen, enter a desired account name. This is the name you will see on the Welcome screen and on the Start menu. Click Next.

4. In the Pick an Account Type screen, choose either Computer Administrator or Limited. Keep in mind that a computer administrator account can create, change, or delete user accounts; make system changes that affect all users, including adding and removing hardware; install programs; and access all files. A limited user, on the other hand, can only manage his or her own account, files, and folders. Click Create Account.

User Accounts

Back   Home

Learn About

[?] User account types

Pick an account type

○ Computer administrator   ⊙ Limited

With a limited account, you can:
- Change or remove your password
- Change your picture, theme, and other desktop settings
- View files you created
- View files in the Shared Documents folder

Users with limited accounts cannot always install programs. Depending on the program, a user might need administrator privileges to install it.

Also, programs designed prior to Windows XP or Windows 2000 might not work properly with limited accounts. For best results, choose programs bearing the Designed for Windows XP logo, or, to run older programs, choose the "computer administrator" account type.

< Back   Create Account   Cancel

5. The new user account is created and now appears in the User Accounts window.

I can't delete an account.

Operating Systems Affected   Windows XP Professional and Home Editions are affected.

Cause   There are two possible problems if you cannot delete an account:

- You are not logged on with an administrator account.

- You are trying to delete your own administrator account.

The Pain Killer   If you need to delete a user's account, you must log on with an administrator account. If you want to delete your administrator account, you'll have to have someone else with an administrator account do it for you, or you will need to create a new administrator account, log on with that account, and then delete the old one. There must be at least one administrator account on any Windows XP computer.

I can't make a limited account become an administrator account.

Operating Systems Affected   Windows XP Professional and Home Editions are affected.

Cause   If you have created a limited account, you can change that account to an administrator account at a later time if you like. However, in order to change the account, you must log on with an administrator account to change the limited account.

The Pain Killer   To change the limited account to an administrator account, follow these steps:

1. Log on to Windows XP with an administrator account.

2. Click Start | Control Panel | User Accounts.

3. In the User Accounts window, choose the account that you want to change, and then click the Change an Account option.

4. In the What Do You Want to Change About Your Account screen, click the Change My Account Type option, as shown in the illustration.

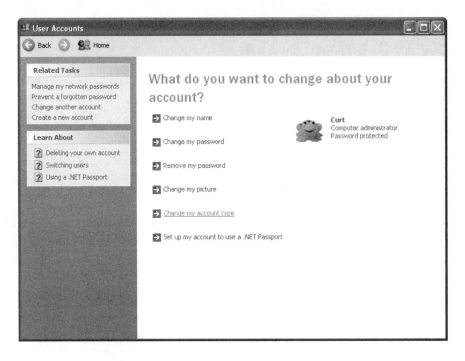

5. In the Pick a New Account Type screen, choose Computer Administrator and click the Change Account Type button.

My account does not work with .NET Passport.

Operating Systems Affected   Windows XP Professional and Home Editions are affected.

Cause   The .NET Passport feature enables you to integrate your user account with Internet sites in a safe way. Essentially, the .NET Passport allows you to sign into various web sites that support .NET Passport with a single user name and password. The idea is to make Web usage easier and uniform with your user account. By default, accounts are not configured for .NET Passport support, but you can easily configure your account.

TIP   *The .NET Passport enables you to store information about yourself that you can provide to web sites without having to type all of the information in those aggravating web forms. It's safe and secure, and is also a great way to surf the Internet.*

The Pain Killer   To configure your account for .NET Passport support, follow these steps:

1. Click Start | Control Panel | User Accounts.

2. In the User Accounts window, click the Change an Account option.

3. If there is more than one user account on your computer, a window appears that allows you to click the account you want to configure. Click the desired account.

NOTE   *This window only appears if you are logged on with the computer administrator account. Additionally, you cannot enable someone else's account for .NET Passport support unless you are logged on with the computer administrator account.*

4. Click the Set Up My Account to Use a .NET Passport option.

5. The .NET Passport Wizard appears. In the first screen, click Next. An Internet connection will be launched if you are not connected already.

6. In the Do You Have an E-mail Address screen, you can choose to use your existing e-mail address or create a new one for free at MSN.com. Make a selection, and then click Next.

.NET Passport Wizard

Do you have an e-mail address?

With a Microsoft® .NET Passport, you can use your e-mail address and a single password to sign in to all participating Web sites and services.

Do you have an e-mail address?

⦿ Yes.

◯ No, I would like to open a free MSN.com e-mail account now.

Don't want free MSN.com e-mail? Just open an e-mail account with another provider and then return to this wizard to register it as your .NET Passport.

[< Back] [Next >] [Cancel]

7. Depending on your selection, you will need to enter your e-mail address or sign up for a free e-mail address. Follow the instructions that appear.

I want a second person to be able to use the computer without the first person having to log out completely.

Operating Systems Affected   Windows XP Professional and Home Editions are affected.

Cause   In some cases, user accounts are necessary, but are a real pain. For example, let's say that a single Windows XP computer is used in an office. Two different people use this computer at various times during the day. However, each person has a different user account. This causes one person to have to close all programs and log off so that the other person can use the computer. Doing this several times a day becomes a real drag.

The Pain Killer   The good news is that Microsoft thought of this problem before they sold XP to you. They provided a good solution called Fast User Switching, which enables one person to log off so that another person can log on with a different account. However, the first person's programs and files remain open. When that user logs back on, everything is just as he or she left it, which is a great feature. To use Fast User Switching, you simply need to turn the feature on. Follow these steps:

1. Log on with an administrator account.

2. Click Start | Control Panel | User Accounts.

3. In the User Accounts window, click the Change the Way Users Log On or
   Off option. In the Select Logon and Logoff Options window, click the Use
   Fast User Switching check box, as shown in the illustration, and then click
   the Apply Options button.

NOTE *Fast User Switching is not compatible with Offline Folders. If you want to
use Offline Folders, you can't use Fast User Switching. See Chapter 2 to
learn more about Offline Folders.*

I don't want to use the Welcome screen.

Operating Systems Affected   Windows XP Professional and Home Editions are
affected.

Cause   By default, Windows XP provides you with the Welcome screen, which
gives an icon and a list of all users. In order to log on, you simply click your user
name and provide your password, if necessary. However, you don't have to use the
Welcome screen if you don't want to. Once removed, a standard Windows logon
dialog box appears, in which you will have to type your user name and password.

TIP *In cases where several people use a computer, such as in an office, you might want to remove the Welcome screen for added security. If you remove the Welcome screen, no one will know the user names of other people who log on to the computer.*

The Pain Killer   To remove the Welcome screen, follow these steps:

1. Log on with an administrator account.

2. Click Start | Control Panel | User Accounts.

3. In the User Accounts window, click the Change the Way Users Log On or Off option. In the Select Logon and Logoff Options window, clear the Use the Welcome Screen check box and click the Apply Options button.

Password Headaches

Dealing with passwords is rather easy in Windows XP, because each user manages his or her own password. In fact, you don't even have to use a password if you don't want to. However, a computer administrator can control passwords and require users to configure a password if necessary. You are unlikely to have many problems working with passwords, but I've included a few Headaches in this section that you might encounter.

Users are able to log on without passwords.

Operating Systems Affected   Windows XP Professional and Home Editions are affected.

Cause   By default, Windows XP allows the creation of user accounts without passwords. Users simply log on by clicking their account on the Welcome screen. Of course, this setup is not at all secure, and if you want to make sure no one logs on with someone else's account, then all users need a password.

The Pain Killer   To configure a password, follow these steps:

1. Log on with the desired account.

2. Click Start | Control Panel | User Accounts.

3. Click the Create a Password option.

4. In the Create a Password for Your Account screen, type your desired password, type it again for confirmation, and then enter a password hint if you like. This hint appears on the Welcome screen to help you remember your password; but all users can see the hint, so be careful that the hint does not give your password away.

User Accounts

Back   Home

Learn About
 Creating a secure password
 Creating a good password hint
 Remembering a password

Create a password for your account

Type a new password:

●●●●●●

Type the new password again to confirm:

●●●●●●

If your password contains capital letters, be sure to type them the same way every time you log on.

Type a word or phrase to use as a password hint:

Favorite pet and favorite numbers

The password hint will be visible to everyone who uses this computer.

[Create Password]   [Cancel]

5. Click Create Password.

Remember, passwords are case sensitive. If you are having problems logging on with your password, make sure the CAPS LOCK *key is not turned on.*

I can't enforce password restrictions.

Operating Systems Affected   Windows XP Professional and Home Editions are affected.

Cause   The default XP behavior allows users to create and modify their own passwords. As an administrator, you can access the User Accounts tool in Control Panel to create a password for a user. However, the user can change the password with the User Accounts tool after he or she logs on. If you are using Windows XP

Home Edition, I'm afraid you are stuck. Users can always create a different password with the User Accounts tool, and there are no direct rules you can enforce. However, if you are using Windows XP Professional, you have an additional tool that you can use to enforce password restrictions.

The Pain Killer   To configure additional password restrictions in Windows XP Professional, follow these steps:

1. Log on with an administrator account.

2. Click Start | Control Panel | Administrative Tools | Computer Management.

3. In the left pane of the Computer Management console, expand Local Users and Groups and select the Users container. You can see a listing of user accounts on your computer in the right pane.

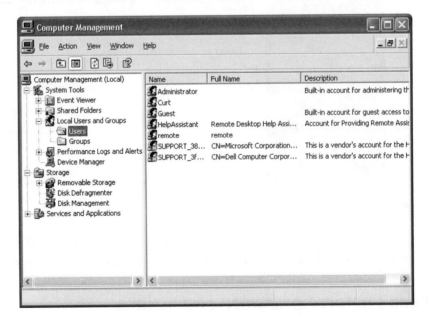

4. Right-click the desired user account and click Properties.

5. On the General tab, you see a list of restriction options. You can make sure that the user has to change his or her password at the next logon, that the user cannot change his or her password, or that the password never expires, as shown in the illustration. Click the desired check box and click OK.

NOTE *If you like using the Local Users and Groups console, you can also create and delete user accounts here without using User Accounts in Control Panel. Just right-click the Users container and click New User. You can delete an account or manage its properties by right-clicking the account icon in the right window pane.*

Curt Properties

General | Member Of | Profile

Curt

Full name:

Description:

☐ User must change password at next logon

☐ User cannot change password

☐ Password never expires

☐ Account is disabled

☐ Account is locked out

OK | Cancel | Apply

When I try to reset a password, a message appears telling me that data will be lost.

Operating Systems Affected Windows XP Professional and Home Editions are affected.

Cause For security reasons, Windows XP ties certain user information directly to the account and password. If a user forgets his or her password, you can choose to reset the password. However, data will be lost if you do so. Specifically, user certificates and web-related passwords, along with basic computer settings, will be lost once the password is reset. There is no workaround for this problem once the password has been forgotten, but you can prevent the loss of data and the reset problems by creating a password reset disk.

The Pain Killer To reset a password without a password reset disk, follow these steps:

1. Log on with an administrator account.

2. Click Start | Control Panel | User Accounts.

3. Select the account that you want to reset.

4. Click the Create a Password option.

5. In the Create a Password screen, create a new password for the user. This will cause the user to lose personal certificates and stored passwords for web sites and network resources.

To create a password reset disk so that manual resetting and loss of data does not occur, follow these steps:

1. Log on with the desired account.

2. Open User Accounts in Control Panel.

3. In the Related Tasks box that appears in the left pane, click the Prevent a Forgotten Password option.

NOTE *You cannot create a password reset disk for another user. You can only create the password reset disk for the account you are currently logged on with. If you try to create it for someone else, the option does not appear in the Related Tasks window.*

4. The Forgotten Password Wizard appears. Click Next on the Welcome screen.

5. Choose the drive, such as your floppy drive, where you want to create the password reset disk and click Next.

6. Enter the current user account password and click Next.

7. The password reset disk is created. Click Next and then click Finish.

TIP *The password reset disk should be kept in a secure place. If someone else gets their hands on your disk, he or she can change your password and access your account!*

In the event that you need to use the password reset disk, follow these steps:

1. On the Welcome screen, click the question mark button next to your user account.

2. The Did You Forget Your Password message appears. Click the Use Your Password Reset Disk option and follow the instructions that appear.

What Makes a Good Password?

A password has to be something you can easily remember, but something other users cannot easily guess. As a general rule, passwords should be "complex," which means they should be at least eight characters long and should use both letters (upper- and lowercase) and numbers. The names of your kids or pets, phone numbers, and other commonly known items should not be used as your password. Often, it is best to combine a couple of common items, such as your favorite pet, food, or automobile with some random numbers that you can remember. Here are some examples of good passwords:

- Parrot4598

- OceAn45surf

- JiMMy72ball

- 14573porchE

Account Feature Headaches

Aside from the basic pains of user accounts and passwords, there are some additional account features or necessary tasks that can cause you some Headaches. Keep in mind that if you are using Windows XP Home Edition, your work with user accounts is limited to the User Accounts tool found in Control Panel. However, if you are using Windows XP Professional, there are some additional account management features that you may find very helpful, especially when XP Professional is used in small office situations.

I don't like the account icon feature.

Operating Systems Affected   Windows XP Professional and Home Editions are affected.

Cause   By default, Windows XP assigns a random icon to your user account. This icon appears with your user name on the Welcome screen and also on the Start menu, as you can see in Figure 3-2. However, you can change the icons and icon behavior using the User Accounts tool in Control Panel, if the computer is not a member of a Windows 2000/.NET domain, which is a large Windows network controlled by network administrators.

Account icon on the Start menu

The Pain Killer   To change the icon feature, follow these steps:

1. Log on with the desired account; or, if you are an administrator, you can change other users' accounts.

2. Click Start | Control Panel | User Accounts.

3. In the User Accounts window, choose an account that you want to change.

4. In the What Do You Want to Change About Your Account screen, click the Change My Picture option.

5. In the Pick a New Picture for Your Account screen, select a picture that you want to use and click the Change Picture button, shown in the illustration.

6. You are not stuck with the default picture list; you can use your own pictures or pictures you download from the Internet. Click the Browse for More Pictures option, and an Open window appears in which you can locate and use a picture of your own. Windows XP can use virtually any picture file format for the icon (for example, BMP, GIF, JPEG, PNG, and so on). This feature allows you to use custom pictures and even photos of real people. For example, you could use a picture of an actual person for each user account. Be creative!

I can't stop a user from logging on without deleting the account.

Operating Systems Affected   Windows XP Professional and Home Editions are affected.

Cause   For Home Edition users, there is no cure for this problem; you must delete the user account if you want to stop a user from logging on, or you can reset the password without giving the user the new password. For XP Professional users, you can disable an account instead of deleting it, but you have to use the Local Users and Groups console to configure this option.

Disabling an account is usually done for specific reasons, namely for security. For example, let's say you have very sensitive data stored on Windows XP. A particular user may be out of the office for a month. You do not want to delete the account, but you can disable it in order to provide extra security while the user is away.

The Pain Killer   To disable an account, follow these steps:

1. Click Start | Control Panel | Administrative Tools | Computer Management.

2. Expand Local Users and Groups and select the Users container.

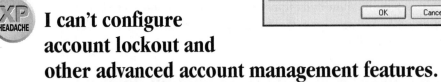

3. In the right pane of the console, right-click on the user account that you want to disable and click Properties.

4. On the General tab, click the Account is Disabled check box to disable the account, as shown here.

5. Click OK.

I can't configure account lockout and other advanced account management features.

Operating Systems Affected   Windows XP Professional Edition is affected.

Cause   Windows XP Professional provides some additional account management features that you can implement if you want to finely control user account logons. However, these options are not intuitively apparent, and that is because you configure them locally through Group Policy.

Group Policy is a feature that allows an XP administrator to configure all kinds of settings and account options that are applied to all users. Users cannot override the settings and are forced to live with what you configure. Group Policy is provided for uniformity and to apply standards that you want to enforce to all user accounts.

TIP *It is beyond the scope of this book to explore Group Policy in its entirety, but you can learn more about it in Windows XP Help or at http:// www.microsoft.com.*

The Pain Killer   To use Group Policy to configure account restrictions, follow these steps:

1. Click Start | Run.

2. Type **gpedit.msc** and click OK. Keep in mind that this command will only work in Windows XP Professional.

3. The Group Policy console opens, as you can see in the illustration.

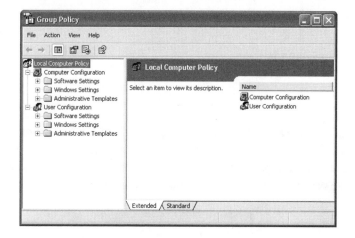

4. Under Computer Configuration, expand Windows Settings. Then, expand Security Settings and select Account Policies, as shown in the illustration.

5. In the right pane, you see containers for Password Policy and Account Lockout Policy. You can double-click a container to see the available policy options. For example, you see the options to configure minimum and maximum ages, complexity requirements, and others.

6. To configure a policy, double-click it and a policy configuration window will appear. As you can see in the following illustration, I am configuring the minimum password length. Once configured, all users will be forced to use passwords that are at least eight characters long.

7. When you have finished, click OK and exit Group Policy.

TIP

You should only configure policies that you want to use. Group Policy is powerful, and it should be managed with care. Again, if you are interested in using Group Policy to invoke a number of settings and restrictions on local users, you should spend some time studying this feature and how it works.

Chapter 4

Windows XP Accessory and Software Headaches

In this chapter, you'll cure...

- ■ Struggles with software

- ■ Getting rid of spyware and adware

- ■ Controlling startup items

We all love software, and after all, software is probably the main reason you have a computer in the first place. With Windows XP, you can easily install new software that you purchase or download from the Internet. Of course, software can also give you plenty of headaches as well, and in this chapter, you'll see how to solve common software Headaches. We'll also see how to destroy adware and spyware as well as manage startup items.

Difficulties with Software

Windows XP comes with a number of tools, utilities, and accessories to meet your needs. However, most of us are going to install and use additional software. For example, I use Microsoft Office to write books and manage documents. Office is not included with Windows XP, so I have to purchase and install it separately. The same is true for all kinds of additional software, from games to antivirus programs, to spreadsheets, to photo editors—you name it and you can probably find it in the software market.

If you are thinking about buying software, which can range from about $20–$800, depending on what you want, there are two main things you need to consider before you ever buy the software:

- ■ **Compatibility** The software should say "compatible with Windows XP" on the box. If it does not, Windows XP still may be able to run the software, but you are likely to have more problems.

- ■ **System requirements** Some software, especially graphics programs, require a lot of memory and system resources. Read the outside of the software box and check the system requirements, and then make sure your computer meets those minimum requirements. You can usually see how much RAM your computer has and how fast the processor is by opening Control Panel | System Properties and reading the information on the General tab, as you can see in Figure 4-1.

FIGURE 4-1   System Properties

TIP   *In my explanations, I will always assume you are using the Classic view of Control Panel. If you are not sure if you are using the Classic view of Control Panel, click Start | Control Panel. In the left window pane, click the Switch to Classic View option.*

Once you have purchased the software that you want to use, you may experience a few Headaches dealing with that software, and the rest of this section explores those issues.

NOTE   *Some programs cannot be installed by a limited user, but require administrative control. If you are having any problems with software, always log on with an administrator account first before trying to fix the problem.*

I can't install a program.

Operating Systems Affected   Windows XP Professional and Home Editions are affected.

Cause   If you cannot install a program, there are few possible explanations, which are

- You are not logged on with an administrator account.

- The program is not compatible with Windows XP.

- There is something wrong with the program or CD that is preventing installation from completing.

A typical program installs from a CD-ROM. Most CD-ROMs today have an auto-start file, which allows the setup program to begin automatically when you put the CD in the CD drive. This makes life easier on you. However, if this does not happen, you can try using Add/Remove Programs in Control Panel. If this does not work, check the CD-ROM drive with a different CD to make sure the CD-ROM is working. If the setup routine keeps failing and you are sure that you are logged on with an administrator account and that the software is compatible with Windows XP, it is time to call the software manufacturer's technical support line and get help. The CD may be faulty!

The Pain Killer   To use Add or Remove Programs, follow these steps:

1. Log on with an administrator account.

2. Click Start | Control Panel | Add Remove Programs.

3. In the Add/Remove Programs window, you can see a list of all of the programs currently installed on your computer. Click the Add New Programs button.

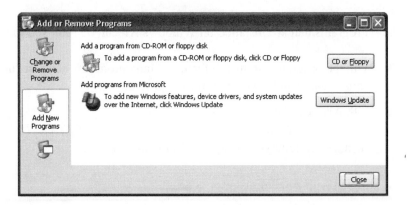

4. A window appears that enables you to install the new program from a CD or floppy disk, or you can install a new program from the Windows Update web site (which I'll get to a little later in this chapter). Click the CD or Floppy button, shown in the illustration.

5. Another window appears, telling you to insert the CD-ROM or floppy disk and click Next. If your computer resides on a Windows domain, you may also see a From Network option.

6. Windows XP looks at your drives and finds the setup program (which is called setup.exe). A window appears showing you what was found and asking if this is the correct program that you want to install. Click Finish.

Run Installation Program

If this is the correct installation program, click Finish. To start the automatic search again, click Back. To manually search for the installation program, click Browse.

Open:

"E:\ServerCert 2000.5.0\Setup.exe"   Browse...

< Back   Finish   Cancel

7. At this point, your application's setup routine will start. You will probably need to answer some setup prompts—refer to the manufacturer's setup instructions for more information.

NOTE

As you can see, the Add/Remove Programs feature really just helps you find the setup.exe program so that a software setup can begin. You can also start any setup.exe file by just double-clicking it instead of using Add/Remove Programs.

I can't remove a program.

Operating Systems Affected   Windows XP Professional and Home Editions are affected.

Cause   Programs that are installed on Windows XP can be removed in two ways:

- With the program's uninstall feature. Many programs have an "uninstall" feature, which helps you remove the program.

- With Add/Remove Programs.

The Pain Killer   To remove a program, follow these steps:

1. Log on with an administrator account.

2. Click Start | All Programs. Then, point to the program that you want to remove. A separate menu may appear with the option to uninstall. If it does, click the option. If not go to step 3.

3. Click Start | Control Panel | Add/Remove Programs.

4. In the Program list, shown in the illustration, select the program that you want to remove. Then, click the Remove button. Follow any instructions that appear.

	Add or Remove Programs			

Currently installed programs:		Sort by:	Name	

Adobe Acrobat 5.0   Size   15.68MB
Click here for support information.   Used   rarely
Last Used On   1/29/2002
To change this program or remove it from your computer, click Change or Remove.   [Change] [Remove]

Association 105 Part 1

Association 105 Part 2

Camtasia   Size   8.53MB

Conexant HCF V90 56K RTAD Speakerphone PCI Modem   Size   0.37MB

Dell Picture Studio - Image Expert 2000   Size   52.16MB

Dell Solution Center

DellTouch   Size   1.54MB

Easy CD Creator 5 Basic

EPSON Printer Software

Ink Monitor   Size   0.34MB

LiveReg (Symantec Corporation)   Size   1.98MB

LiveUpdate 1.6 (Symantec Corporation)   Size   2.92MB

[Close]

I can't remove a program with Add / Remove Programs.

Operating Systems Affected   Windows XP Professional and Home Editions are affected.

Cause   In some cases, you may have trouble removing a program with Add/Remove Programs. You may get a message that the program is busy and can't be uninstalled. This Headache occurs when a program is doing something and the uninstall routine can't run. Even though you make sure all programs are closed, the program can still be running in the background. To remove this offending program, you'll need to use Safe Mode.

The Pain Killer   To remove a program using Safe Mode, follow these steps:

1. Restart your computer and hold down the F8 key when you see the initial screen.

2. When the Startup menu appears, choose the Safe Mode option.

3. Log on with your administrator account.

4. Go to Add/Remove Programs and uninstall the program as usual.

5. Restart your computer.

When I uninstall a program, I receive warnings about shared files.

Operating Systems Affected   Windows XP Professional and Home Editions are affected.

Cause   In order to reduce the thousands and thousands of files that Windows XP has to house, programs often share files with each other. These files allow the program to interact with Windows XP in some way. When you remove a program, you may see a message about deleting shared files and that deleting shared files may make other programs stop functioning. In many cases, you can remove these files anyway, but to be safe it is best to leave them on your computer so that other programs are not damaged, especially if you have several programs from the same company/developer installed on your computer.

The Pain Killer   The safest action is to choose to leave any shared files so that they are not uninstalled. This will not harm your computer or other programs in any way.

I need to use an older program that is not compatible with Windows XP.

Operating Systems Affected   Windows XP Professional and Home Editions are affected.

Cause   Programs are written to specifically work with certain operating systems. As operating systems are updated and changed, the program may not work with the new operating system. As a general rule, you need to purchase a program upgrade so that you will have a compatible program. However, what should you do if the program you need to use is no longer available? The answer is to use Windows XP's Program Compatibility feature.

Windows XP offers a new Program Compatibility feature that allows many programs that are compatible with previous versions of Windows to work on Windows XP, even though the programs are not technically compatible. Basically, when you use the Program Compatibility feature, Windows XP "acts" like an earlier operating system so that the program will be happy and work the way it is supposed to act. The good news too is that the Program Compatibility Wizard is very easy to use.

TIP   *Let me offer a disclaimer here. The Program Compatibility Wizard will enable many noncompatible programs to work under Windows XP, but this does not mean that all programs will work. In fact, programs written for other platforms, such as Apple's Macintosh, will simply not work on a Windows computer. If the program worked with an earlier version of Windows, such as Me or 9x, you may have better luck, even though the results are not guaranteed.*

The Pain Killer   To use the Program Compatibility Wizard, follow these steps:

1. Log on with an administrator account.

2. Click Start | All Programs | Accessories | Program Compatibility Wizard.

3. The Help and Support Center opens and you see a Welcome screen. Click Next.

NOTE   *Note the warning on the Welcome screen—the Program Compatibility Wizard is not designed for use with antivirus programs and backup devices. You must upgrade in order to use these programs with Windows XP. Trying to use them with the Program Compatibility Wizard may cause you serious other Headaches.*

4. In the next window, shown on the following page, pick the program you want to run with Program Compatibility. You can select from a list, use the one in your CD-ROM drive, or browse for it manually. Select a radio button and click Next.

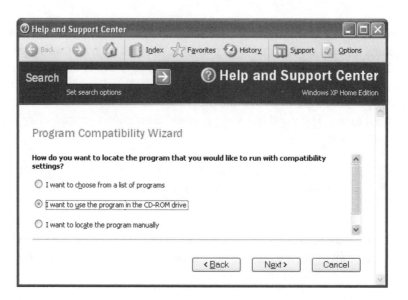

5. In the Select a Compatibility window, select the radio button for the operating system the program was designed for and click Next.

6. In the Settings window, you can also restrict display settings if necessary. Some older programs only work in 256 colors or with a 640 × 480 screen display. See the program's documentation to find out if you need to use these features or not. Click Next.

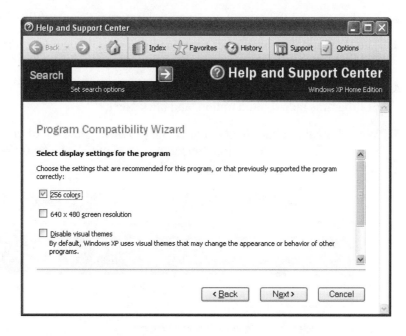

7. You now arrive at a test window. Click Next.

8. Run the software and see if it functions correctly. If so, complete the wizard by accepting the Yes option and click Finish. If not, click No. This will allow you to try different compatibility settings. Now, every time you launch this program, compatibility settings will be used.

I need to stop using compatibility settings on a certain program.

Operating Systems Affected   Windows XP Professional and Home Editions are affected.

Cause   Once you configure compatibility settings for a program, they run every time you launch the program. However, there may come a time when you need to remove those settings.

The Pain Killer   To remove compatibility settings from a program, follow these steps:

1.   Log on with an administrator account.

2.   Click Start | All Programs | Accessories | Program Compatibility Wizard.

3.   The Help and Support Center opens and you see a Welcome screen. Click Next.

4.   In the program selection window, choose the I Want to Choose From a List of Programs radio button option, and click Next.

5.   Windows XP searches the computer and provides you a list of programs, as you can see in the illustration. Select the program for which you want to remove compatibility settings and click Next.

6.   In the compatibility mode window, choose the option to Do Not Apply a Compatibility Mode and click Next.

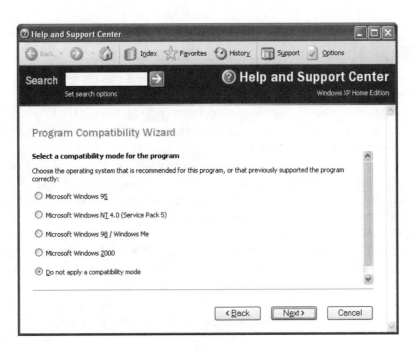

7. Clear any visual settings you have configured and click Next.

8. Click Next to apply and test the removal of settings.

9. Click Yes and click Finish to complete the removal of compatibility settings.

Windows XP keeps downloading stuff from Windows Update without my permission.

Operating Systems Affected   Windows XP Professional and Home Editions are affected.

Cause   Microsoft maintains a Windows Update web site, where fixes to Windows XP are posted and can be downloaded for free. As a general rule, you should visit this site and download the latest stuff regularly, since it is provided to help resolve XP problems, security holes, and generally make XP run faster. However, Windows XP tries to do all of this for you automatically. That may be OK with

What About Downloaded Programs?

Downloaded applications and programs have a self-executing launcher. Generally, you download the program and it appears as an icon on your desktop or in My Documents. Just double-click the program to start the installation. If this does not seem to work, check the web site where you downloaded the file for specific setup instructions.

On a related note, there are lots of cool things that you can download from the Internet and use on XP, and most are safe. However, you should always maintain and run a copy of an antivirus program, such as Norton Antivirus or McAfee, in order to prevent a virus attack. Don't let the fear of viruses, however, scare you from using the Internet. Just get protected and get to surfing! If you are looking for cool and fun stuff for Windows XP, start by checking out http://www.tucows.com, where you can find lots of Windows downloads—many of them free! However, make sure you download items from reputable sites or from the manufacturer's web site. Always, *always* make sure you are running antivirus software when you download anything from the Internet.

you, and the feature is safe, but if you are a little squeamish about Windows XP automatically downloading stuff, or you don't want XP automatically dialing your Internet connection, you can easily stop this behavior.

The Pain Killer   To stop XP from automatically downloading updates, follow these steps:

1. Log on with an administrator account.

2. Click Start | Control Panel | System.

3. Click the Automatic Updates tab.

4. You have the following options:

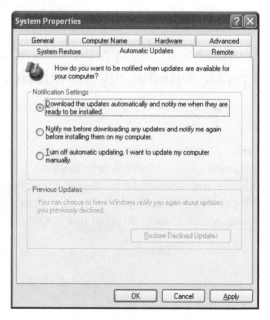

- **Download automatically**   This setting automatically downloads new updates when they are available and prompts you to install them.

- **Notify**   This option lets you know when new updates are available, but it does not download them unless you want to.

- **Turn off**   You turn off automatic updates altogether.

Make a selection by selecting the correct radio button and click OK.

> NOTE   *Automatic Updates work great, but if you access the Internet with a modem, instead of broadband connection such as DSL or cable, download may take some time. Also, if you have only one phone line, Windows XP will automatically dial out periodically to check without your notification. So, choose the setting that works best for you, but automatic updates with a modem connection can cause you some pain, and for this reason many people choose to turn it off completely and check for updates manually, which you can easily do any time by clicking Start | All Programs | Windows Update.*

Removing Spyware and Adware

Imagine this scenario: You recline on your couch and put a movie in your DVD player. The movie has just started, and you receive a phone call asking if you would like to change your long-distance provider. You decline and return to your movie. Ten minutes later, you receive a call, asking if you would like to apply for a new credit card. Sound familiar? I thought so. We are so bombarded with advertisements that they interrupt the things we want to do. Surfing the Internet is no exception.

Have you had the experience of trying to surf the Internet, but you keep seeing these pop-up Windows advertising all kinds of junk? Or, have you set your home page in Internet Explorer only to find that it gets changed to something else every time you open IE? If so, you are the victim of little programs called spyware or adware. These programs are downloaded to your computer without your knowledge, and they run a routine that brings junk from the Internet to you, or worse, they spy on what you are doing on the Internet and report the information back to someone in cyberland.

This Headache is very common, and to get rid of spyware or adware, you'll need a third-party utility that can hunt these programs down and delete them from your computer (you'll need the software—you can't do this yourself). I can recommend two programs for this purpose.

The first is Spybot, which is available for download from http://www.safer-networking.org. Spybot is a small, safe utility, recommended by *PC Magazine,* which will periodically scan your system for personal invasion programs and delete them from your system. Spybot provides you with a simple interface that enables you to scan your system and remove offending applications.

Another great utility is Ad-Aware. This utility, available for free at http://www.lavasoftusa.com/software/adaware, essentially performs the same functions as Spybot, also with a simple-to-use interface. You can scan your system for problems and then choose to fix those problems once the scan completes.

Controlling Startup Programs

If it seems that your Windows XP computer takes some time to boot up, startup programs may be to blame. When you install programs on your computer, some of those programs are configured to start when Windows XP starts. Naturally, Windows XP has a number of its own programs that start when the computer boots, but programs that you install may do the same thing. That can be a real Headache if there are too many of them. Antivirus software is a good example. In order to keep your computer protected at all times, virtually all antivirus software automatically loads when your computer boots. This allows the software to work without your intervention and removes the possibility of your forgetting to start it. However, a number of unnecessary programs may also start. That's fine if you use them, but you may be waiting too long for XP to boot because too many programs are starting up—programs you may not even use that often.

 ## Too many programs start when Windows XP starts.

Operating Systems Affected   Windows XP Professional and Home Editions are affected.

Cause   You can easily reduce the number of programs that start, and if you want to increase boot speed as far as programs are concerned and reduce the amount of program clutter that automatically ends up in the notification area, it's a good idea to examine all of the programs that start when your computer starts and stop programs from loading on startup if you don't really need them. After all, you can always start those programs yourself as they are needed. The good news is you can easily control which programs start when you start your computer.

The Pain Killer   To control which programs automatically start, follow these steps:

1. Click Start | Run. Type **msconfig** and click OK.

2. The System Configuration Utility appears. Click the Startup tab.

3. The Startup tab, shown in Figure 4-2, shows you every service and program that starts when your computer starts. As you can see, I have some internal items and program helper DLLs, but I also have some programs that are designed to startup. You can stop a program from starting by simply clearing the check box next to it and clicking OK.

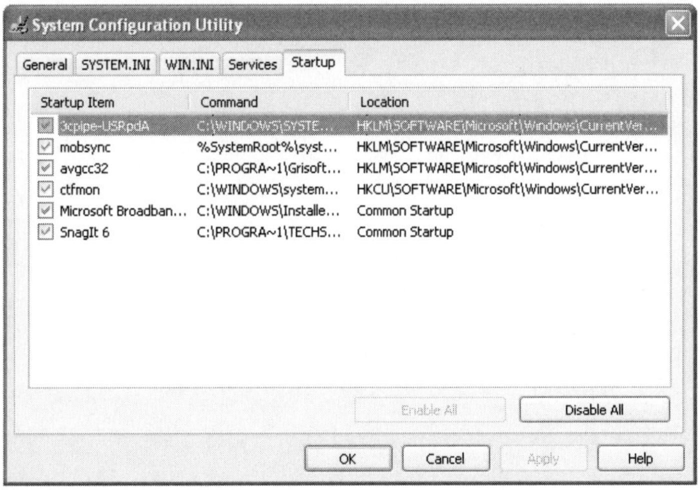

FIGURE 4-2   MSCONFIG

Chapter 5

Windows XP Hardware Headaches

In this chapter, you'll cure...

- ■ Difficulties in installing and removing hardware

- ■ Problems with drivers

- ■ Aggravation with hardware management

Hardware is one of those terms that typically strikes fear into the heart of any computer user—at least it used to. In the past, Windows had a lot of problems with computer hardware, and getting new hardware to work with Windows could be a serious migraine headache. You had to know some things about awful hardware details, such as IRQ (interrupt request) numbers, DMA (direct memory access) channels, memory allocations... you get the picture.

You can rest easy—hardware management in Windows XP is easier than it has ever been. With new advancements in Plug and Play, Windows can usually detect new hardware and install it without any help from you at all. If you have problems, there are a number of features that can help you out.

Before we get started, let's make sure we have a firm definition of hardware. Hardware is any physical device that you attach to or insert into your computer system. Sound cards, video cards, modems, keyboards, mice, printers, scanners, digital cameras, and game controllers are all hardware devices. There are a lot of them these days, which is really great, but Windows has a lot to keep up with. No problem, though, in most cases; Windows will take care of your hardware needs automatically. When it doesn't, then you have this chapter to help you out!

Installing and Uninstalling Hardware

Let's say you buy a new mouse for your computer. You open up the box, read the instructions, attach to the correct port on your computer, and begin using the mouse right away. How? Simple enough. Windows XP works with your computer hardware to detect changes. When you attached that mouse to the port on the computer, Windows XP

- ■ Detected that a new hardware device had been attached to the port.

- ■ Understood that the device was a mouse.

- ■ Grabbed a file, called a *driver,* from an internal Windows XP database that enables XP to manage and use the mouse. This driver is a generic driver designed to work with several mice. You may have better results installing the manufacturer's driver, which you'll learn how to do later in this chapter.

■ Installed the driver for the device.

To you, it looks like nothing happened. You plugged in the mouse and began using it, and that's the way it should be. However, in some cases, Windows XP is not able to detect the hardware device you attach, or the hardware device may not work well without the correct driver. Again, a *driver* is a piece of software that enables Windows to communicate and manage, or drive, the device. You can think of a driver as the steering wheel in your car. The steering wheel enables you to drive the wheels so that the car goes where you want it to go. In the computer system, a driver enables Windows XP to drive the hardware so that you can use it with the operating system.

With all that said, you can experience some problems installing and uninstalling hardware, so this section reviews some common Headaches you might run into.

I can't connect my new device to my computer.

Operating Systems Affected   Windows XP Professional and Home Editions are affected.

Cause   Hardware devices attach to a computer in some way. Some devices, such as sound cards and video cards, are installed into internal slots inside of the computer's case; most attach to ports that are available on the back (or even front) of your computer. Common ports used on Windows XP are

■ **Parallel**   Parallel ports are mostly used for printers. They are wide ports with rows of pins that look like teeth.

■ **Serial**   Serial ports are small and square, with pins inside of them. Mice, keyboards, external modems, and other devices may connect to serial ports, especially if you are using older mice and keyboards.

■ **Keyboard and Mouse PS/2**   These connections are often round with small pins inside. These kinds of connections are more commonly used today instead of serial ports.

■ **Universal Serial Bus (USB)**   First used in Windows 98, USB ports are square and flat. You can connect all kinds of devices to USB ports— everything from printers to digital cameras.

- **Infrared**   Many computers today ship with an infrared port, which allows you to use wireless keyboards, mice, and game controllers.

- **FireWire (IEEE 1394)**   FireWire ports work like USB ports, but they are capable of very high data transfer. Some new computers now support FireWire.

The Pain Killer   In order to attach the device to the correct port, you need to open up the device manufacturer's instructions and follow them. Most instruction booklets tell you exactly what to do and where to attach the new device.

> TIP
>
> *If you need to install a new internal device, such as a video card, you need to know what you are doing before proceeding. Opening the case and tinkering with the inside can cause all kinds of problems and may even nullify your warranty. Also, if you choose to install an internal device, UNPLUG THE POWER! Even if the computer is turned off, you may get shocked from touching internal components that are connected to a power source!*

I don't know if a device I bought will work with Windows XP.

Operating Systems Affected   Windows XP Professional and Home Editions are affected.

Cause   Like all operating systems, most hardware works with Windows XP and some does not. Although many hardware devices are compatible with Windows, some simply are not designed for Windows XP. However, under most circumstances, the hardware devices that you purchase will be Windows compatible. Before buying hardware, you can save yourself a lot of grief if you do just a bit of homework first.

The Pain Killer   There are two main ways to determine if a device is compatible with Windows XP:

- Look on the box while your money is still safe in your pocket. While you are at the store, read the outside of the box. It should say "Compatible with Windows XP" right on the box. If it does not, look for a "Compatible with Windows 2000" label. If you do not see either of these, try to find a device that has one of these labels. You'll save yourself a lot of problems. If you are not sure, ask someone in the store for help.

■ Microsoft maintains a list of hardware that has been tested with Windows XP, called the Hardware Compatibility List (HCL). The HCL tells you what hardware is certain to work with XP, a good reason to check before ever upgrading a computer to Windows XP. However, this does not mean that if something is not listed on HCL that it will not work; it just means that Microsoft has not tested it. Still, the HCL is a great site to check before you buy a device. Check it out at http://www.microsoft.com/hcl. You can search by device and even brand name to see what items are listed.

NOTE   *If there is a device you want, but its compatibility with Windows XP is questionable, you can also try the manufacturer's web site for the latest information about compatibility with Windows XP.*

Windows XP does not detect my new device.

Operating Systems Affected   Windows XP Professional and Home Editions are affected.

Cause   If you attach a new device to your computer and Windows XP does not detect and automatically install the new device, there are several different possible solutions. First, you need to carefully check the device to make sure you have plugged it into the correct port. Devices usually work with some type of port found on the back (or even the front) of your computer. Common examples are parallel ports (printers), serial ports (mice, keyboards, modems, and so on), and USB ports (for all kinds of devices). Some devices even work with infrared wireless ports (called IrDA ports), if your computer has one. The trick is simply this: you have to plug the device into the right port in order for it to work, so check the device documentation to make sure you have it hooked up correctly before going any further. See the first Headache in this section.

Once you are sure that the device is attached correctly, restart the computer. Even though Windows XP can usually detect devices without a reboot, the reboot may help get the device installed. If this doesn't help, do the following:

1. Check the device's documentation for instructions. If a device came with a CD or floppy disk, follow the manufacturer's instructions to install it.

2. Check the HCL (see the second Headache in this section).

3. If both of these options do not help, use the following Pain Killer.

The Pain Killer   To install a device manually, follow these steps:

1. Log on with an administrator account.

2. Ensure that the device is turned on and working.

The following steps assume you are using the Classic view of Control Panel. If you are not sure if you are using the Classic view of Control Panel, click Start | Control Panel. In the left window pane, click the Switch to Classic View option.

3. Click Start | Control Panel | Add Hardware.

4. The Add Hardware Wizard appears. Click Next on the Welcome screen.

5. Windows XP begins a search for any new hardware. If it finds the hardware, it will then install it. If not, a window appears, asking if you have connected the hardware. Make sure the hardware is connected to the computer correctly and click Next.

6. Windows XP then provides you with a list of hardware that is installed on your computer. Scroll to the bottom of the list and select Add a New Hardware Device, as shown in the illustration. Click Next.

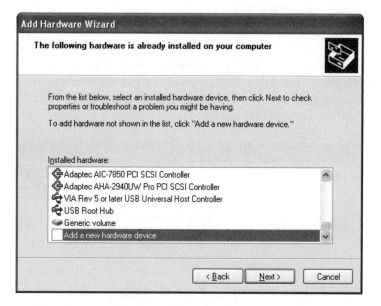

7. In the What Do You Want the Wizard to Do screen, choose the Search For and Install the Hardware Automatically option and click Next. Windows XP will then perform an exhaustive system search.

8. If the hardware is still not found, Windows tells you that you can select the hardware from a list. Click Next.

9. In the provided list, shown here, select the type of hardware device that you want to install and click Next.

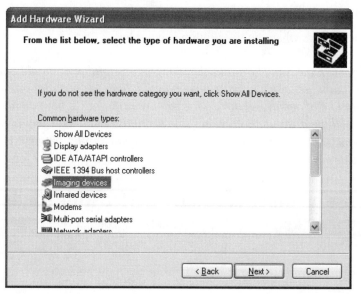

10. If you choose to install a scanner, printer, or modem, a different wizard may appear to help you; just follow the steps. For other devices, you'll see a selection window, as shown in the illustration. Choose the manufacturer and the device and click Next. If you have an installation CD or floppy disk from the manufacturer, you can use it here by clicking the Have Disk button and following the instructions.

```
┌─ Add Hardware Wizard ─────────────────────────────────────┐
│                                                            │
│   Select Infrared Device                          ┌─────┐  │
│      Which infrared device do you want to install?│     │  │
│                                                   └─────┘  │
│                                                            │
│   ┌──┐  Click the Infrared Device that matches your hardware, then click OK. If you have an │
│   │  │  installation disk for this component, click Have Disk.                              │
│                                                            │
│   Manufacturer          ▲    Infrared Device:              │
│   (Standard Infrared Port)   ▤ ACTiSYS IR-200L Serial Infrared Device  │
│   ACTiSYS                    ▤ ACTiSYS IR-220L Serial Infrared Device   │
│   AMP                        ▤ ACTiSYS IR-220L+ Serial Infrared Device  │
│   Extended Systems                                         │
│   Greenwich Instruments Ltd ▼                              │
│                                                            │
│   ▤  This driver is digitally signed.          ┌─────────┐ │
│      Tell me why driver signing is important   │Have Disk...│ │
│                                                └─────────┘ │
│                                                            │
│                        ┌──────┐ ┌──────┐ ┌──────┐         │
│                        │< Back│ │Next >│ │Cancel│         │
│                        └──────┘ └──────┘ └──────┘         │
└────────────────────────────────────────────────────────────┘
```

11. Click Next. Windows XP will install the software for your hardware device.

12. Click Finish when the installation is complete.

NOTE   *Although the Add Hardware Wizard is very helpful, you should always check the manufacturer's instructions and guidelines for installation; this is your first line of defense. If the device you are installing is new, do not hesitate to call the manufacturer's help line for assistance. Some devices, such as some USB devices, require certain drivers and utilities before ever plugging the device into the port. So, check the documentation carefully for instructions.*

I can't use an older hardware device with Windows XP.

Operating Systems Affected   Windows XP Professional and Home Editions are affected.

Cause　In order for any hardware device to work with Windows XP, there must be a driver that will work with Windows XP. The problem with older hardware devices is that a new driver for the device may not be available. You can check out the manufacturer's web site and see if a new driver software is available. If not, you may simply be stuck.

The Pain Killer　If you can't get a new driver, your only solution is to buy a new device that is compatible with Windows XP. Just as with a steering wheel, you can't drive a car without one; and Windows XP cannot drive a hardware device without a driver.

I can't uninstall a device.

Operating Systems Affected　Windows XP Professional and Home Editions are affected.

Cause　At some point, you may want to uninstall a device from Windows XP. For example, let's say that you replace your keyboard with a newer model. Windows XP should detect that the old keyboard is no longer attached to the system and remove it. Sometimes, though, Windows XP may not get the message that a hardware device has been removed, and the device may keep showing up on your computer. This is an easy Headache to fix, however.

The Pain Killer　To manually uninstall a device, follow these steps:

1. Log on with an administrator account.

2. Make sure the device you want to uninstall is physically removed from the computer.

3. Click Start | Control Panel | System.

4. Click the Hardware tab, and then click the Device Manager button.

5. In Device Manager, expand the category of your hardware device, as shown in the illustration. You'll see the device in that category. Right-click the device's icon and click Properties.

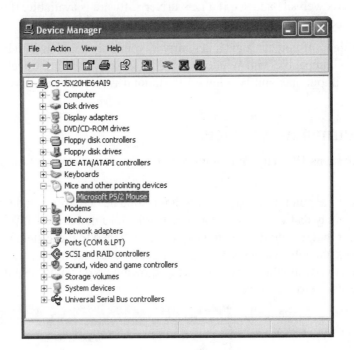

6. On the device's properties pages, click the Driver tab, and then click the Uninstall button.

7. Click OK and close Device Manager.

NOTE   *Keep in mind that the driver is the clue to many device problems. For a device to work, you must have a proper driver. If you want to remove the device from the computer, first remove the device, and then uninstall the driver.*

Solving Problems with Drivers

If you have read the previous section, you know that a driver is a piece of software that Windows XP must have in order to communicate and run a hardware device. Without a driver, Windows XP cannot do anything with the device and will not even know that the device is attached to the computer. Windows XP has its own internal database that contains hundreds of generic drivers to allow Windows XP

What's All This Stuff About "Driver Compatibility"?

Over time, operating systems change. The way Microsoft writes the Windows program code changes the way Windows works and behaves. For example, the Windows XP operating system is very different from older Windows operating systems, such as Windows 98 and Me—*very* different. Because of this, the program code that runs the operating system is different, and that's where you get into "driver compatibility" problems. A driver that was written for an older operating system, such as Windows 9*x* and Windows Me or even NT and 2000, may expect the operating system to act differently than it does—or vice versa. When the program code between the system and the driver do not agree, you end up with driver problems that prevent your hardware device from working. The end result? Device manufacturers have to update drivers for new operating system releases, and you need the newest driver—one that works with Windows XP—in order to avoid hardware problems.

to automatically install hardware that you attach to your computer. That's good news; however, it is the responsibility of the device manufacturer to create drivers that work well with Windows XP. So even if Windows XP assigns a driver for your device, there could be another driver that will make the device work better.

Either way, Windows XP must have a compatible driver. In the following sections, I'll address some common driver problems you might experience and tell you how to solve those problems.

I don't know how to install a new driver.

Operating Systems Affected   Windows XP Professional and Home Editions are affected.

Cause   If a new driver becomes available for a hardware device, Windows XP will help you install it so that you can begin using the new driver.

The Pain Killer   To install a new driver, follow these steps:

1. Log on with an administrator account.

2. Download the new driver from the manufacturer's web site, or if you have a CD or disk, insert it into the CD or floppy drive, respectively. If you download the driver from the Internet, the driver may be *self-installing,*

which means you can open the downloaded file and have a setup routine walk you through the steps. Follow the web site's instructions for installation, if this is the case. If the driver is not self-installing, it will probably be downloaded to you in a compressed (zipped) folder. You can unzip the driver files and put them in a folder on your desktop so that Windows XP can easily use them.

3. Click Start | Control Panel | System.

4. Click the Hardware tab, and then click Device Manager.

5. In Device Manager, expand the category of your hardware device. Then, right-click the device whose driver you want to upgrade and click Properties.

6. Click the Driver tab and click the Update Driver button.

7. The Hardware Update Wizard appears. On the Welcome screen, click the Install the Software Automatically radio button, shown here, and click Next. Windows XP will check your CD-ROM drive and your floppy disk drive for the driver and then install it. If you downloaded the driver, go to step 8.

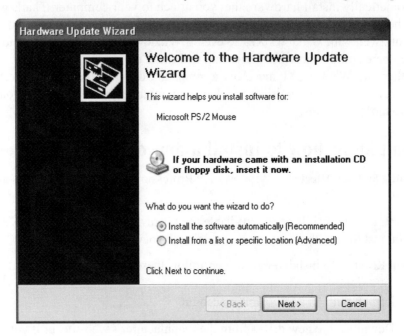

8. If the driver that you downloaded from the Internet is not self-installing, make sure you have unzipped the driver files if they were compressed. You can put them in a folder on your desktop for easy use. Then, on the Hardware Update Wizard Welcome screen, click the Install From a List or Specific Location radio button and click Next.

9. In the Choose a Search window, click the Don't Search radio button, shown in the illustration, and click Next.

10. In the selection window, click the Have Disk button, and then click the Browse button in the Install from Disk screen.

11. A browse window appears. You can browse to the driver file and select it for installation. Click OK once and then again. Follow the rest of the wizard steps to complete the installation.

NOTE   *The driver file should have an .inf extension, such as driver.inf.*

I installed a new driver, but now the device does not work, or does not work well.

Operating Systems Affected   Windows XP Professional and Home Editions are affected.

Cause   If this happens, you either installed the wrong driver, or the driver is corrupt. In either case, you want to go back to the original driver so that you can try to install it again, or try to use a different driver. Fortunately, Windows XP has a rollback feature that will make this process easy.

The Pain Killer   To roll back a driver, follow these steps:

1. Log on as an administrator.

2. Click Start | Control Panel | System.

3. Click the Hardware tab, and then click the Device Manager button.

4. In Device Manager, expand the desired category; then right-click the desired device and click Properties.

5. Click the Driver tab.

6. Click the Roll Back Driver button. Follow any instructions that appear.

The Roll Back Driver feature will not work unless you have installed a new driver, replacing an existing old driver. If the device does not work or does not work well, you must try to install new driver; see the preceding Headache for instructions.

I need to download a new driver, but Internet Explorer will not let me.

Operating Systems Affected   Windows XP Professional and Home Editions are affected.

Cause   Internet Explorer 6, which is included with Windows XP, has some security features that try to keep you from downloading "unsigned" drivers. This is a security feature that helps prevent the downloading of viruses and other malicious code. Normally, Internet Explorer will prompt you before downloading an unsigned driver, but if the setting has been configured to "block," then you will not be able to download the driver.

The Pain Killer   To enable Internet Explorer to prompt you for driver download action, follow these steps:

1. Log on with an administrator account.

2. Click Start | Control Panel | System.

3. Click the Hardware tab and click the Driver Signing button.

4. In the Driver Signing Options window that appears, click the Warn radio button so that Internet Explorer will warn you before downloading unsigned driver files, rather than blocking the downloading. If you want this setting to apply to all users on the computer, click the Make This Action the System Default check box. Click OK.

Driver Signing Options

During hardware installation, Windows might detect software that has not passed Windows Logo testing to verify its compatibility with Windows. (Tell me why this testing is important.)

What action do you want Windows to take?

○ Ignore - Install the software anyway and don't ask for my approval

◉ Warn - Prompt me each time to choose an action

○ Block - Never install unsigned driver software

Administrator option

☑ Make this action the system default

OK   Cancel

Managing Hardware

The concept of managing hardware refers to a number of different settings and potential problems. In this section, we'll take a look at some common Headaches and problems users experience from time to time.

My device does not act the way I want it to.

Operating Systems Affected   Windows XP Professional and Home Editions are affected.

Cause   Once installed correctly, a device may or may not behave in the way that you want. Most devices have properties sheets that you can access to configure how the device behaves. To make the device do what you want, you'll need to access the correct property sheet and also check the device manufacturer's instructions.

The Pain Killer   Read the documentation that came with the device and check for a solution. Then, you'll need to access any available properties for the device so you can change the behavior. Common devices, such as mice, keyboards, game controllers, modems, and printers, all have configuration icons in Control Panel.

> **TIP**   *See Chapter 7 to learn more about peripheral Headaches.*

 # I need to stop a device from working without uninstalling it.

Operating Systems Affected   Windows XP Professional and Home Editions are affected.

Cause   Windows XP gives you the option to disable a device for a period of time instead of uninstalling it. This feature gives you the chance to troubleshoot problems or make configuration changes.

The Pain Killer   To disable a device, follow these steps:

1. Log on with an administrator account.

2. Click Start | Control Panel | System.

3. Click the Hardware tab and click the Device Manager button.

4. Expand the desired category; then right-click the desired device and click Disable. Click Yes to the message that appears. You can return to the device at any time, right-click it, and then click Enable to begin using it again.

> **CAUTION**   *Do not try to disable a device by removing its driver. This uninstalls the device from your computer. If you do, Plug and Play will redetect it on the next reboot, so it will end up working again anyway. Always use the Disable option.*

My USB scanner does not work.

Operating Systems Affected   Windows XP Professional and Home Editions are affected.

Cause   USB works with *hubs,* attachment ports to which you can attach USB devices. A USB hub can either be self-powered or bus-powered. A self-powered hub has a wall outlet that you plug in, in order to power the devices attached to the hub. Bus-powered hubs get their juice from the computer. Some devices, such as scanners and portable hard disks, need more power than the USB bus-powered hub can provide.

The Pain Killer   Either purchase and begin using a self-powered hub or provide outlet power to the device. See the device manufacturer's instructions for specific information. Also, you can simply try moving the device to a different port on the hub; sometimes that helps, too.

Devices and PC cards used on my laptop computer keep draining the battery when I am not connected to a power source.

Operating Systems Affected   Windows XP Professional and Home Editions are affected.

Cause   A number of PC cards and different peripherals work very well with laptop computers. However, when the laptop is running batteries, these devices put a drain on battery power, which makes the battery run down faster than it should. The good news is that you can easily create a hardware profile to use when you are not connected to a power source. This feature allows you to disable certain devices when you are running on batteries so that you can conserve battery power.

The Pain Killer   To create a hardware profile that you can use when you are mobile, follow these steps:

1. Log on with an administrator account.

2. Click Start | Control Panel | System.

3. Click the Hardware tab and click the Hardware Profiles button. The Hardware Profiles window appears, as shown in this illustration.

> **Hardware Profiles**   [?][X]
>
> You can set up hardware profiles for different hardware configurations. At startup, you can choose the profile you want to use.
>
> Available hardware profiles:
>
> Profile 1 (Current)
>
> [Properties] [Copy] [Rename] [Delete]
>
> Hardware profiles selection
> When Windows starts:
>
> ○ Wait until I select a hardware profile
> ◉ Select the first profile listed if I don't select a profile in
> [30] seconds
>
> [OK] [Cancel]

4. You see the current default profile. If you click the Properties button, you can see the basic properties of the default profile, shown in this illustration. You have two basic options here. You can identify the profile as one for a portable computer, and you can choose always to include the profile as an option when Windows starts.

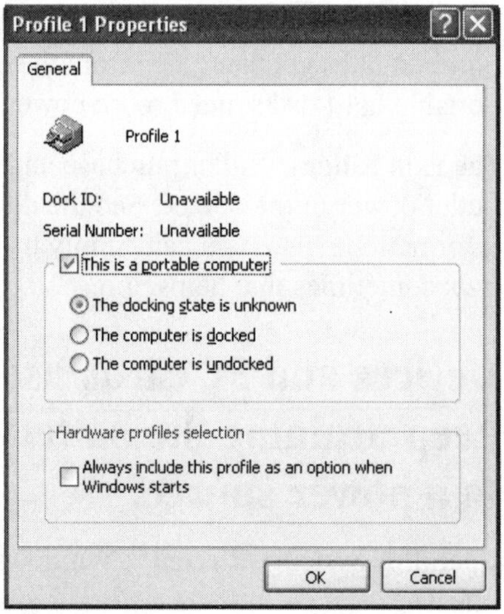

5. To create a new profile, click the Copy button. The Copy Profile dialog box appears. Enter a desired name for the new profile and click OK. You might want to call the profile something like "Mobile" or "Batteries." The current configuration from the default profile is copied to the new profile. At this point, you now have two profiles that are the same.

6. You can now select the new profile and click Properties. In the provided dialog box, you can choose the portable computer option, and you can choose always to include the profile option when Windows starts, as shown here.

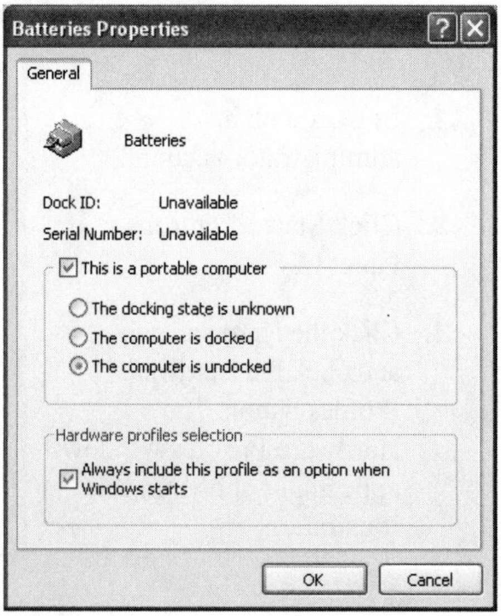

7. In the Hardware Profiles window, you now see the two profiles. When you restart the computer, you'll see a boot menu so that you can select the profile you want. Click OK in the Hardware Profiles window and restart Windows XP.

8. During startup, a Hardware Profile menu appears. Select the new hardware profile that you want to use and allow Windows XP to start up using that hardware profile. Log onto the computer with an administrator account.

9. Click Start | Control Panel | System.

10. Click the Hardware tab, and then click the Device Manager option.

11. Now that you are in Device Manager, access the properties page for each of the devices that you do not want to use under the new profile. On the General tab of each device, choose the Do Not Use This Device in the Current Hardware Profile (Disable) option from the drop-down menu. Continue this process until you have disabled any and all devices that should not be a part of the portable hardware profile.

12. As you complete step 11 for each device, close the properties page for it. Notice that the devices you have disabled now appear in Device Manager with a red X over them, indicating that the device is disabled, as shown here.

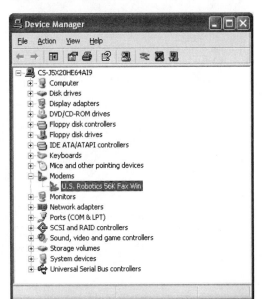

13. At any time, you can create additional hardware profiles by following these steps, or you can delete a hardware profile by returning to the Hardware Profile window.

Chapter 6

Windows XP Disk Headaches

In this chapter, you'll cure...

■ Problems with hard disks

■ Difficulties with floppy disks

■ Problems with CD and DVD-ROM drives

Windows XP, like all operating systems, has to have a way to store information. Much like a filing cabinet, a computer has to have an organized way to store data so that the data can be retrieved when it is needed. All computer systems store data on a disk of some kind—typically an internal hard disk or a removable disk, such as a floppy disk, a Zip or Jaz drive, or a read-write CD-ROM drive, called a Compact Disc-ReWritable (CD-RW) drive. Again, the purpose of these options is simply to store information, which is a large part of what computing is about in the first place.

In the past, it wasn't necessary for PCs to store a lot of information because they could not manage that much information to begin with. Today, computer systems commonly have hard drives in excess of 50GB plus an additional removable drive feature that gives you a number of ways to save data. From files to pictures to video, the disk is your way of protecting your data, and you can't do much without it.

On a positive note, you don't need to spend too much of your time worrying about disks because the technology is stable and it works well. The problems you may experience are usually easily fixed, and in this chapter, we'll explore those issues.

> **TIP** *Keep in mind that disks are used to store data, and tinkering with them in the wrong way can cause you to lose data! As you try to solve problems or learn more about disk management in this chapter, be careful and make sure you completely understand any and all actions that you perform with the computer's disks before doing so.*

Problems with Hard Disks

Every computer contains at least one hard disk. The hard disk is inside the computer's case, and it looks somewhat like a big floppy disk. Whenever you save data, that data is written to the hard disk. Whenever you open and read or view data, it is read from the hard disk.

Without getting into the gross details of how hard disks work, the disk is divided into sections so that data can be written to the disk and read from it. Windows XP configures the disk with a *file system* so that XP can use the disk and retrieve information from it. Windows XP supports several different file systems:

- **NTFS**   The New Technology File System (NTFS), which was first seen in Windows NT, is the file system of choice for Windows XP computers. NTFS has the best security and disk management features of any file system.

- **FAT32**   FAT32 (FAT stands for File Allocation Table) was used in Windows Me, 98, and some versions of Windows 95. It is still supported in Windows XP, but it is not as good as NTFS.

- **FAT16**   This previous version of FAT was used by Windows 3.*x* and some versions of Windows 95.

- **CDFS**   The CD File System (CDFS) is used on CD-ROM drives.

In Windows 2000, the concept of *volume management* appeared in the computing world. Using volumes enables you to segment your drive into numerous divisions that act as independent drives. The process of configuring hard drives is beyond the scope of this book, but there are a number of good books on the subject; and you can find information at http://www.microsoft.com if you are interested. In the following sections, I will explore the common problems you are likely to experience with your computer's hard disk.

My drive is not an NTFS drive.

Operating Systems Affected   Windows XP Professional and Home Editions are affected.

Cause   NTFS is the file system of choice for Windows XP. However, if you upgraded from Windows 98/Me, then you probably still have a FAT32 drive. (If you don't know, I'll show you how to find out later in this chapter.) Also, the drive may have come from the computer manufacturer to you as a FAT32 drive. NTFS provides better management features than FAT32, but keep in mind that it is not required for use with Windows XP—a FAT32 drive will work just fine. However, if you really want to use NTFS so that you can take advantage of compression and other features, you can convert the drive to NTFS with no problems and no data loss at all.

The Pain Killer   To convert a drive to NTFS, follow these steps:

1. First, make sure the drive is formatted with FAT32. Click Start | My Computer. Right-click the drive you want to convert (such as your C drive), and then click Properties.

2. On the General tab, under File System, if the file system is already listed as NTFS, then there is nothing more to do. If the file system is listed as FAT32, go to step 3.

3. Before performing the conversion, back up your data just to be safe. You may wish to back up your data to a CD or other removable device.

4. Click Start | Run. Type **Command** in the dialog box and click OK.

5. In the command window, shown in the illustration, type the following command:

    convert *driveletter*: /fs:ntfs

    For example, if I wanted to convert my C drive, I would type **convert c: /fs:ntfs**.

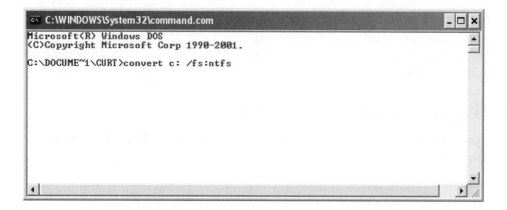

Make sure you punctuate the command correctly and that you leave a space after the driveletter and colon.

6. Click OK.

My computer's hard disk is running out of space.

Operating Systems Affected   Windows XP Professional and Home Editions are affected.

Cause   The hard disk is used to store information. The more information you store, the less extra space the disk has. Like a clothes closet, the more stuff you cram into it, the faster it runs out of room. The hard disk in your computer can hold a lot of data, but if you are storing lots of files, especially picture or video files, you can begin to run low on disk space.

The Pain Killer   To clean up some of the disk and give yourself more room, follow these steps:

1. First, inspect your files and discard anything you really don't need. Click Start | My Documents to see if there are any subfolders in that directory that you can throw away. If you have a Zip disk or a CD-RW disc, you can store data on those as well in order to remove the data from the hard drive.

2. Click Start | My Computer. Right-click the drive you want to clean up, and then click Properties.

3. On the General tab, you can compress the drive by clicking the Compress Drive to Save Disk Space check box at the bottom of the page. (If this option is not available, then the drive is not formatted with NTFS.) This will compress the drive and save disk space, but will not make any difference in your day-to-day use of the drive. Also, consider disabling the indexing feature, which takes up disk space as well.

4. Click the Disk Cleanup button. Windows XP inspects your hard disk and looks for items that you can safely remove to create more room on the disk. As you can see in the illustration, I have more than 2MB in temporary Internet files and over 12MB in my Recycle Bin that I can remove. Click the check boxes next to the items you want to remove, and then click OK.

5. If you click the More Options tab, you can also choose to clean up Windows components and installed programs that you do not use and old System Restore points. Click the Clean Up buttons next to the item(s) that you want to clean up, and follow the instructions that appear.

Disk Cleanup for (C:)

| Disk Cleanup | More Options |

Windows components

You can free more disk space by removing optional Windows components that you do not use.

Clean up...

Installed programs

You can free more disk space by removing programs that you do not use.

Clean up...

System Restore

You can free more disk space by removing all but the most recent restore point.

Clean up...

OK   Cancel

 My hard disk seems to behave erratically, or I get error messages.

Operating Systems Affected   Windows XP Professional and Home Editions are affected.

Cause   A hard disk can develop a number of disk surface and file system errors that can cause you some problems. This happens during use of the disk due to "wear and tear," so to speak. The good news is that Windows XP gives you an Error-checking tool that can solve the problems.

The Pain Killer   To run error-checking on the disk, follow these steps:

1. Click Start | My Computer. Right-click the disk and click Properties.

2. Click the Tools tab, shown here.

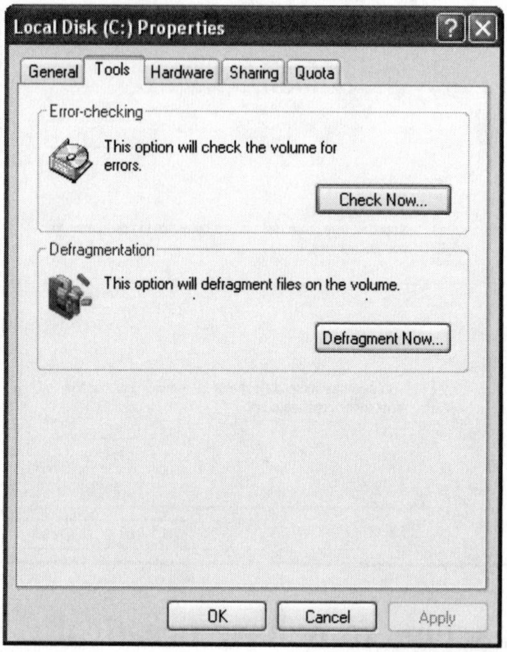

3. Click the Check Now button. A dialog box appears that allows you to automatically fix file system problems and check for and attempt repair of bad sectors. Click both check boxes, and then click Start. Error-checking begins to run, and the process may take an hour or more, depending on the size of the disk.

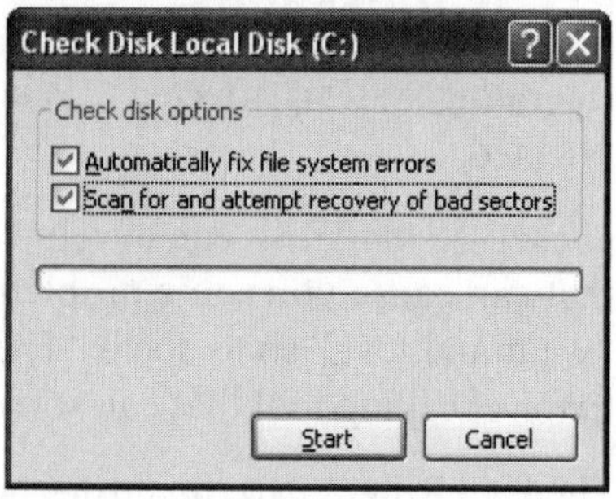

TIP *If the Error-checking tool is not working correctly, see Chapter 15 for more information.*

My hard disk makes strange noises.

Operating Systems Affected   Windows XP Professional and Home Editions are affected.

Cause   Hard disks make noise when they work. Normal noises include a churning sound, or maybe even a sound like a jet engine about to take off. These noises are a normal part of the disk spinning and should be ignored. However, if your disk is making clicking or popping noises, you may have a problem, especially if other read or write errors or failures seem to be occurring.

The Pain Killer   You should get in touch with technical support because you may have a hardware problem. Also, you might try using third-party disk tools, such as Norton Utilities, which may be able to resolve problems with the disk.

My hard disk reads and writes data very slowly.

Operating Systems Affected   Windows XP Professional and Home Editions are affected.

Cause   Over time, your hard disk may become *fragmented;* that is, as files are saved and opened, Windows XP may have stored pieces of the files in different places on the disk, which in turn requires more time to save and open them. Fragmentation is a normal part of excessive disk use, and the primary sign of fragmentation is slow reading and writing. For example, a file might take a little too long to open, or save. The good news is that Windows XP provides the Disk Defragmenter tool to defragment the hard disk and resolve the problem.

The Pain Killer   To defragment the drive, follow these steps:

1. Close all programs, and then click Start | My Computer. Right-click the disk you want to defragment, and then click Properties.

2. Click the Tools tab, and then click the Defragment Now button.

3. In the Disk Defragmenter window, shown here, click the Analyze button
to see if the disk needs to be defragmented.

4. A message appears telling you whether or not you should defragment the
volume. Click Defragment to continue.

5. The defragmentation process begins and may take some time, depending on
the size of the hard disk (possibly several hours). If you are using a laptop,
make sure it is plugged in and not running on batteries.

If your disk is highly fragmented, you can run the Disk Defragmenter tool several times in a row. The tool does not fix all defragmentation, so running the tool several times may give you even better results. However, do not expect your disk to become 100 percent defragmented; again, fragmentation is a normal result and not one that needs to be feared—just controlled.

My computer is not able to boot, and I see "disk missing" messages.

Operating Systems Affected   Windows XP Professional and Home Editions are affected.

Cause   If Windows XP suddenly does not boot one day and you see messages about missing disks, your hard disk has either crashed or is not connected. This generally does not happen; but should a disk fail, you will see this error because Windows XP will not be able to find a disk to boot from.

The Pain Killer   This is a hardware problem, so you'll need to get some help from technical support. See your computer's documentation for more information.

One of my hard disks does not work.

Operating Systems Affected   Windows XP Professional and Home Editions are affected.

Cause   If your computer has multiple hard disks, it's possible that one of them could quit working for a variety of reasons. If the disk does not seem to be working, you can use the Computer Management console to view its status. The Computer Management console has a Disk Management utility that gives you a graphical view of the hard disks and the status of each one, as you can see in Figure 6-1.

Event Viewer, also found in Computer Management, may give you some clues about the problem as well.

The Pain Killer   You must be logged on with an administrator account to use the Disk Management console. You can access the Disk Management console by clicking Start | Control Panel | Administrative Tools | Computer Management. (When you are in Control Panel, remember to work in Classic view in order to be able to see

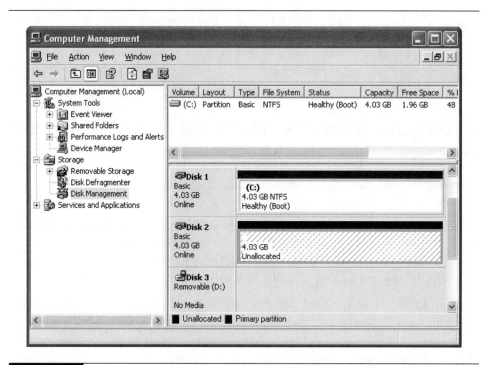

Computer Management console

all the icons.) In Figure 6-1, both hard disks are listed as Online, which means they are functional. However, the following status indicators may also appear:

■ **Audio CD**   This status appears when you have an audio CD in the CD drive.

■ **Foreign**   This status appears when a dynamic disk is moved to a computer running Windows XP Home Edition, or in cases where Windows XP Home Edition is configured to dual-boot with another operating system that supports dynamic disks, such as Windows 2000. Windows XP Home Edition cannot read a dynamic disk; however, you can right-click the Disk Status box and then click Revert to Basic Disk. Proceed carefully, though, because if you do this, all data on the disk will be destroyed.

- **No Media** This status appears on removable drives (floppy, CD, Zip disks, and so on) when there is no disk in the drive.

- **Not Initialized** This status appears when the disk does not contain a valid signature. Windows XP must write a master boot record before the disk is ready to use. You can right-click the Disk Status box and then click Initialize Disk to start the process.

- **Unreadable** This status appears when the disk is not accessible, such as in the case of a hardware failure. Click Action and then click Rescan Disks to try to bring it back online, or try restarting the computer.

I can't create a new partition.

Operating Systems Affected Windows XP Professional and Home Editions are affected.

Cause If your computer has multiple hard disks or has unallocated space on the first disk, you can create additional partitions. Having partitions works like having different hard disks, by enabling you to store data in a more organized manner. Different partitions on the same disk can use different file systems and can be used for different purposes. To create a new partition, you must have unallocated space from which to create the partition, you must be logged on as an administrator, and you must use the Disk Management utility to create the partition.

The Pain Killer To create a new partition, follow these steps:

1. Log on with an administrator account.

2. Click Start | Control Panel | Administrative Tools | Computer Management.

3. In the Computer Management console, right-click the unallocated space on the desired disk where you want to create the new partition and click New Partition, as shown in the illustration.

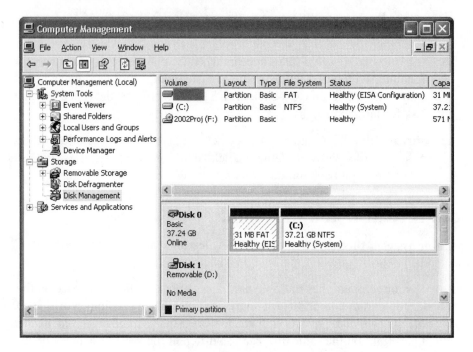

4. The New Partition Wizard appears. Click Next on the Welcome screen.

5. In the Select Partition Type screen, click either Primary Partition, Extended Partition, or Logical Drive. See the Windows XP Help and Support Center for more information about partition types. Click Next.

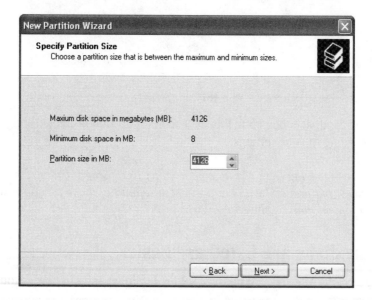

6. In the Specify Partition Size screen, choose the size in megabytes for the partition. As you can see, this screen shows the minimum and maximum sizes you can choose. Click Next.

7. In the Assign Drive Letter and Path screen, you can choose a drive letter or mount the drive to an empty NTFS folder. (See the Windows XP Help and Support Center to learn more about mounting to an empty NTFS folder.) Click Next.

8. In the Format Partition screen, choose the file system you want to use. This screen also allows you to choose to run a quick format, which is faster than a full format (full is usually better), and enable file and folder compression. Make your selections and click Next.

New Partition Wizard ☒

Format Partition
To store data on this partition, you must format it first.

Choose whether you want to format this partition, and if so, what settings you want to use.

○ Do not format this partition

⦿ Format this partition with the following settings:

File system:	NTFS ▾
Allocation unit size:	Default ▾
Volume label:	New Volume

☐ Perform a quick format

☐ Enable file and folder compression

[< Back] [Next >] [Cancel]

9. Click Next, and then click Finish. The new partition is created and formatted according to your settings.

 You can use the Disk Management utility to reformat drives and delete drives; but proceed with caution because both of those functions destroy all information on the chosen drives!

 ## All of my disks are listed as "basic."

Operating Systems Affected   Windows XP Professional and Home Editions are affected.

Cause   Windows XP Professional supports both basic and dynamic disks (see the sidebar to find out more about basic and dynamic disks). XP Home Edition, however,

Why Doesn't Windows XP Home Edition Support Dynamic Disks?

Dynamic disks give you more configuration options and dynamic volume support, which is a new way to manage hard disk divisions. However, dynamic disks are not supported in Windows XP Home Edition. Why, you might ask? That's a question best left for the "powers that be" at Microsoft; however, I'm willing to take a couple of guesses:

- Most home users have only a single hard disk that is preconfigured before you buy the computer. In short, since most home users will not actually configure dynamic volumes, there is no need to provide the option.

- Dynamic volumes can be great, but they can lead to a lot of configuration problems if you don't know what you're doing. In other words, dynamic volume configuration is best left to advanced users.

supports only basic disks. If you are using Windows XP Professional and you want to convert the disks to dynamic disks so that you can take advantage of volume management, you can easily convert them.

The Pain Killer   To convert a basic disk to a dynamic disk, follow these steps:

1. Log onto the Windows XP Professional computer with an administrator account.

2. Click Start | Control Panel | Administrative Tools | Computer Management.

3. In the Computer Management console, select Disk Management in the left console. You'll see your disks listed in the right pane. Right-click the disk status box in the left pane of the disk you want to convert, and click Convert to Dynamic Disk. This process will not damage any data. You will be prompted to reboot your computer once the conversion is complete.

Difficulties with Floppy Disks

Floppy disks have been around for years, and they provide a great way to move information from one computer to another easily, or even to store smaller files.

Since the creation of CD-RW drives, floppy disks are not used as much, but they still have a valid place in the computing world and can be quick and easy to use. The following Headaches explain the problems that can occur when working with floppy disks, as well as the cures for solving them.

I can't open a floppy disk.

Operating Systems Affected   Windows XP Professional and Home Editions are affected.

Cause   Floppy disks can be opened, assuming the disk is working correctly, by following the steps in the Pain Killer.

The Pain Killer   To open a floppy disk, follow these steps:

1. Insert the disk into the floppy disk drive.

2. Click Start | My Computer.

3. Double-click the floppy disk drive in the My Computer window, as shown in the illustration. If you cannot open the disk or you receive an error message, see the next Headache.

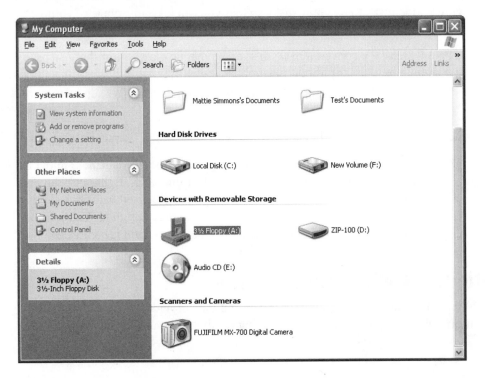

When I try to open a floppy disk, an error message appears.

Operating Systems Affected   Windows XP Professional and Home Editions are affected.

Cause   If you followed the steps in the previous Headache but still cannot open a floppy disk, there are a few possible explanations:

- The floppy drive has failed.

- The disk is formatted for an unsupported operating system, such as for the Macintosh Operating System (Mac OS).

- The disk is corrupt.

The Pain Killer   To solve the problem, try the following:

- First, try a different disk in the floppy drive to see if the floppy drive is working. If it is not, try restarting the computer. If the floppy drive still does not work, you'll need to get help from your computer manufacturer's technical support.

- If the floppy drive works on other disks, you can try to open the disk again. If this does not work, the disk is probably corrupt or there is some mechanical problem with the disk or disk drive. You can try to reformat the disk so that you can use it, but this will destroy all data on the disk.

I want to use NTFS on my hard disk, but I'm afraid that will prevent my system from being able to read floppy disks, which are formatted with FAT.

Operating Systems Affected   Windows XP Professional and Home Editions are affected.

Cause   Floppy disks use the FAT file system, while your internal hard disks can use either FAT or NTFS. However, if your computer uses NTFS, you can still use and read floppy disks because Windows XP can read both file systems. So relax, converting to NTFS on the internal hard disks will not affect the use of the floppy drive.

The Pain Killer   You don't need to do anything—you're safe!

TIP

The same concept is true of network access. You can access a shared NTFS drive or folder from a Windows 9x or Me computer over the network. A service called a network redirector handles the translation, so there are no worries about accessing NTFS drives over a network; and there is nothing for you to configure.

XP HEADACHE A floppy disk will not hold a file I need to move to another computer.

Operating Systems Affected   Windows XP Professional and Home Editions are affected.

Cause   Floppy disks can only hold only a tiny 1.38MB of information, which is the physical limitation of the storage space, so anything you try to store on the floppy disk must be smaller than 1.38MB.

The Pain Killer   If you need to move a file to another computer, you'll need to use an alternative storage device, such as a Zip drive or a CD-RW drive. You can also try to compress the file so that it takes up less room. To compress a file using Windows file system compression, follow these steps:

1. Right-click an empty area of your desktop and click New | Compressed (Zipped) Folder. The new compressed folder appears on your desktop.

2. Drag the file into the compressed folder.

3. Right-click the compressed folder and click Properties. On the General tab, check out the size of the folder. If it is under 1.38MB, you can now store it on the floppy disk.

New Properties

General | Security | Summary

New

Type of file: Compressed (zipped) Folder

Opens with: Compressed (zipped) F   [Change...]

Location: C:\Documents and Settings\Curt\Desktop

Size: 283 KB (290,500 bytes)

Size on disk: 284 KB (290,816 bytes)

Created: Today, February 11, 2002, 10:33:22 AM

Modified: Today, February 11, 2002, 10:33:31 AM

Accessed: Today, February 11, 2002, 10:33:31 AM

Attributes: ☐ Read-only   ☐ Hidden   [Advanced...]

[OK] [Cancel] [Apply]

NOTE
There are other compression utilities available at your favorite computer store and on the Internet that perform a number of important compression features. WinZip is the most common one, which you can download from www.winzip.com.

TIP
When storing a large file on a floppy disk, open the disk first to make sure there are no other files taking up room on the disk.

Problems with CD and DVD-ROM Drives

Under most circumstances, you are not likely to have problems with your Compact Disc (CD) or Digital Video Disc–Read-Only Memory (DVD-ROM) drives. If a particular drive does not work, the problem is usually associated with a corrupt driver (see Chapter 5) or a hardware failure. However, there are a few aggravations that you can easily solve.

Windows Media Player keeps opening automatically when I insert a CD.

Operating Systems Affected   Windows XP Professional and Home Editions are affected.

Cause   Windows XP tries to guess what you want to do with an audio CD or DVD when you insert it, so it opens Windows Media Player for you to use. However, you may not want this to happen. No problem—you can change it.

The Pain Killer   To stop Windows Media Player from opening when you insert a CD, follow these steps:

1. Click Start | My Computer. Right-click the CD or DVD-ROM drive that you want to configure, and then click Properties.

2. Click the AutoPlay tab. Under Actions, you can choose the Take No Action option so that Windows Media Player will not open and Windows XP will not prompt you for any action. If you want to be prompted, just click the

Prompt Me Each Time to Choose an Action radio button at the bottom of the window and click OK.

![Audio CD (E:) Properties dialog box showing the AutoPlay tab with content type "Music files" and actions Play, Open folder to view files, and Take no action selected]

I can't hear any sound when I play a DVD.

Operating Systems Affected   Windows XP Professional and Home Editions are affected.

Cause   In order for your DVD player to play sound, your computer must have a sound card and it must be configured correctly for sound playback. Obviously, you should first make sure the sound on the PC is actually turned on. There are other reasons for no sound, some of them seemingly obvious, but worth mentioning. Your volume wheel, or the system's volume slider, may be turned down. Your plugged-in earbuds may have stopped working because you got them from the vendor and they're super cheap. And the volume wheel on your external speakers may be turned down.

The Pain Killer   See Chapter 15 to learn more about sound cards and sound configuration.

When I try to play my DVD, the screen becomes black.

Operating Systems Affected   Windows XP Professional and Home Editions are affected.

Cause   In order for DVD playback to work correctly, you need to ensure that two or more programs using video overlay are not running at the same time (for example, WebTV and Microsoft NetMeeting).

The Pain Killer   Make sure all of your programs are closed, and then try running the DVD again.

 ## I receive a region error message when I try to use the DVD player.

Operating Systems Affected   Windows XP Professional and Home Editions are affected.

Cause   DVD players function by regions, because many DVDs are imprinted with a code that controls which geographical region they can be played in. To make sure your DVD is using the correct region, see the following Pain Killer.

The Pain Killer   To make sure your DVD drive is using the correct region, follow these steps:

1. Click Start | Control Panel | System.

NOTE
These steps assume you are using the Classic view of Control Panel, which shows you all the icon options. If you are not sure you are using the Classic view of Control Panel, click Start | Control Panel. In the left window pane, click the Switch to Classic View option.

2. Click the Hardware tab and click the Device Manager button.

3. Expand the DVD/CD-ROM Drives category. Right-click the icon for your DVD player, and then click Properties.

4. On the DVD Region tab, the current region is displayed. Click a geographic area in the list and look in the New Region field to see the region code of

the geographic area you need to use to change the currently configured code. Click OK when you are done.

5. A message appears asking, "Are you sure you want to change your DVD drive region setting to region *x*?" Click OK.

TIP   *If you cannot change the code, then your DVD does not support other regions. The only solution is to purchase a DVD-ROM drive for the region in which you now reside.*

Chapter 7

Windows XP Peripheral Headaches

In this chapter, you'll cure...

■ Problems with peripherals

■ Difficulties with game controllers

Like all computers today, Windows XP supports a number of different peripherals and game controllers. The term "peripheral" loosely refers to hardware devices that are used to interact with your computer. Keyboards, mice, and game controllers are all examples of peripherals. All peripherals allow you to manage and interact with your computer. Without them, you could see what is on your computer screen, but you would be powerless to interact with it.

Peripherals are generally easy to use and easy to install. Normally, you just connect them to the correct port and off you go. However, you may have some possible installation Headaches, depending on the peripheral; for those problems, see Chapter 5. The rest of the Headaches you are likely to experience relate to using the peripherals and getting them to work the way you want. Technically, although game controllers are peripherals, I have separated them in this chapter for organizational purposes.

Windows XP Peripheral Problems

There are a number of different peripherals you can use, such as keyboards, mice, trackballs or trackwheels, and a variety of freehand writing and drawing devices. Keyboards and mice are the most common and necessary, and a number of different Headaches concerning keyboards and mice can arise, so I'll focus on those in this section. The Headaches you are likely to experience with keyboards and mice are usually easy to solve, and in the following sections, I'll give you the cure for the most common problems.

My keyboard does not work.

Operating Systems Affected   Windows XP Professional and Home Editions are affected.

Cause   If your keyboard does not respond at all, there is a communication problem between the keyboard and your computer, and a few possible explanations.

The Pain Killer   Try these solutions:

1. Check the connection on the keyboard port. The keyboard may not be plugged in. If your keyboard has worked previously, this most often is the cause of the problem. Just plug the keyboard in securely, and the keyboard should start working.

2. If the keyboard is plugged in correctly but still not working, reboot your computer and see if Windows XP can redetect and install it.

3. If this does not work, you may need to get a keyboard driver from the keyboard manufacturer or get technical support help to solve the problem. See Chapter 5 for more information about solving hardware installation problems.

NOTE   *Keep in mind that you cannot install new hardware unless you are logged on with an administrator account. See Chapter 3 for more information about user accounts.*

 ## The keyboard works too slowly.

Operating Systems Affected   Windows XP Professional and Home Editions are affected.

Cause   Keyboard settings determine how fast keystrokes appear on your screen when you touch the keyboard. If the keyboard is working too slowly, you can adjust the keyboard stroke speed.

TIP   *All Control Panel instructions in this chapter assume you are using the Classic view. If you are not, just Click Start | Control Panel, and then click the option in the left portion of the window to use Classic view.*

The Pain Killer   To adjust the keyboard speed, follow these steps:

1. Click Start | Control Panel | Keyboard.

2. On the Speed tab, adjust the Repeat Delay and Repeat Rate settings so that they are longer or shorter and slower or faster, respectively. You can use the repeat box, shown in the illustration, to test the repeat rate setting.

Keyboard Properties

Speed | Hardware

Character repeat

Repeat delay:
Long ———————⬤——— Short

Repeat rate:
Slow ———————————⬤ Fast

Click here and hold down a key to test repeat rate:

Cursor blink rate

| None ——————⬤——— Fast

OK | Cancel | Apply

3. Click OK when you are done.

Keep in mind that you can return to this window and adjust the settings again if you still do not like the performance.

My cursor blinks too fast/slow.

Operating Systems Affected   Windows XP Professional and Home Editions are affected.

Cause   The cursor's blink rate is usually set to a middle configuration between no blinking at all and fast blinking. However, you can adjust how your cursor blinks so that it works the way you want it to.

The Pain Killer   To adjust the cursor blink rate, follow these steps:

1. Click Start | Control Panel | Keyboard.

2. On the Speed tab, you'll see a Cursor Blink Rate slider bar. Adjust the slider bar until the cursor blinks at a rate that is pleasing to you. Click OK when you are done.

The cursor blink rate does not affect how fast you can type. In other words, a slow cursor blink rate simply means that the cursor blinks slowly; it does not mean that the keyboard responds slowly.

My keyboard one-touch buttons do not work.

Operating Systems Affected Windows XP Professional and Home Editions are affected.

Cause Depending on your computer manufacturer, you may have some additional buttons on your keyboard for "one-touch" access. For example, you may have a single button that puts the computer into standby, or you may have an Internet button that connects you to the Internet. These buttons are manufacturer specific and vary from keyboard to keyboard. If you are having problems, there is most likely a configuration change of some kind that you can make.

The Pain Killer To change the one-touch configuration, click Start | Control Panel | Keyboard. You may see an additional tab that concerns these keys. For example, in the illustration, you can see that I can configure my DellTouch keys using the window provided. You'll need to check your manufacturer's documentation for specific information and steps for configuring these keys on your keyboard model.

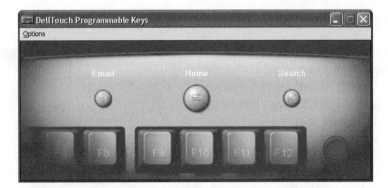

Because of a disability, I can't use my keyboard correctly. How can I get help?

Operating Systems Affected Windows XP Professional and Home Editions are affected.

Cause Windows XP provides a number of features that can help people with certain disabilities use the computer more easily. You can learn about some of them in Chapter 1, but there are a few additional help features that work specifically on the keyboard. Because the keyboard is built for two-handed use, this creates Headaches for users with disabilities. So, Windows XP provides the following support features:

- **StickyKeys**   StickyKeys "stick" when you press them. For example, in order to press CTRL+ALT+DEL, you need two hands. For some users, two-handed use is impossible or is very difficult. A solution is to turn on the StickyKeys feature, which allows you to press CTRL first, then ALT, and then DEL. Windows XP will hold the keystrokes and still open the Close Program window, even though you did not actually press them all at once.

- **FilterKeys**   FilterKeys is a feature that allows Windows XP to ignore brief or repeated keystrokes. If you have problems pressing keys without accidentally hitting them twice, then this feature can help you.

- **ToggleKeys**   ToggleKeys play tones when you press CAPS LOCK, NUM LOCK, and SCROLL LOCK. This feature is helpful to persons with vision impairment.

The Pain Killer   To turn on any of these features, follow these steps:

1. Click Start | Control Panel | Accessibility Options.

2. On the Keyboard tab, click the check boxes next to the keyboard accessibility features you want to use. Click the Settings button for each feature to further determine how the feature works. The options in each Settings window are self-explanatory. When you are done, click OK.

My mouse keeps sticking.

Operating Systems Affected   Windows XP Professional and Home Editions are affected.

Cause   If your mouse pointer seems to stick on the screen when you move the mouse, there are two possible problems:

■ The mouse ball has collected gunk over time and needs to be cleaned.

■ The mouse ball is wearing out and is not communicating movement to the computer.

The Pain Killer   To fix the problem, you'll need one of these solutions:

■ You can clean the mouse ball gently with an alcohol pad, or you can buy cleaner at a computer store. If this does not work, go to the second solution.

■ Mice get a lot of use and abuse and do not last forever. If you are having a lot of tracking problems, you might just want to buy a new one. A good mouse usually costs under $30. Make sure you buy one that is compatible with Windows (most are). Also, consider buying an optical mouse, which is not as susceptible to gunk buildup and wear and tear.

 # I am left-handed, and I find right-clicking difficult.

Operating Systems Affected   Windows XP Professional and Home Editions are affected.

Cause   Mouse keys provide right and left buttons; but to left-handed people, who use the mouse on the left side, it sometimes feels wrong to find the right-click features on the right side. The good news is that you can easily reverse the keys so that the left key is the primary key and the right key is the secondary key. This means that right-click features will work on the left key and left-click features will work on the right key.

The Pain Killer   To change the primary and secondary button configuration on your mouse, follow these steps:

1. Click Start | Control Panel | Mouse.

2. On the Buttons tab, select the Switch Primary and Secondary Buttons check box and click OK.

Mouse Properties

Buttons | Pointers | Pointer Options | Wheel | Hardware

Button configuration

☑ Switch primary and secondary buttons

Select this check box to make the button on the
right the one you use for primary functions such
as selecting and dragging.

Double-click speed

Double-click the folder to test your setting. If the
folder does not open or close, try using a slower
setting.

Speed: Slow ————————[]———————— Fast

ClickLock

☐ Turn on ClickLock   [Settings...]

Enables you to highlight or drag without holding down the mouse
button. To set, briefly press the mouse button. To release, click the
mouse button again.

[OK]   [Cancel]   [Apply]

Double-clicking does not work well.

Operating Systems Affected   Windows XP Professional and Home Editions are
affected.

Cause   The double-click response rate is determined by a setting in the Mouse
Properties window. If the double-click feature is too fast or too slow, you can
adjust it to meet your needs.

The Pain Killer   To adjust the double-click speed, follow these steps:

1. Click Start | Control Panel | Mouse.

2. On the Buttons tab, adjust the Double-Click Speed slider bar until you find
   the setting that is right for you, and click OK.

My mouse pointer is too small/large.

Operating Systems Affected   Windows XP Professional and Home Editions are
affected.

Cause   The mouse pointers that you see on your computer screen are the pointers
for the default Windows mouse pointer scheme. The scheme tells Windows the
kind of pointer to display when you are moving your mouse, when the system is

What Is ClickLock?

ClickLock is a feature that lets you drag items without holding down the mouse button. You turn on ClickLock by holding down the left mouse key for a moment; then you can let go of the key and still drag items. To release it, all you have to do is click the button again. This feature can be very helpful if you have problems holding down the left mouse key because of physical difficulties, or you simply may find that ClickLock is easier to use when dragging and dropping.

If you click Start | Control Panel | Mouse and click the Button tab, you can turn on ClickLock by selecting the Turn On ClickLock check box at the bottom of the window. If you click the Settings button, you see a small dialog box, shown in the illustration, which lets you set how long you need to hold down the mouse key until ClickLock is turned on or off. If you use a laptop computer, you should certainly try ClickLock; you'll find the option easier than dragging with the touch pad. Experiment with this feature and see if you like it!

busy, when you are working in the background, and in a number of other situations as well. If you do not like the default Windows scheme, you can choose another one or even customize different pointer options so that the mouse pointers work well for you.

The Pain Killer   To change the mouse pointers, follow these steps:

1. Click Start | Control Panel | Mouse.

2. Click the Pointers tab. The Pointers tab shows you the default scheme and the appearance of the pointers under that scheme, as shown in the illustration. The Windows Default scheme is automatically configured, but you can click the Scheme drop-down menu and select one of the many other schemes available. Some schemes make pointers larger or smaller, and some simply make the pointers more fun. For example, in the illustration, I have selected the Dinosaur scheme.

3. Once you find a scheme that you like, just click OK to begin using it. You can return to the Pointers tab at any time and change the scheme to something else.

4. Another possibility is that you might find a scheme you like, but decide one of the pointer options is not right for you. You can customize that particular pointer and save your own scheme. First, select the pointer that you want to change in the Customize box, and then click Browse.

5. The Browse window appears, showing all of the available cursor files. Choose a pointer that you want to use and click Open. This will return you to the Pointers tab, and the cursor you selected will now be in place.

6. Click the Save As button, give your modified scheme a name (anything will do), and click OK. You now have your own customized scheme.

You can also use pointer files that you download from the Internet, but Windows will only use pointers that are animation files or cursor files. In other words, if you download a pointer called CoolPointer from the Internet, the pointer must be a CoolPointer.ani or CoolPointer.cur file in order to work with Windows XP. If you like the idea of cool and interesting mouse pointers, check out http://www.pcworld.com/downloads and look for a link for "Cursors" to get you started. Or, check other sites by using your favorite search engine to search for "Windows mouse pointers."

My mouse pointer creates a trailing effect when I move it.

Operating Systems Affected   Windows XP Professional and Home Editions are affected.

Cause   Your mouse pointer can be configured to trail when it is moved, which just gives it a blurring movement effect. Some people like this; others get a feeling of motion sickness. If you don't like it, you can easily stop the behavior.

The Pain Killer   To stop the mouse trail effect, follow these steps:

1. Click Start | Control Panel | Mouse.

2. Click the Pointer Options tab. Under Visibility, clear the Display Pointer Trails check box and click OK.

My mouse pointer disappears when I am typing.

Operating Systems Affected
Windows XP Professional and Home Editions are affected.

Cause   Mouse pointers typically remain available when you are typing on the keyboard; however, a setting can be selected that makes the mouse pointer disappear when you are typing.

The Pain Killer   To prevent the mouse pointer from disappearing, follow these steps:

1. Click Start | Control Panel | Mouse.

2. Click the Pointer Options tab. Under Visibility, clear the Hide Pointer While Typing check box and click OK.

NOTE   *Some laptops have an annoying button between the two mouse buttons that will lock your taskbar so that you can't move the cursor when you're typing. You should be able to click the button again to unlock it.*

My mouse wheel makes entire pages scroll by.

Operating Systems Affected   Windows XP Professional and Home Editions are affected.

Cause   Most mice have a scroll wheel that is located between the two keys. This makes scrolling through documents and Web pages easier. However, if the setting it too high, you may have difficulty scrolling.

The Pain Killer   To prevent the mouse wheel from scrolling too quickly, follow these steps:

1. Click Start | Control Panel | Mouse.

2. Click the Wheel tab. Instead of using the One Screen at a Time button, choose the Following Number of Lines at a Time option and configure it for three lines at a time. This scroll setting works best for most people. Click OK.

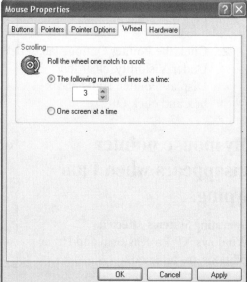

I am having problems with a wireless mouse/ keyboard.

Operating Systems Affected   Windows XP Professional and Home Editions are affected.

Cause   A number of wireless mice and keyboards are available, all of which work with your computer's infrared port. These devices are great because they allow you flexibility and a computing experience without aggravating wires. However, you can have some problems with infrared devices.

The Pain Killer   There are some common reasons and solutions for infrared problems:

- **Distance/obstruction**   For infrared devices to work, the mouse or keyboard must be within range of the infrared port, and other objects must not be blocking the infrared beams.

- **Unconfigured infrared port**   If the devices do not work at all, you may need to configure your infrared port. You'll need to check both your computer's documentation and your keyboard or mouse documentation for configuration assistance.

Chapter 8

Windows XP Printer, Scanner, and Camera Headaches

In this chapter, you'll cure...

- ■ Problems with printer setup
- ■ Frustrating printer problems
- ■ Difficulties with scanners and cameras

When computers first began to become popular in offices and homes, analysts thought we would one day have a paperless society. After all, with computer networks and e-mail, why use paper? The truth, of course, is completely opposite. Most home users have a printer, and we use millions of sheets of paper a year— there's just something about printed hardcopy that is always better than what you see on the screen.

So, if you have a printer, what Headaches might you encounter? There are a number of potential problems that might come your way. Before we get into the specifics of printer Headaches, as well as scanner and camera Headaches, let me first of all say that your product documentation should be your first line of defense. Always refer to the documentation and the printer manufacturer's web site, which can probably offer you helpful troubleshooting tips and address known issues and problems. For the rest, read on.

Printer Setup Problems

Printers work like any other hardware device. You connect the printer to the correct port on your computer, and Windows XP generally installs necessary drivers. Referring back to Chapter 5, a driver is a piece of software that allows Windows XP to work with a device, such as a printer. Without the correct driver, the device will not work. Most printers come to you with a software CD, which installs tools, utilities, and a driver. Again, save yourself some Headaches and read the manufacturer's setup instructions. Follow the instructions exactly, and you should be home free.

NOTE *Most printers do not ship with the USB cable you'll need to connect the printer to the PC, which is a real pain. However, the good news is that installation is typically a breeze with Windows XP, since Windows XP has most of the drivers already installed.*

Windows XP does not detect my printer.

Operating Systems Affected   Windows XP Professional and Home Editions are affected.

Cause   Windows XP's Plug and Play normally does a good job of detecting new hardware. Once you plug the printer into the correct port (usually an LPT port or a USB port), Windows XP can detect the printer. However, if you are having problems installing a printer, first make sure the printer is compatible with Windows XP. If you are sure it is, you can use the Add a Printer Wizard.

> **NOTE**   *The Add a Printer Wizard is designed to help you set up printers when you are having problems. Under most circumstances, you do not need to use this wizard.*

The Pain Killer   To use the Add a Printer Wizard, follow these steps:

1. Click Start | Control Panel | Printers and Faxes.

> **NOTE**   *These steps and other discussions assume you are using the Classic view of Control Panel, which shows you all the icon options. If you are not sure you are using the Classic view of Control Panel, click Start | Control Panel. In the left window pane, click the Switch to Classic View option.*

2. In the Printers and Faxes window, click the Add a Printer option.

3. Click Next on the Welcome screen.

4. In the Local or Network Printer screen, select the Local Printer Attached to This Computer option, and select the check box to let Windows XP detect your device.

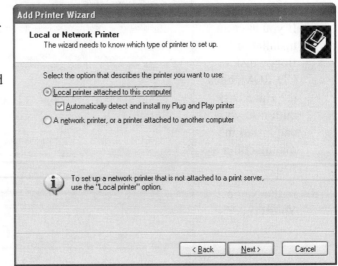

5. Windows XP searches for the printer attached to your computer. If the printer is found, it is installed. If not, the wizard tells you that a printer was not found, and you can install the printer manually. Click Next.

Make sure the printer is turned on when you are trying to install it!

6. In the Select a Printer Port screen, use the drop-down menu to choose the port where the printer is connected. Before continuing, make absolutely certain that the printer is connected to the port correctly. See your printer's documentation for specific instructions. Click Next.

Add Printer Wizard

Select a Printer Port
Computers communicate with printers through ports.

Select the port you want your printer to use. If the port is not listed, you can create a new port.

○ Use the following port: `LPT1: (Recommended Printer Port)`

Note: Most computers use the LPT1: port to communicate with a local printer. The connector for this port should look something like this:

○ Create a new port:
Type of port: `Local Port`

< Back   Next >   Cancel

7. In the Install Printer Software screen, choose the manufacturer and model of your printer and click Next. If you have an installation floppy disk or CD-ROM, click the Have Disk button so you can install the manufacturer's software.

8. In the Name Your Printer

Add Printer Wizard

Install Printer Software
The manufacturer and model determine which printer software to use.

Select the manufacturer and model of your printer. If your printer came with an installation disk, click Have Disk. If your printer is not listed, consult your printer documentation for compatible printer software.

Manufacturer	Printers
AT&T	Canon Bubble-Jet BJ-10e
Brother	Canon Bubble-Jet BJ-10ex
Bull	Canon Bubble-Jet BJ-10sx
Canon	Canon Bubble-Jet BJ-20
Citizen	

This driver is digitally signed.
Tell me why driver signing is important

Windows Update   Have Disk...

< Back   Next >   Cancel

screen, give the printer a friendly name, and choose whether or not to use the printer as the default printer. Click Next.

9. In the Print Test Page screen, you can choose to print a test page if you click the Yes radio button. Click Yes or No, and then click Next.

10. Click Finish. The new printer now appears in the Printers and Faxes window, as shown in the illustration.

If you follow these steps and the printer does not work, double-check the documentation and possibly the manufacturer's web site to make sure that you have followed the instructions correctly. If you have, it may be time to call the printer manufacturer's hotline for support.

I cannot get an older printer to work with Windows XP.

Operating Systems Affected   Windows XP Professional and Home Editions are affected.

Cause   Hardware, such as a printer, has to be compatible with Windows XP. You may be able to get an older model printer to work with Windows XP, but you will often need an updated driver.

The Pain Killer   To get an updated driver, visit the manufacturer's web site and see if a new driver for the printer model has been developed. If there is a printer driver for Windows 2000 but not for XP, the 2000 driver may work on XP. Download the new driver, and follow the manufacturer's instructions for installation.

TIP

Always remember, the driver is the key to good compatibility with virtually all hardware. If Windows XP does not have a good driver for the hardware you are trying to use, you will probably have difficulties.

My USB printer does not work, even though other USB devices connected to the USB hub work.

Operating Systems Affected   Windows XP Professional and Home Editions are affected.

Cause   USB hubs allow a number of different devices to connect to them, but some devices can pull too much power, causing other devices not to work or not to work well.

The Pain Killer   Plug the printer into a different USB port. If that does not work, unplug some of the other USB devices. If the printer now works, you may need to consider installing an additional USB hub or a self-powered USB hub. See the Windows XP Help and Support Center to learn more about USB devices and also see Chapter 5 for more information about self-powered hubs.

I can't connect to a network printer.

Operating Systems Affected   Windows XP Professional and Home Editions are affected.

Cause   The good thing about networked printers is that several different people can use the same printer, and that saves money and desk space. In an office environment, a networked printer can mean the need for only one printer for an entire department. In a home environment, you can create a small home network so that a single printer can be shared among computers.

   If a printer is shared on the network, you can access it and use it, assuming the owner of the printer has given you permission to do so. If you are having problems connecting to a shared printer, the Add a Printer Wizard can help you.

The Pain Killer   To use the Add a Printer Wizard to connect to a network printer, follow these steps:

1. Click Start | Control Panel (Classic view) | Printers and Faxes.

2. In the Printers and Faxes window, click the Add a Printer option.

3. Click Next on the Welcome screen.

4. In the Local or Network Printer screen, choose the Network printer radio button and click Next.

5. In the Specify a Printer screen, you can click the Browse for a Printer radio button to look for the printer, or you can connect to a specific printer by providing the network path, using the format *servername*\ *printername*. If you don't know the network path, click the Browse for a Printer radio button and then click Next.

> **Add Printer Wizard**
>
> **Specify a Printer**
> If you don't know the name or address of the printer, you can search for a printer that meets your needs.
>
> What printer do you want to connect to?
>
> ◉ Browse for a printer
>
> ○ Connect to this printer (or to browse for a printer, select this option and click Next):
>
>   Name: [   ]
>
>   Example: \\server\printer
>
> ○ Connect to a printer on the Internet or on a home or office network:
>
>   URL: [   ]
>
>   Example: http://server/printers/myprinter/.printer
>
> [< Back] [Next >] [Cancel]

6. In the Browse for Printer screen, find the computer and expand it in the list. This will allow you to see the printers that are shared. Select the printer you want to connect to and click Next.

> **Add Printer Wizard**
>
> **Browse for Printer**
> When the list of printers appears, select the one you want to use.
>
> Printer: [\\CSIMMONS\HP]
>
> Shared printers:
> - CURT
>   - CSIMMONS
>   - **HP**
>   - PRINTER
>   - PRINTER2
>   - PRINTER3
>   - PRINTER4
>
> Printer information
> Comment:
> Status: Ready   Documents waiting: 0
>
> [< Back] [Next >] [Cancel]

7. You can choose whether or not to print a test page by clicking Yes or No. Click Next.

8. Click Finish.

TIP   *See the next section to learn more about sharing a printer so that other users can access it.*

Solving Printing Problems

Once the printer is up and running, your work with it will probably be trouble free. However, there are some common Headaches you might experience, and the following sections explain those problems and how to solve them.

My printer prints garbled text.

Operating Systems Affected   Windows XP Professional and Home Editions are affected.

Cause   If your printer prints garbled text, it is almost always a sign of a bad or corrupt driver. Even if you installed the correct driver, it may have become corrupt over time. In this case, you need to reinstall the driver for the printer.

The Pain Killer   To update the printer driver, follow these steps:

1. Download a new copy of the printer driver from the manufacturer's web site. You can also use the installation CD; but if you have Internet access, always check the manufacturer's Web site first because you will get the latest driver and information from the site.

2. Click Start | Control Panel (Classic view) | Printers and Faxes.

3. Right-click the desired printer icon and click Properties.

4. Click the Advanced tab and then click the New Driver button.

5. The Add Printer Driver Wizard appears. Click Next.

6. In the Printer Driver Selection screen, choose the manufacturer and model of your printer, or click the Have Disk button to install the driver from the floppy or CD-ROM drive (or from the hard drive, if you downloaded the driver). Click Next.

7. Click Finish.

NOTE   *Remember, any time you have garbled text or the printer just does not work well with the computer (such as in the case of communication errors), the driver is commonly the problem.*

A certain file will not print.

Operating Systems Affected   Windows XP Professional and Home Editions are affected.

Cause   If a certain file type will not print, but other documents print fine, there is probably some kind of software problem between the application you are using and your operating system. This happens sometimes with games and programs that have print features, especially if those games were written for a different operating system. Case in point, my daughter has a My Pretty Pony CD that works fine on Windows 9x/Me. It also works on XP, but when she tries to print something, it just prints a bunch of lines.

The Pain Killer   Since this is a software compatibility problem, I'm afraid there is not much you can do except to try and get a software upgrade so that the software will work fully with Windows XP.

No documents or files are printing, even though the printer was working fine previously.

Operating Systems Affected   Windows XP Professional and Home Editions are affected.

Cause   When you choose to print documents or files, they are held in a print queue on the computer's hard disk until the printer can take the jobs. Sometimes, software problems can cause the queue to become clogged. When that happens, print jobs cannot flow to the printer. In this case, you need to flush out the queue so that you can get the printer going again. Once you remove the current jobs from the queue, you'll need to reprint all of the print jobs that were waiting.

The Pain Killer   To flush out the queue, follow these steps:

1. In the notification area of the Windows XP taskbar (at the lower-right corner of your screen), right-click the printer icon and click the Open option.

2. The printer queue window appears, as you can see in the illustration. You can see the current documents waiting to be printed that are stuck in the queue. To clear the queue, click the Printer menu and then click Cancel All Documents.

🖨 Canon Bubble-Jet BJ-10ex					⊟ ⊡ ☒
Printer Document View Help					
Document Name	Status	Owner	Pages	Size	Subr
🔳 Untitled - Notepad	Error - Print...	Curt	1	1.07 KB/1.09 KB	9:51:
🔳 Untitled - Notepad		Curt	1	1.09 KB	9:51:
🔳 Untitled - Notepad		Curt	1	1.09 KB	9:51:
‹					›
3 document(s) in queue					

I can't stop a document from printing.

Operating Systems Affected   Windows XP Professional and Home Editions are affected.

Cause   If you chose to print a document and now you want it to stop printing, you can use the print queue. The print queue is particularly helpful when you have a long document that you no longer want to print.

The Pain Killer   To stop a document from printing, follow these steps:

1. In the notification area of the Windows XP taskbar (at the lower-right corner of your screen), right-click the printer icon and click Open All Active Printers and Faxes.

2. Select the document you want to stop from printing; then click the Document menu and choose Cancel. If your printer has memory, another page or two may still print after you have clicked Cancel. You can easily stop this by removing the paper from the tray.

My printer color or fonts do not look good.

Operating Systems Affected   Windows XP Professional and Home Editions are affected.

Cause   This problem typically occurs if incorrect settings are configured for the printer or setup has gone haywire.

The Pain Killer   Since the solution to these kinds of problems varies from printer to printer, you'll need to check the printer manufacturer's instructions or the manufacturer's web site for help. Usually, there are settings that you can change in order to improve the quality or actions you can take, such as replacing the ink cartridge.

My printer works very slowly.

Operating Systems Affected Windows XP Professional and Home Editions are affected.

Cause If printing files seems to be very slow, you may be running low on system resources, such as RAM or hard disk space.

The Pain Killer Try closing other programs when you print to see if it makes a difference. If you continue to have problems, you may need some hardware upgrades. If your computer barely meets the recommended hardware requirements for Windows XP, printing will slow everything down, I'm afraid.

My computer stops responding when I print something and begins to respond again only when the print job is finished.

Operating Systems Affected Windows XP Professional and Home Editions are affected.

Cause Print jobs should be handled by a process called the Windows spooler, which processes and holds print jobs until they are printed. This frees up the computer so that you can continue to work and play while the printer is working. If the spooler is not used, however, the computer will not respond until the print job is finished.

Which Spool Setting Option Should I Use?

You can see on the Advanced tab of Printer Properties that if you choose the Spool Print Documents So Program Finishes Printing Faster option, you can select one of two radio buttons: Start Printing After Last Page Is Spooled and Start Printing Immediately. The default setting is Start Printing Immediately, which allows the printer to get started and returns the application to you faster. However, this setting could cause you to experience communication errors in some cases. If you want to make sure that the entire print job gets to the spool before printing starts, choose the Start Printing After Last Page Is Spooled radio button. This will slow down the return of your application, however. For most users, the Start Printing Immediately setting is best.

The Pain Killer   To make sure you are using the spooler, follow these steps:

1. Click Start | Control Panel (Classic view) | Printers and Faxes.

2. Right-click the desired printer icon and click Properties.

3. Click the Advanced tab. Make sure the Spool Print Documents So Program Finishes Printing Faster option is selected—*not* the Print Directly to the Printer option.

My printer keeps printing in landscape instead of portrait orientation.

Operating Systems Affected   Windows XP Professional and Home Editions are affected.

Cause   You can configure your printer to print in either landscape or portrait orientation by default, but programs can also determine how the page setup works. If your printer always prints landscape instead of portrait, no matter what printer you are using, see the following Pain Killer for instructions. If the problem seems to happen only when you use a certain application, see the application's help files for instructions about how to correct the problem.

The Pain Killer   To configure the printer to print in portrait instead of landscape orientation, follow these steps:

1. Click Start | Control Panel (Classic view) | Printers and Faxes.

2. Right-click the desired printer icon and click Properties.

3. Click the General tab and click the Printing Preferences button.

4. On the Layout tab, change the Orientation setting to Portrait instead of Landscape.

I can't share my printer so that other users on my network can use it.

Operating Systems Affected   Windows XP Professional and Home Editions are affected.

Cause   In order to share a printer, you can access the Sharing tab on the printer's properties pages. However, if the sharing option does not seem to be available, then you have not yet set up networking on your Windows XP computer.

The Pain Killer   For instructions on configuring networking components on your computer, see Chapter 12.

I want to make a shared printer available only at certain times, but I can't do it without also restricting myself.

Operating Systems Affected   Windows XP Professional and Home Editions are affected.

Cause   If you have a shared printer, there may be cases where you only want the printer available at certain times to network users, but all the time for yourself. You can do this by creating two separate printers for the same physical printer. Sound confusing? It's not.

In the Printers and Faxes window, you have an icon that represents your printer. Actually, that icon represents the software *for* the printer. In Microsoft terms, that icon is called the *printer,* while the device that sits on your desk is called a *print device*. So, you can configure two different printers for the same print device—one is shared while the other is not. The shared printer has a time restriction, and the nonshared printer (used by you only) has no restrictions. It is the same print device, but two different software configurations exist for it.

The Pain Killer   To configure different printers with different restrictions, follow these steps:

1. Use the Add a Printer Wizard to create a second printer for the print device. See the first Headache in this chapter for step-by-step instructions.

2. When you create the second printer, access the properties pages.

3. Share the printer and configure permissions as needed. (See Chapter 11 for more information about network setup.)

4. Click the Advanced tab. Choose the Available From option and configure the time limit range as you like, as shown here.

5. Click OK. Now the printer will be available to network users under the time constraints you configured, but you still have your original printer that is not shared, allowing you access all the time.

Solving Problems with Scanners and Cameras

Scanners and cameras work like any other hardware device; that is, you must connect the scanner or camera to the correct port, and you will probably need to use the software that came with the camera or scanner to set up the connection.

Beyond the Headaches listed in the next few pages, you are not likely to have many problems with these devices. Remember to always check the manufacturer's documentation for instructions and troubleshooting issues—and always buy products that are compatible with Windows XP.

I can't get my scanner or camera to install.

Operating Systems Affected   Windows XP Professional and Home Editions are affected.

Cause   If you are having problems installing the scanner or camera, make certain that you are following the manufacturer's instructions provided with the device and that the scanner or camera is connected to the computer correctly. USB devices may require that you install the drivers before plugging in the device, so check the documentation for details. If you are sure that you have followed the instructions and that your device is compatible with Windows XP, you can use the Add an Imaging Device Wizard to help you.

The Pain Killer   To add an imaging device, follow these steps:

1. Click Start | Control Panel (Classic view) | Scanners and Cameras.

2. In the Scanners and Cameras window, click the Add an Imaging Device option under Imaging Tasks.

3. The Scanner and Camera Installation Wizard appears. Click Next on the Welcome screen.

4. In the provided list, shown in the illustration, choose the manufacturer and model of the scanner or camera that you want to install. If you have an installation disk, click the Have Disk button. Click Next.

Scanner and Camera Installation Wizard
Which scanner or camera do you want to install?
Select the manufacturer and model of your device. If you have an installation disk, click Have Disk.
Manufacturer	Model
Agfa	FUJIFILM MX-700 Digital Camera
Casio	
Epson	
FUJIFILM	
Hewlett Packard	
This driver is digitally signed.	Have Disk...
Tell me why driver signing is important	
< Back	Next >	Cancel

5. In the next screen, make sure the device is connected to your computer and choose the Automatic Port Detection option. Click Next.

6. Type a name for the device, and then click Next.

7. Click Finish.

My scanner/camera does not work correctly or works only intermittently.

Operating Systems Affected   Windows XP Professional and Home Editions are affected.

Cause   If the device is installed but does not work the way it should or works only intermittently, it usually means you have a driver problem. Either you need an updated driver that works with Windows XP, or the current driver is becoming corrupt.

The Pain Killer   You'll need to update the driver to try to correct the problem. See Chapter 5 for instructions about updating device drivers.

> TIP
> *Remember, read the manufacturer's instructions concerning scanners and cameras. They usually contain valuable information, as well as specific instructions and issues you should be aware of in order to make your scanner or camera work the way it should.*

Chapter 9

Windows XP Internet Connection Headaches

In this chapter, you'll cure...

- Problems with Internet connections

- Aggravating modem behavior

- Difficulties with Windows Firewall

The Internet has become a very important part of all of our lives, and the odds are very good that if you own a Windows XP computer, you also have a connection to the Internet. The Internet provides a rich landscape of information and multimedia—but enough advertising. The connection issues with Windows XP and the Internet can give you such a Headache that you can't even have fun. In truth, connections to the Internet are easier to configure and use on Windows XP than they have been on any older version of Windows. Still, Internet connections can be tricky, and there are a number of Headaches with the connection and modems that you might encounter.

An updated feature in Service Pack 2 is Windows Firewall. Windows Firewall helps protect your computer from hackers on the Internet, but you might run into some Headaches with Windows Firewall as well. In this chapter, we'll explore connections, modems, and Windows Firewall Headaches and find the cures you need!

Windows XP Internet Connection Headaches

In order for your computer to connect to the Internet, you need three main things:

- **A physical connection**   You'll need either a modem, DSL hardware, cable connection, or Internet satellite hardware.

- **A configured connection**   The connection tells your computer how to use the connection hardware, the number to dial or access, your user name and password, and so forth.

- **Software for the Internet   You'll need a web browser to access web pages** and an e-mail client to send and receive e-mail. Windows XP includes Internet Explorer for your browser and Outlook Express for your e-mail client. See Chapters 10 and 11 to learn more.

Your computer probably already has an internal modem, as most do. You may want a broadband connection to the Internet, which provides very fast access and

Which ISP Should I Use?

If you have not yet signed up with an ISP, you can try to do that when you are using the New Connection Wizard, but you may want to sign up with one beforehand. There is no right or wrong answer concerning the ISP you want to use. You must find one that provides local access numbers and the services you like. Most of them offer competitive rates, and you can choose to go with a national ISP, such as MSN or AOL, or you can find a local provider in your area. Do not assume that national ISPs will give you better service though—many local providers have great service and even lower prices. Ask around and get input from friends and your family before making a decision. Then, all you need to do is call the ISP to get an account, or if you have Internet access through another account or a friend's computer, you can probably sign up online.

downloads as well as an "always on" feature (you don't dial any numbers). Broadband connections—such as cable modems, DSL connections, and Internet satellite—have a number of advantages over modems, but they do cost more. Because these connections are vendor specific, you'll need to refer to the provider's documentation or turn to them for help if you are having problems. If you are using a modem, we'll cover modem configuration a little later in this chapter.

For now, let's turn our attention to the Internet connection. Your computer has everything you need to create a connection to the Internet, but you have to create it and configure it. That's where the problems can come in, and in the following sections I'll explore the Headaches you are likely to get.

I don't know how to create an Internet connection.

Operating Systems Affected   Windows XP Professional and Home Editions are affected.

Cause   Internet connections can be created with a wizard. You can click Start | Control Panel | Network Connections. You see an option to Create a New Connection in the Network Tasks window. You can start this wizard and configure the connection.

TIP   *The following steps and other discussions assume you are using the Classic view of Control Panel, which shows you all the icon options. If you are not sure if you are using the Classic view of Control Panel, click Start | Control Panel. In the left window pane, click the Switch to Classic View option.*

The Pain Killer   To use the New Connection Wizard, follow these steps:

1. Click Start | Control Panel | Network Connections. Click the Create a New Connection link in the Network Tasks pane. Or, you can also access the wizard by clicking Start | All Programs | Accessories | Communications | New Connection Wizard. Either way is fine.

2. The New Connection Wizard Welcome screen appears. Click Next.

3. In the Network Connection Type window, click the Connect to the Internet radio button and click Next.

4. In the Getting Ready window, you can choose to see a list of Internet service providers and sign up with one. If you already have a provider (such as MSN, AOL, Earthlink, or even a local company), you can choose to set up the connection either manually or with a CD. If you have a setup CD from your ISP, choose that option and follow the instructions that appear. If you want to set up the connection manually, read on.

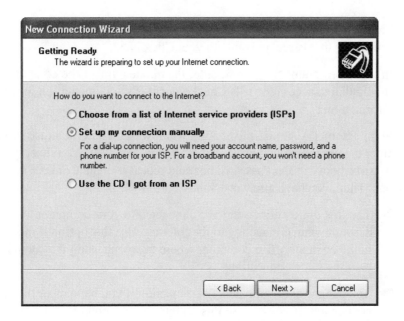

5. In the Internet Connection window, choose the type of connection that you are using, such as dial-up (modem), broadband (user name/password required), or always on. I'll assume you are using a modem for this example. Make your selection and click Next.

6. Enter a name for the connection. The name can be anything—just something that is recognizable to you. Click Next.

7. In the Phone Number window, enter the phone number the computer should dial to access the ISP. Check your ISP's documentation for more information.

8. In the Internet Account Information window, shown in the illustration, enter the user name and password created by your ISP. You must type your password once in the Password box and repeat it in the Confirm Password box. Then, you have a few check box options:

■ The first option allows anyone connected to your computer to use the account when connecting to the Internet. Use this option if this is a home or small office computer where everyone using the computer uses the same connection.

■ You can make this the default connection if you have more than one connection. If you choose this option, the computer will always try to use this connection first.

■ You can choose to turn on ICF for the connection if you like. We'll get to ICF issues later in this chapter. Make your selections and entries and click Next.

9. Click Finish. The new connection now appears in your Network Connections folder. You'll also see the Connection window so that you can test the connection.

Connect My Connection [?][X]

User name: csimmons

Password: *[To change the saved password, click here]*

☑ Save this user name and password for the following users:
  ○ Me only
  ⦿ Anyone who uses this computer

Dial: 5551212

[Dial] [Cancel] [Properties] [Help]

I do not want other users accessing my Internet connection, but they can.

Operating Systems Affected Windows XP Professional and Home Editions are affected.

Cause When you created the Internet connection, you could specify if other users could access the connection or not (see the previous Headache). If you enabled the option, you can change it so that only you are allowed to access your connection.

The Pain Killer To make your connection private, follow these steps:

1. Click Start | Network Connections | *the desired connection.*

2. In the Connection window, click the Me Only radio button so that only you will be able to access the connection. Click Dial.

3. If you had previously allowed other users to use the connection, you'll see a message telling you that your user name and password will be saved, but deleted for all other users. Click Yes.

 # I need to configure more than one dial-up number.

Operating Systems Affected   Windows XP Professional and Home Editions are affected.

Cause   When you create a new connection, you must provide the dial-up access number for modem connections. However, many ISPs give you multiple numbers. This way, if one line is busy, you can try a different number. Even though the wizard does not give you the option to enter additional numbers, you can easily add them once the connection is created.

The Pain Killer   To add alternative numbers, follow these steps:

1. Click Start | Connect To | Show all Connections.

2. In the Network Connections window, right-click the desired connection and click Properties.

3. On the General tab, click the Alternates button.

4. In the Alternate Phone Numbers window, click the Add button.

5. In the Add Alternate Phone Number window, enter the additional phone number you want to use. If you want to use dialing rules, click the check box and choose the country/region code from the drop-down menu. If you are having problems with dialing rules, see the "Modems" section later in this chapter. Click OK when you are done.

6. The new number now appears on the Alternate Phone Numbers page, shown in the illustration. You can continue to add new numbers, or you can edit or delete them at any time using this page.

TIP

If you want the dial-up connection to automatically try the next number when the first one fails, click the check box option at the bottom of the window. You can also choose to automatically move the successful number to the top of the list. These settings can be really helpful, and I recommend that you select them both. However, make sure the additional numbers you configure to dial are not long-distance calls!

I am having problems with dialing options or idle time hang-up.

Operating Systems Affected   Windows XP Professional and Home Editions are affected.

Cause   When you create an Internet connection, Windows XP assigns some default settings. In other words, Windows XP makes a basic guess about what you might want. By default, there are three redial attempts when you try to generate an Internet connection; there is 1 minute placed between each attempt and there is a 20-minute idle time hang-up configured. In other words, if you stay connected to the Internet but are not doing anything, Windows XP will let you stay connected for 20 minutes of idle time before you are automatically disconnected. Fortunately, all of these options can be reconfigured to meet your needs.

The Pain Killer   To reconfigure redial and hang-up options, follow these steps:

1. Click Start | Connect To | Show all Connections.

2. In the Network Connections window, right-click the desired connection and click Properties.

3. Click the Options tab. You see the Redialing Options section. Use the drop-down menus to change the redial attempts, time between redial attempts, and idle time as desired. Click OK when you are done.

Dial-up to my corporate network requires additional security settings that I do not understand.

Operating Systems Affected   Windows XP Professional and Home Editions are affected.

Cause   Dial-up connections support a number of complicated security features under Windows XP. You can require encryption and the use of certain security protocols. For a dial-up connection to an ISP, you seldom need to configure these, and in fact if you do configure them, your connection will probably fail if the ISP does not support the increased security (which they usually do not). However, if you use a computer to access a corporate network in order to access the Internet, you may need to configure different options. In this case, you need to follow the specific instructions provided to you by network administrators.

The Pain Killer   Follow your network administrators' instructions. You'll access the connection's properties pages and use the Security tab to configure the desired security settings.

 Again, do not make any changes on the Security tab of the connection's properties unless you have been explicitly instructed to do so by a network administrator or your ISP. Making incorrect changes here will stop your connection from working.

I need a different connection to work as the default connection.

Operating Systems Affected   Windows XP Professional and Home Editions are affected.

Cause   Windows XP assigns one Internet connection as the default connection. This means that when you launch a program, such as Internet Explorer, which needs an Internet connection, Windows XP will always try to dial the default connection. If you have more than one connection, however, you may want a different connection to serve as the default. No problem—you can easily change it.

The Pain Killer   To change the default connection, follow these steps:

1. Click Start | Connect To | Show all Connections.

2. In the Network Connections window, right click the current default connection and click Cancel as Default Connection. Then, right-click the connection you want to be the default and click Set as Default Connection.

TIP   *The default connection always appears with a check mark over it in the Network Connections window.*

Solving Problems with Modems

Modems are great little devices, but they have a tendency to cause problems for even the most devoted computer user. This is probably due to the fact that the modem has a lot of work to do and problems can occur. The modem's job is to modulate and demodulate data. This means that the modem takes the digital communication coming from your computer and turns it into analog waves for the phone line and vice versa.

If you use a modem that is supported under Windows XP, Windows XP should install and configure your modem automatically. You may also have better drivers you can install from the manufacturer, but beyond this issue, installation of modems is like most other hardware devices (see Chapter 5). However, because the modem is a somewhat different device, Windows XP does provide a wizard to help you set up the modem. Again, however, you should never need to use the wizard if the modem is compatible with Windows XP. If you are having installation trouble, see Chapter 5—and you may also need to get help from the modem manufacturer.

For all other Headaches, read on...

When my modem dials, the connection noise is too loud.

Operating Systems Affected   Windows XP Professional and Home Editions are affected.

Cause   Modems let you hear the connection noise so you know if the connection is working or not. However, you can reduce the loudness of the connection noise, and even turn it off if you want to.

The Pain Killer   To change the connection noise volume, follow these steps:

1. Click Start | Control Panel | Phone and Modem Options.

2. Click the Modems tab. Select your modem in the list and click Properties.

3. Click the Modem tab. Adjust the speaker volume using the slider bar as desired. Click OK.

U.S. Robotics 56K Fax Win Properties

General | Modem | Diagnostics | Advanced | Driver | Resources

Port: COM3

Speaker volume

Off   High

Maximum Port Speed

115200

Dial Control

☑ Wait for dial tone before dialing

OK   Cancel

My modem seems to be really slow when I am sending data.

Operating Systems Affected   Windows XP Professional and Home Editions are affected.

Cause   If your modem seems to be really slow when you are sending data, there are two primary settings you should check. First, you want to check the port speed, which determines how fast applications can send data to the modem, and you also want to check some advanced port settings to make sure your modem is configured to operate at its peak.

The Pain Killer   To check these two settings, follow these steps:

1. Click Start | Control Panel | Phone and Modem Options.

2. Click the Modems tab. Select your modem in the list and click Properties.

3. Click the Modem tab. The Maximum Port speed should typically be set to at least 115200. If it is not, increase it to this amount using the drop-down menu.

4. Click the Advanced tab. Click the Advanced Port Settings button.

5. In the Advanced Settings window, shown in the illustration, make sure the Use FIFO check box is selected and make sure the Receive and Transmit Buffer setting slider bars are set to the High position. Click OK and OK again.

Advanced Settings for COM3

☑ Use FIFO buffers (requires 16550 compatible UART)

Select lower settings to correct connection problems.
Select higher settings for faster performance.

Receive Buffer: Low (1) ———————————⬡ High (14) (14)

Transmit Buffer: Low (1) ——————————⬡ High (16) (16)

COM Port Number: COM3 ▾

[OK]
[Cancel]
[Defaults]

TIP *If the connection is still slow, don't worry too much. The odds are good that phone line traffic and static are causing your problems. These are beyond your control, and you may have better luck trying again later.*

My modem keeps disconnecting after a certain period of idle time. My connection is not set to disconnect if idle.

Operating Systems Affected Windows XP Professional and Home Editions are affected.

Cause The Disconnect If Idle feature works on both the modem configuration and the connection configuration. If your modem is disconnecting after a period of idle time and you want to change the behavior, first check the connection properties (see the previous section). If the connection properties are not set to disconnect, then you can check the modem settings.

The Pain Killer To check the modem settings for Disconnect If Idle, follow these steps:

1. Click Start | Control Panel | Phone and Modem Options.

2. Click the Modems tab. Select your modem in the list and click Properties.

3. Click the Advanced tab, and then click the Change Default Preferences button.

4. On the General tab, clear the Disconnect a Call If Idle... check box, or change the value if desired. Click OK and OK again.

NOTE   *Some ISPs also have disconnect if the call is idle. If the settings are correct on your end, then your ISP may be disconnecting you. If this is the case, then you can have your e-mail program check for mail automatically every 5 minutes—this will keep your connection alive so that it does not time out.*

My connection requires different compression and flow control settings. How can I change these?

Operating Systems Affected   Windows XP Professional and Home Editions are affected.

Cause   In order for two modems to communicate with each other, such as the modem in your home computer and the modem at your ISP, they must use the same protocol, compression, and flow control settings. Under most circumstances, all modems use a default setting and you do not have to adjust these. However, if your ISP requires you to change them, you can easily do so following your ISP's instructions.

The Pain Killer   To change the data connection preferences, follow these steps:

1. Click Start | Control Panel | Phone and Modem Options.

2. Click the Modems tab. Select your modem in the list and click Properties.

3. Click the Advanced tab, and then click the Change Default Preferences button.

4. On the General tab, use the drop-down menus provided under Data Connection Preferences to change the settings to match your ISP's settings.

NOTE   *Do not change these settings unless you are explicitly told to do so by your ISP. Incorrect changes in these settings will stop your modem from connecting to other modems.*

Downloading information from the Internet is slow.

Operating Systems Affected   Windows XP Professional and Home Editions are affected.

Cause   Your modem can only work as fast as the modem at your ISP will let it work. If you get connected to a slow modem, the download rate will be slow. When you are connected, you should see an icon in your notification area. Hold your mouse over the icon and a pop-up will tell you how fast your connection is working.

The Pain Killer   There is no way to solve the problem since the problem is on your ISP's end. You can try disconnecting and reconnecting, hoping you'll get a faster modem connection, but if the problem persists, you should contact your ISP for assistance. Also, the web site itself could be very busy and simply slow—you can try using a different web site and see if that helps.

My modem works sporadically or keeps disconnecting randomly.

Operating Systems Affected   Windows XP Professional and Home Editions are affected.

Cause   Modems will work sporadically or disconnect randomly if the connection is bad or certain commands are not configured correctly. Normally, you don't have to do anything with commands, but sometimes additional "initialization commands" can help you solve connection problems.

The Pain Killer   You'll need to check your modem documentation to see if there are additional initialization commands that you can enter for your modem. Your ISP support line may also be able to help you with these connection problems. Also, check your phone line. If you seem to have a lot of static on the line when you make voice calls, it may be time for a service call from your phone company.

My modem keeps dialing a 1 in front of my ISP's number, or it does/does not dial the area code.

Operating Systems Affected   Windows XP Professional and Home Editions are affected.

Cause   Your computer has no way of knowing whether certain area codes and phone numbers are local or not, so it uses a default area code rule configuration. You'll need to configure area code rules in order to make the modem dial the number correctly.

The Pain Killer   Dialing rules can be configured from the Dialing Rules tab found in Phone and Modem Options. You'll need to check your Windows XP documentation or another general user book for step-by-step instructions, since they are rather involved and contain a lot of options that space does not permit us to cover here. Once configured correctly, though, your computer will know what to do with the area code and the 1 option.

Problems with Windows Firewall

Windows XP provides the Windows Firewall, which is updated in Service Pack 2 from the older Internet Connection Firewall. A firewall is either a hardware or software solution that can help protect your computer from Internet attacks and hackers. This may sound like something out of a science fiction movie, but firewalls have been around on corporate networks for some time, and now personal firewalls designed for home users have become more popular and important.

Without jumping into techno-babble land, Internet traffic is broken down into Internet Protocol packets. The packets enter your computer and are assembled to provide you with the data you want, such as a web page or an e-mail. Windows Firewall is able to inspect these packets as they arrive at your computer and determine if they are allowed or not. Packets that are not allowed are simply dropped and do not enter your computer. In order to determine what packets are allowed, Windows Firewall keeps an internal log of your requests. For example, if you type www.osborne.com in your web browser, you are sending a request to that web site for the page. Windows Firewall notes this in its table. When the Osborne.com web site packets begin arriving, Windows Firewall inspects and determines that you requested them, so they are allowed to pass through. Anything arriving that you did not explicitly request is denied.

I should note here that third-party companies, such as Symantec and McAfee, also sell personal firewalls for XP. This software usually costs around $30 and provides more options than the free Windows Firewall software included with Windows XP. Still, if you want protection without spending additional money, Windows Firewall will certainly help you. For the most part, Windows Firewall usage is completely trouble free, but you might run into the problems explored in the following sections.

CAUTION   *Windows Firewall does not provide any antivirus protection. You must use third-party antivirus software, such as McAfee or Symantec, in order to protect your computer from viruses. Also, Windows Firewall only protects data from coming into your computer—it does not protect data leaving your computer. The result is that Windows Firewall is useful, but not as powerful as third-party firewall products.*

I don't know how to turn on Windows Firewall.

Operating Systems Affected   Windows XP Professional and Home Editions are affected.

Cause   The new Security Center in Windows XP Service Pack 2 attempts to keep your computer protected by making suggestions to you. One of those is that you turn on Windows Firewall for all connections.

The Pain Killer   To turn on Windows Firewall, click the Windows Security Center icon in the Notification Area. In the Security Center, as shown in the illustration, the window will tell you if the firewall is turned on or off. If it is off, follow the instructions on the Windows Security Center to turn it on.

I want to see what Windows Firewall is dropping from the Internet.

Operating Systems Affected Windows XP Professional and Home Editions are affected.

Cause Windows Firewall works in the background without disturbing you, and that is good news. Essentially, you click the check box to turn it on and you are done. However, if you want to see what Windows Firewall is doing, you can view a log file and configure what is recorded.

The Pain Killer To use the Windows Firewall log file, follow these steps:

1. Click Start | Connect To | Show All Connections.

2. Right-click the desired firewalled connection and click Properties.

3. Click the Advanced tab, and then click the Settings.

4. Click the Advanced tab, and then click the Setting buttons under the Security Logging category. By default, the security log is stored in C:\Windows and is named pfirewall.log, but you can click the Save As button so that it is saved in a different place if you like. You can choose to log dropped packets or successful connections, but as a general rule, logging only dropped packets is your best choice—it tells you what did not get through the firewall and nothing else. Make your selections and click OK.

5. At any time, you can access the log file and view it. The log file will open with Notepad.

I use firewall exceptions when I use my laptop at home, but when I travel, I do not want to allow exceptions. How can I easily configure this?

Operating Systems Affected   Windows XP Professional and Home Editions are affected.

Cause   Windows Firewall allows exceptions to the firewall rules. This enables you to use file and printer sharing and other programs, such as Remote Desktop. You may use these in a secure location, but if you travel with a computer, you may wish to turn them off for additional security purposes. You can easily disallow exceptions as needed.

The Pain Killer   To disallow exceptions, follow these steps:

1. Click Start | Connect To | Show All Connections.

2. Right-click the desired firewalled connection and click Properties.

3. Click the Advanced tab, and then click the Settings.

4. On the General tab, click the Don't Allow Exceptions check box and click OK. When you want to reenable exceptions, simply return to this tab and clear the check box and click OK.

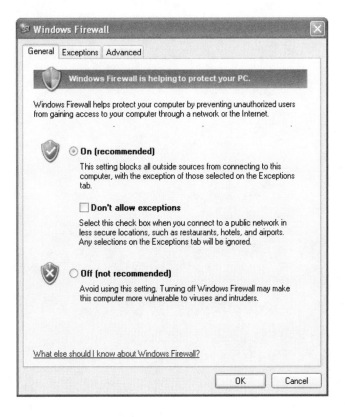

NOTE

If your computer is on a network, never turn on the firewall on the network adapter card—this will prevent other users from connecting to and using resources on your computer. See Chapter 12 to learn more about networking. If you are having problems with Windows Firewall and your e-mail, see Chapter 11.

Chapter 10

Windows XP Internet Explorer Headaches

In this chapter, you'll cure…

■ Problems with IE connections

■ IE configuration difficulties

■ Aggravating security issues

Internet Explorer (IE) is a web browser. A web browser is a program that enables you to download and view web pages. The concept of a web browser is probably old news to you—you've been on the Net for some time now and you are familiar with its ins and outs. If you are new to the Internet, IE is the web browser Microsoft provides for you. In fact, IE is built into the Windows XP operating system, which makes web surfing easy to do and easy to manage.

This, however, does not mean that you cannot use a different web browser, such as Netscape or Opera. If you want to use something different, no problem— just install it on XP and get to surfing. For everyone who wants to use IE, this chapter explores some Headaches you might run into while using Internet Explorer 6!

IE Connection Problems

IE works with your Internet connection, such as your modem connection or broadband connection, so that web pages can be retrieved from the Internet and displayed to you. Web browsers like Internet Explorer use the HTTP (Hypertext Transfer Protocol) to access web pages, and they can read and display HTML (Hypertext Markup Language) to you. All web pages on the Internet are built on the HTML programming language. You can think of IE as an interpreter—its job is to download web pages using HTTP, interpret the HTML, and display the interpretation to you in the easy-to-read graphical format that you are accustomed to with web pages.

However, you may have some connectivity problems with IE, just as you would any browser, and there are a few different things that can cause connection problems— mainly settings configured on IE and the Internet itself. The following Headaches explore possible connection problems and how to solve them.

I get a Cannot Find Server message.

Operating Systems Affected   Windows XP Professional and Home Editions are affected.

Cause   If you receive a Cannot Find Server page, such as the one shown in Figure 10-1, there is a problem with the connection—either on your end or on the Internet. This message occurs for one of the following reasons:

- You don't have a connection to the Internet (modem has disconnected or some other problem has occurred).

- The web page is offline or has moved.

- Heavy traffic on the Internet has caused your request to time out.

- You typed the wrong address or misspelled it.

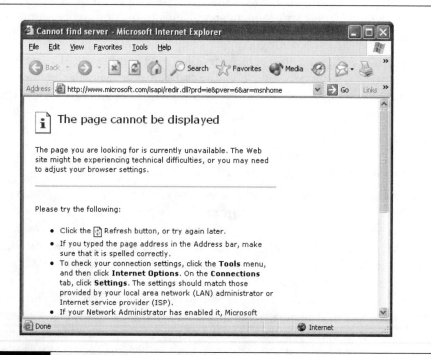

FIGURE 10-1   Cannot Find Server error message

The Pain Killer   To solve the problem, follow these steps:

1. Make sure your connection is working—if you can access other web pages okay, you know the problem is not on your end. If it is, Headaches later in this section address the issue.

2. Check your spelling of the address in the Address line and click the Refresh button on the toolbar.

3. If neither solution works, you can try again later, or the web site may simply be down or unavailable.

IE provides intermittent pages, but fails on many others.

Operating Systems Affected   Windows XP Professional and Home Editions are affected.

Cause   If you are using the Internet and some pages load while others do not, or if the wait time seems very long, the problem is traffic or the connection to the Internet—not IE directly.

The Pain Killer   To solve the problem, try disconnecting from the Internet and connecting again. If this does not work, wait awhile before using the Internet again. If this happens often, you should check with your Internet service provider (ISP) for assistance.

How does IE find web sites?

Humans are language-based creatures. However, computers communicate using numbers. In order to make the Internet easier, you simply have to type a web address (such as www.osborne.com) to access a web site. However, your computer must have a numeric address to find the web site. In order to find the correct number, a system called Domain Name System (DNS) is used on the Internet. Computers query DNS servers in order to resolve domain names (such as Osborne.com) to a TCP/IP address (such as 131.107.2.200). Once your computer has the IP address, it can locate the Osborne.com servers, who can then respond to your request to see the web page. Of course, all of this happens in the background without any help from you—which makes it really nice!

TIP   *You can learn more about Internet connections and ISPs in Chapter 9.*

I have two Internet connections, but IE automatically dials the one I do not want to use.

Operating Systems Affected   Windows XP Professional and Home Editions are affected.

Cause   If you have more than one Internet connection, Windows XP assigns a default to one of them. Then, programs like IE will always use the default connection. In order to stop this behavior, you must change the default connection.

The Pain Killer   To change the default connection, you will need to access Network Connections and change the default. See Chapter 9 for step-by-step instructions.

IE does not automatically dial my Internet connection, or I do not want IE to dial a connection.

Operating Systems Affected   Windows XP Professional and Home Editions are affected.

Cause   By default, IE will try to dial your default connection when you open IE if a connection to the Internet does not currently exist. You can change this behavior, however, as needed.

The Pain Killer   To change the dialing behavior of IE, follow these steps:

1.   Click Start | Control Panel | Internet Options.

NOTE   *The following steps assume you are using the Classic view of Control Panel, which shows you all the icon options. If you are not sure if you are using the Classic view of Control Panel, click Start | Control Panel. In the left window pane, click the Switch to Classic View option.*

TIP   *You can also access Internet Options from within IE by clicking the Tools menu and clicking Internet Options.*

2. Click the Connections tab.

3. As you can see in the illustration, you have three radio button options that allow IE to Never Dial a Connection, Dial Whenever a Network Connection Is Not Present, or Always Dial My Default Connection. Choose a setting that you want and click OK.

NOTE *When you are solving connection problems, it is always important to keep in mind that IE can only connect based on the Internet connection's configuration. In other words, the Internet connection manages the connection to the Internet and IE uses that connection—IE does not directly affect the connection's configuration. If you are having a number of different connection problems, always remember that the problem will be the connection, not software using the connection (such as IE), and the resolution lies with connection properties or even your ISP—not IE. See Chapter 9 to learn more about solving problems with Internet connections.*

IE dials a connection, even when I have a different connection established or when using a broadband connection.

Operating Systems Affected   Windows XP Professional and Home Editions are affected.

Cause   IE is set to Always Dial My Default Connection. Let's say you have two connections—connection1 and connection2. Connection1 is the default, but you are currently connected with connection2. If you open IE, IE will see that connection1 is not connected and try to connect, even if you already have connection2 available (I know, the explanation here is enough to give you a Headache!). The point is, IE only cares about the default connection, and if it is not connected, IE will attempt to make the connection.

The Pain Killer   Access the Connections tab again (see the previous Headache for steps) and click the Dial Whenever a Network Connection Is Not Present option so that the Always Dial My Default Connection option is not selected. Now, when you open IE, it will use any connection currently open. If no connection is open, only then will it dial the default connection.

I cannot configure IE to connect through a proxy server or broadband hardware.

Operating Systems Affected   Windows XP Professional and Home Editions are affected.

Cause   Besides using an Internet connection, you may access the Internet when you are on a local network, or you may even have an Internet connection that uses a network adapter card. For example, I have an Internet satellite connection that uses a network adapter card in my computer. I have to have IE configured to use that kind of connection instead of a modem connection.

In corporate networks, users often connect through a proxy server, which is a computer that manages Internet connections. When you need something from the Internet, your computer connects to the proxy server, who then gets what you need from the Internet for you. Proxy servers are security features that are used often in corporate networks.

In order to get IE to work with these kinds of connections, IE has to be configured correctly.

The Pain Killer   The actual configuration for local network or broadband hardware connection varies, so you'll need to follow the exact setup instructions provided by your broadband company or your network administrator.

Regardless, you will configure IE to connect this way on the Connections tab. If you click the Settings button, you see a page that gives you the option to connect using a proxy server or configuration script, as you can see in Figure 10-2. Again, your network administrator will need to help you configure these settings.

On the Connections tab, you also see that you have a LAN Settings button. LAN stands for local area network, and if you are using a DSL or satellite connection (or even cable), you will probably need to configure settings here, as shown in Figure 10-3. Again, you'll need to check with the ISP for specific instructions.

TIP   *Do not enable any of these settings unless you have instructions to do so. Enabling these settings when they are not needed will probably stop IE from connecting to the Internet.*

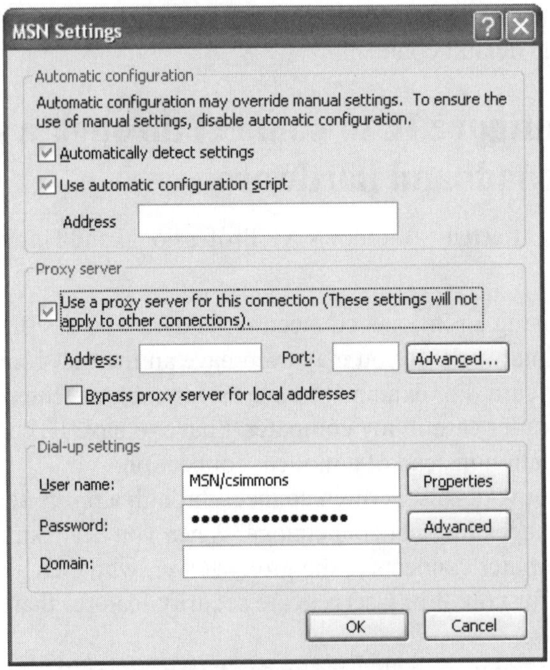

FIGURE 10-2   Use a proxy server or configuration script.

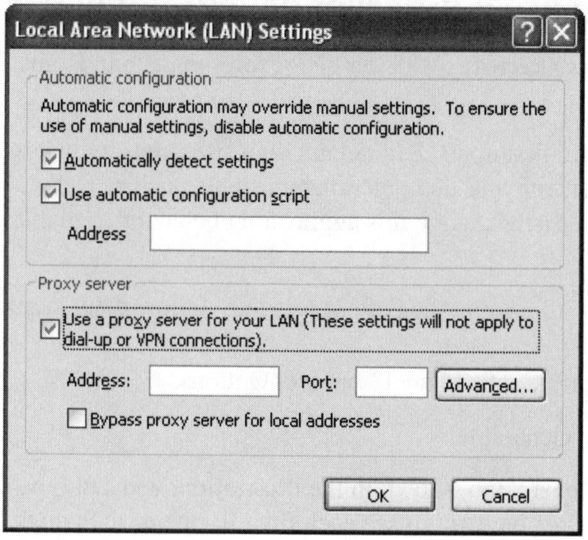

Local Area Network (LAN) Settings   [?] [X]

Automatic configuration

Automatic configuration may override manual settings. To ensure the use of manual settings, disable automatic configuration.

☑ Automatically detect settings

☑ Use automatic configuration script

Address [   ]

Proxy server

☑ Use a proxy server for your LAN (These settings will not apply to dial-up or VPN connections).

Address: [   ]   Port: [   ]   [Advanced...]

☐ Bypass proxy server for local addresses

[OK]   [Cancel]

FIGURE 10-3   LAN Settings options

Solving IE Configuration Problems

Internet Explorer is configured automatically with a number of preset options—most of which you will find useful. However, you will probably run into settings that are a real pain. The good news is that you can change just about anything that you want—if you know how. In this section, I'll explore some common Headaches you are most likely to experience.

I don't like the setup of the IE toolbar.

Operating Systems Affected   Windows XP Professional and Home Editions are affected.

Cause   IE has a default toolbar configuration with default bars and buttons. However, IE works just like any folder in Windows XP, and you can change the way the toolbars look easily and quickly.

The Pain Killer   To change the IE toolbar, use the View menu to make specific changes or customize the options. You can learn more about configuring toolbars in Chapter 2.

I want IE to use a different default home page.

Operating Systems Affected   Windows XP Professional and Home Editions are affected.

Cause   When you first open IE, a default web site opens, which may be MSN— or it may be the site of your computer manufacturer, such as Dell, Gateway, HP, and so forth. You can easily change this aggravating behavior so that the web site you want opens first.

The Pain Killer   To change the default web site, follow these steps:

1. Click Start | Control Panel | Internet Options.

2. Click the General tab.

3. On the General tab, shown in the illustration, you can type the address of the web site you want to see each time IE opens, then click OK. If you are currently at that web site, just click the Use Current button. If you don't want to see a default web site at all, click Use Blank.

I want IE to keep more temporary Internet files, or I want IE to not use temporary Internet files.

Operating Systems Affected   Windows XP Professional and Home Editions are affected.

Cause   Internet Explorer saves web pages that you visit in a temporary files folder. This helps speed up your web surfing because you can reuse those pages when you visit the site again (if the pages have not changed) instead of downloading new copies each time. You can increase the disk space allowed for temporary Internet files, or you can stop IE from using temporary Internet files altogether if you like. For most users, however, the default settings are good, so don't change them unless you have a specific reason for doing so.

The Pain Killer   To change the temporary Internet files settings, follow these steps:

1. Click Start | Control Panel | Internet Options.

2. Click the General tab. Under Temporary Internet Files, click the Settings button.

3. In the Settings window, you can choose to never use temporary Internet files if you like—or if you want to continue using them with more room to grow, simply use the slider bar to increase the amount of disk space that can be used. Be careful not to increase this setting too much, however, because you will eat up a lot of disk space that can be used for other purposes. When you are done, click OK.

I want IE to keep History entries for a longer/shorter period of time.

Operating Systems Affected   Windows XP Professional and Home Editions are affected.

Cause   Internet Explorer keeps a history of the web sites that are accessed for 20 days, by default. This feature is helpful so that you can go back and find web pages you want to revisit (or to see what your children are doing on the Internet). Depending on your needs, you can easily increase/decrease the 20-day default setting.

The Pain Killer   To increase/decrease the history time, follow these steps:

1. Click Start | Control Panel | Internet Options.

2. Click the General tab. In the History section, change the configuration box to the number of days that you want. If you do not want to keep a history at all, choose 0 and click OK.

I want to stop pornographic or violent content from being displayed in IE.

Operating Systems Affected   Windows XP Professional and Home Editions are affected.

Cause   Unfortunately, the Internet is full of pornographic, violent, racist, and other hate content that you may not want displayed on IE. I have two kids myself, so I know how important this can be. My daughter loves to play at Barbie.com, but I don't want her accidentally jumping from this safe and fun site to something she doesn't need to see. Unfortunately, nothing is foolproof and I always suggest that you use the Internet with kids in much the same way as you would a public amusement park—you hold their hands and you watch everything. Let me reiterate this soap box one more time—leaving children unattended with the Internet is like leaving them unattended to play in the street—something bad *will* happen eventually.

You can configure some content settings on IE that enable you to block objectionable material, if the web site has identified itself as such. If the site has not identified itself as such, IE has no way of knowing what it is downloading. There are some additional security applications that you can purchase that can further help control objectionable material. Some examples are NetKeys Internet Security and Norton Internet Security, Family Edition. Also, specific blocking products work well, such as Net Nanny (www.netnanny.com), Safe Surf (www.safesurf.com), and Cyber Sitter (www.cybersitter.com). You can find these products and more at your favorite computer store, but again, they are not foolproof. In the meantime, you can turn on IE's content option, which will provide you some protection.

The Pain Killer   To use IE's content feature, follow these steps:

1. Click Start | Control Panel | Internet Options.

2. Click the Content tab, and then click the Enable button under Content Advisor.

3. On the Ratings tab, click through each category and set the slider bar to the level that you want. The first level is None, followed by other levels that allow the content to a degree. Choose the levels you want to enforce for each category.

4. Click the Approved Sites tab. You can choose override settings on the Ratings page by entering the address of any sites that are allowed or not allowed at all. Simply enter the address and click the appropriate button, as shown in the illustration. Allowed sites appear with a green check mark, while blocked sites appear with a red minus sign.

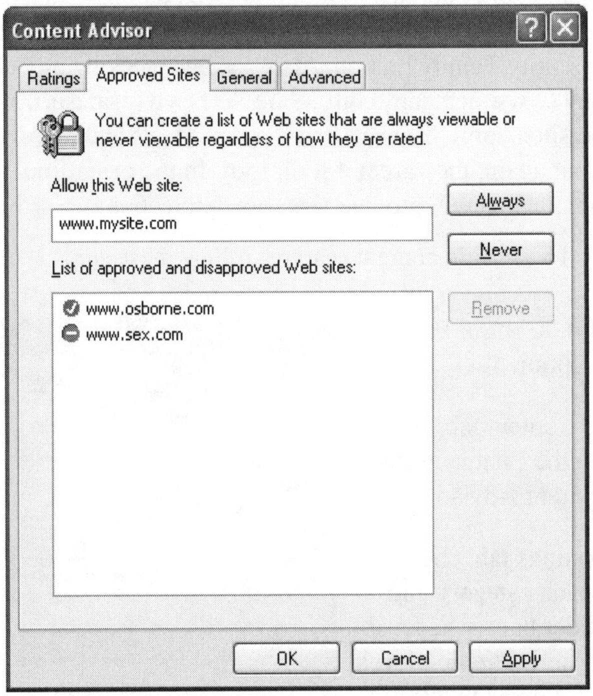

5. Click the General tab. You have two important settings at the top of the page, shown here. First, if you want users to be able to see sites that have no rating, click the check box option—but if not, keep it unchecked. Users will not be able to view any and all unrated web sites (no matter if it has objectionable content). Again, this may not be foolproof, so don't put all of your trust in this setting. Secondly, you definitely want to use the option to Create a Supervisor Password so that no one else can override your settings. Click the button option to create one. Click OK when you are done.

Content Advisor ? ✕

| Ratings | Approved Sites | General | Advanced |

User options

☐ Users can see sites that have no rating

☑ Supervisor can type a password to allow users to view restricted content

Supervisor password

The supervisor password allows you to change Content Advisor settings or turn Content Advisor on or off. To change the supervisor password, click Change Password.

[Create Password...]

Rating systems

The rating systems you use are provided by other companies and organizations. To view or modify the list, click Rating Systems.

[Find Rating Systems] [Rating Systems...]

[OK] [Cancel] [Apply]

NOTE   *If you are interested, you can also learn more about ratings bureaus and organizations with the information on the General and Advanced tabs of the Content Advisor.*

IE keeps trying to complete web addresses and forms for me.

Operating Systems Affected   Windows XP Professional and Home Editions are affected.

Cause   IE has an AutoComplete feature that remembers web addresses and data you have entered on web forms so that IE can try to help you complete the information. This feature is liked by some and hated by others, but if you don't want to use the feature, you can modify it or turn it off.

The Pain Killer   To change AutoComplete, follow these steps:

1. Click Start | Control Panel | Internet Options.

2. Click the Content tab and click the AutoComplete button.

3. In the AutoComplete Settings window, you can choose what you want AutoComplete to help you with. If you don't want to use any AutoComplete features, just clear all of the check boxes and click OK. Notice also the Passwords option. IE can help keep track of the passwords you use on the web, and you can simply click the provided button on this tab to enter or remove passwords.

Whenever I click the Mail icon in IE, Outlook Express opens, but I use another program.

Operating Systems Affected   Windows XP Professional and Home Editions are affected.

Cause   IE chooses certain programs to open by default. For example, if you need to send e-mail and you click the Mail icon on the toolbar, Outlook Express opens (of course). The good news is that you can change this setting so that your Eudora mail opens instead.

The Pain Killer   Assuming the alternate e-mail application is installed, follow these steps:

1. Click Start | Control Panel | Internet Options.

2. Click the Programs tab.

3. In the Programs window, click the drop-down menu under mail (or any other program as well) and choose the application that you want to use. Then click OK.

Internet Options [?][X]

General | Security | Privacy | Content | Connections | Programs | Advanced

Internet programs

You can specify which program Windows automatically uses for each Internet service.

HTML editor: [▼]

E-mail: [Outlook Express   ▼]

Newsgroups: [Outlook Express   ▼]

Internet call: [NetMeeting   ▼]

Calendar: [▼]

Contact list: [Address Book   ▼]

[Reset Web Settings...] You can reset Internet Explorer to the default home and search pages.

[✓] Internet Explorer should check to see whether it is the default browser

[OK] [Cancel] [Apply]

When printing from IE, I don't want background colors and images to print.

Operating Systems Affected   Windows XP Professional and Home Editions are affected.

Cause   IE provides a number of advanced configuration options that control a bunch of different IE settings. You can make changes here easily, including printing options.

The Pain Killer   Open Internet Options and click the Advanced tab, as shown in Figure 10-4. Locate the Printing section and clear the Print Background Colors and Images option. You can scroll through the list of settings here and make additional changes as needed.

NOTE *Most of the default settings here are the best settings for you. Do not change any of these settings unless you are sure you understand the setting you are changing. You can right-click most settings and click What's This for more information.*

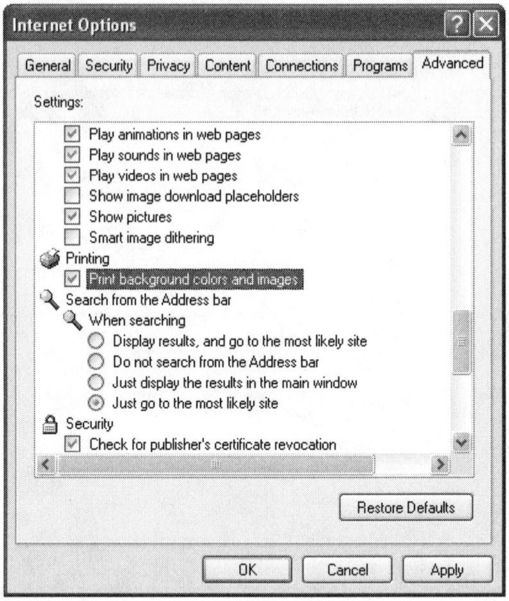

FIGURE 10-4 Advanced tab

Managing Internet Explorer Security

IE 6, which is included with Windows XP, contains a number of security features that are designed to keep you safe from Internet content as well as keep your personal information private. These settings are great and much needed, but they can cause you some configuration Headaches as well. The following sections explore what you are most likely to run into concerning IE security.

IE keeps telling me that sites and/or actions are not allowed.

Operating Systems Affected   Windows XP Professional and Home Editions are affected.

Cause   IE approaches the concept of security through zones. You have an Internet zone, an intranet zone, and zones for trusted sites and restricted sites. High settings in any zone reduce the usability of the Internet, but increase security. On the other hand, low settings let you do whatever you want but are not as safe. You have to strike a balance between security needs and your personal usage needs. Fortunately, you can easily change the security settings at any time.

The Pain Killer   To change the security setting for a zone, follow these steps:

1. Click Start | Control Panel | Internet Options.

2. Click the Security tab. Select the desired zone (Internet, since that is what we are talking about here) and adjust the slider bar to give you more or less security. If you don't see a slider bar, click the Default Level button.

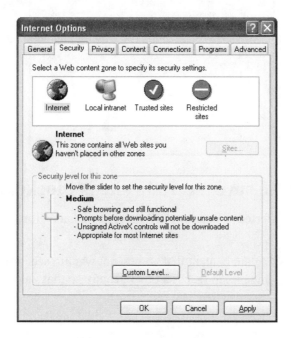

NOTE *The Medium level is the best for most people. If you are unsure, start with Medium—you can always make changes later.*

3. You can manage the security settings by creating a Custom level as well. This feature allows you to pick and choose what is allowed or not allowed. If you want to create a Custom level, click the Custom Level button.

4. This opens the Security Settings window. Click the radio button you want for each setting and click OK.

I need to make sure a certain site is blocked.

Operating Systems Affected   Windows XP Professional and Home Editions are affected.

Cause   Some sites contain content that you do not want to see, or that you do not want anyone else seeing either. IE has a block feature so that you can easily block those sites.

The Pain Killer   To block a site, follow these steps:

1. Click Start | Control Panel | Internet Options.

2. Click the Security tab.

3. Select the Restricted Sites zone and then click the Sites button.

4. Add the web site you want to block to the list and click OK.

 ## Cookies are being blocked without my permission.

Operating Systems Affected   Windows XP Professional and Home Editions are affected.

Cause   A cookie is a text file that IE uses to exchange information about you with another computer on the Internet. In many cases, cookies are very useful. For example, if you visit online stores (such as amazon.com), a cookie is exchanged with the site. The next time you visit the site, the cookie is sent again so that the site can remember who you are, what you have bought, the things you thought about buying, and so forth. In the right hands, cookies can be very beneficial—in the wrong hands, web sites gain information about you and can sell your information to other sites, which accounts for a lot of the junk e-mail you might be receiving.

IE 6 provides a Privacy feature that helps block certain kinds of cookies. However, if the feature is configured too high, even safe cookies are blocked. You can fix the Privacy policy, though, to suit your needs.

The Pain Killer   To configure the Privacy policy, follow these steps:

1. Click Start | Control Panel | Internet Options.

2. Click the Privacy tab.

3. Adjust the slider bar, as shown in the illustration, to the desired level so that cookies are blocked in a desirable fashion. If you need to learn more about cookies first, see the Windows XP Help and Support Center for an overview.

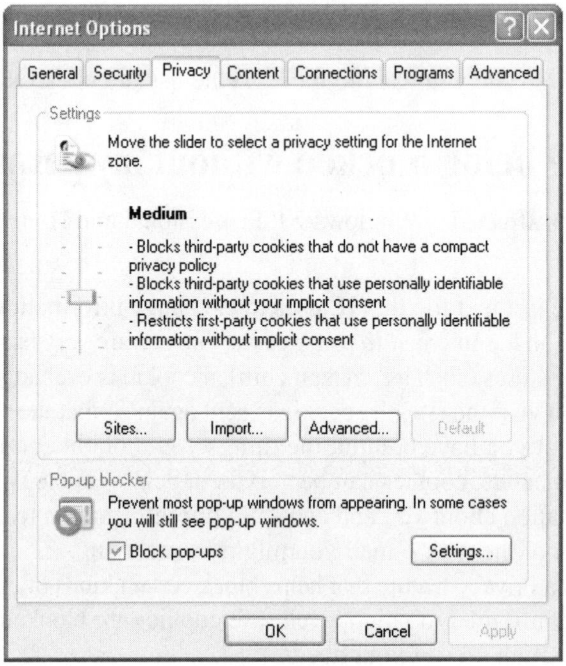

4. If you want to override the default settings, click the Advanced button and choose the Override check box, shown here. You can then choose how first- and third-party cookies are handled.

Advanced Privacy Settings

You can choose how cookies are handled in the Internet zone. This overrides automatic cookie handling.

Cookies

☑ Override automatic cookie handling

First-party Cookies
◉ Accept
○ Block
○ Prompt

Third-party Cookies
◉ Accept
○ Block
○ Prompt

☐ Always allow session cookies

[OK]   [Cancel]

5. If you want to block cookies from being used at certain web sites, click the Edit button at the bottom of the Privacy page and enter the site address.

Pop-up windows are driving me crazy.

Operating Systems Affected   Windows XP Professional and Home Editions are affected.

Cause   Pop-up windows are those annoying little IE boxes that suddenly appear when you use the Internet. Often, the windows are advertising something, and you have to close the window in order to return to what you are doing. In some cases, however, pop-up windows are actually used by the web site you are visiting to provide additional information or services. For example, you may see a pop-up window asking if you want to sign up to receive a newsletter, or the window may alert you to some special sale. Nevertheless, pop-ups can be really frustrating and they can slow down your surfing time. The good news is IE enables you to block pop-ups.

The Pain Killer   To stop pop-up windows, follow these steps:

1. Click Start | Control Panel | Internet Options.

2. Click the Privacy tab.

3. In the Pop-up Blocker portion of the window, click the Block Pop-ups check box to enable the feature, and then click the Settings button.

4. The Pop-up Blocker Settings window enables you to override the blocking of pop-ups from certain sites. For example, if you commonly visit an online store that uses pop-ups, you can simply type the site address and click the Add button. This action puts the site in a safe list so that pop-ups are allowed from that site, as you can see here.

5. Notice that you have a few additional settings at the bottom of the Settings window. You can have a sound played when a pop-up is blocked, block pop-ups opened from links you click (this is not recommended because it may stop you from following links), or show the Information Bar when a pop-up is blocked. Adjust these settings as desired and click Close.

Chapter 11

Outlook Express Headaches

In this chapter, you'll cure...

■ Problems with Outlook Express connections

■ Difficulties using Outlook Express

■ Problems with mail management

Outlook Express is an e-mail client that provides everything you need to manage e-mail. This means that the Outlook Express software is designed to send, receive, and manage e-mail. Without an e-mail client, you cannot send and receive e-mail on the Internet. While it is true that you can use different e-mail clients on Windows XP, such as Netscape and Eudora, Outlook Express is included free as a bonus with Windows XP, so I'll discuss only Outlook Express in this chapter. If you are using a different e-mail client, check the client developer's web site for help and information.

Problems with Outlook Express Connections

Just as a dial-up connection must have certain information to connect, an e-mail client must have certain information for you to be able to send and receive e-mail. This information, called an *account,* enables your computer to interact with a mail server at your Internet service provider (ISP) so that you can send and receive e-mail. An account is usually made up of the following information:

■ Your name

■ Your e-mail address

■ Your user name (assigned by your ISP)

■ Your password (the default is assigned by your ISP)

■ The name of the incoming mail server

■ The name of the outgoing mail server

Before you get ready to set up a mail account, make sure you have this information handy. Once you configure the mail account, you should be ready to send and receive e-mail over your Internet connection. However, there are a few Headaches that can occur, and the following sections cure them for you!

I can't set up an account.

Operating Systems Affected   Windows XP Professional and Home Edition are affected.

Cause   Outlook Express can easily help you set up a mail account, assuming you have available the information that Outlook Express needs. To do this, Outlook Express provides a handy wizard that can guide you through the process. However, you'll need to know how to use that wizard and where to find it to set up the account.

The Pain Killer   To set up a mail account, follow these steps:

1. Click Start | All Programs | Outlook Express.

 TIP   *Outlook Express will probably appear on your Start menu as well.*

2. Click Tools | Accounts.

3. In the Internet Accounts window, click the Mail tab. Click the Add button, and then click Mail.

Internet Accounts	? X
All Mail News Directory Service	Add ▶
Account Type Connection	Remove
	Properties
	Set as Default
	Import...
	Export...
	Set Order...
	Close

4. The Internet Connection Wizard appears. Type your name and click Next.

NOTE   *The name you type is the name that everyone will be able to see when they read your e-mail. This is called your display name.*

5. Next, enter your e-mail address. Click Next.

6. In the E-mail Server Names screen, you'll need to enter the names of your incoming and outgoing mail servers, as well as the type of incoming mail server (usually Post Office Protocol 3, or POP3). Your ISP should have provided you this information. Check your documentation from the ISP, or give them a call if necessary. Enter the correct names, as you see here in the example, and click Next.

Internet Connection Wizard

E-mail Server Names

My incoming mail server is a [POP3 ▼] server.

Incoming mail (POP3, IMAP or HTTP) server:
[mail.myisp.com]

An SMTP server is the server that is used for your outgoing e-mail.

Outgoing mail (SMTP) server:
[mail.myisp.com]

[< Back] [Next >] [Cancel]

7. In the Internet Mail Logon screen, enter your user name and password. You will see that you have an option to use Secure Password Authentication (SPA) security; do not select this check box unless your ISP has told you to do so. Click Next.

NOTE *Remember, passwords are case sensitive, so make sure you are typing the exact password or authentication to your mail server will fail.*

8. Click Finish. The new account appears on the Mail tab of the Internet Accounts window. Click Close.

I can't change information about my account without creating a new account.

Operating Systems Affected   Windows XP Professional and Home Editions are affected.

Cause   From time to time, information in your account may change. Your ISP may give you a new password, or the name of one of the mail servers may change. The good news is that you can make editorial changes to your account without deleting and creating a new one. To make those changes, you'll need to access the Properties dialog box of the existing account.

The Pain Killer   To make changes to an account, follow these steps:

1. In Outlook Express, click Tools | Accounts.

2. Click the Mail tab. Select your account and click the Properties button.

3. On the General tab, you can make changes to your name, organization, e-mail address, and so on.

4. If you need to make changes to your user name, your password, or the mail server name, click the Servers tab and make the change, as shown in the illustration. Make sure your ISP has

directed you to make changes before doing so, or your connectivity will be disrupted. Once you are done, just click OK.

I always have to type my password when I am trying to download mail.

Operating Systems Affected   Windows XP Professional and Home Editions are affected.

Cause   A small check box setting on your account determines whether Outlook Express will prompt you for or remember your password.

The Pain Killer   To make Outlook Express remember your password so you don't have to type it each time, follow these steps:

1. In Outlook Express, click Tools | Accounts.

2. Click the Mail tab. Select your account and click the Properties button.

3. On the Servers tab, select the Remember Password check box found directly under the password dialog box, and then click OK.

Solving Problems Using Outlook Express

Outlook Express is a fairly involved program that performs a lot of different functions related to e-mail. If you want to use Outlook Express and you are not sure how, you need to get familiar with it using the Windows XP Help and Support Center or a book that shows you how to use its features. Since there are a number of potential issues and difficulties that you might run into, the following sections point out the most common Headaches and how to solve them. If you are experiencing something that is not explored here, refer to Outlook Express Help by clicking Help | Contents and Index in Outlook Express.

When I try to download mail, I sometimes get a server timeout message.

Operating Systems Affected   Windows XP Professional and Home Editions are affected.

Cause   Outlook Express provides a timeout message after a certain period of time when there is no activity with the mail server. If you are getting this message, you can increase the timeout value.

The Pain Killer   To increase the timeout value, follow these steps:

1. In Outlook Express, click Tools | Accounts.

2. Click the Mail tab. Select your account, and click the Properties button.

3. Click the Advanced tab, shown here. In the Server Timeouts section, increase the value by moving the slider bar to the right. Click OK when you are done.

I can't get a new mail message I am creating to show me a Blind Carbon Copy field.

Operating Systems Affected   Windows XP Professional and Home Editions are affected.

Cause   When you open a new mail message, you have a To and CC (Carbon Copy) field. However, you can also use a BCC (Blind Carbon Copy) so that you can copy other recipients without the To and CC recipients' awareness. This field does not appear by default, but you can easily enable it.

The Pain Killer   To enable the BCC field, follow these steps:

1. In Outlook Express, click the Create Mail button to open a new message.

2. In the New Message window, click View | All Headers. The BCC field now appears.

I can't use stationery, fonts, or colors in my messages.

Operating Systems Affected   Windows XP Professional and Home Editions are affected.

Cause   In order to use stationery and format different fonts and colors, your message has to be configured to use rich text, or HTML. Plain text messages do not allow these formatting options.

The Pain Killer   To use rich text, follow these steps:

1. In Outlook Express, click the Create Mail button on the toolbar.

2. In the New Message window, click Format | Rich Text (HTML). You can now apply stationery, fonts, and colors to the message. The following illustration shows an example using stationery (the pattern you see in the background of the message area) and different fonts.

![New Message window showing a Rich Text email]

In the message body:

This *message* is written using Rich Text, which is HTML. It allows many creative options!!

> **NOTE** *Although using stationery, as well as different fonts and colors, is nice, keep in mind that these items increase mail transmission time and cannot be seen by a recipient that is not using an HTML-enabled e-mail client.*

I can't send an encrypted or digitally signed message.

Operating Systems Affected   Windows XP Professional and Home Editions are affected.

Cause   As e-mail usage has become more common, the need for secure transmissions has become important as well. Outlook Express 6 supports both encrypted messages and digitally signed messages:

■ An encrypted message cannot be read by another user while in transit, but the receiver of the message can decode and read the message automatically, assuming that the receiver is using Outlook Express 6. Encryption does not require any additional work on your part; you simply select the Encrypt button on the message toolbar, and the message is encrypted while it is sent.

■ A digital signature requires a digital certificate. A *digital certificate* is a digital file that tells who you are and where the mail is coming from, much like a driver's license or social security card confirms your identity. In order to use a digital certificate with Outlook Express, you must purchase one from a digital certificate authority, such as VeriSign. You can learn more about digital certificates at www.verisign.com or using Outlook Express Help.

The Pain Killer   In order to use the encryption or digital signature feature, click the Tools menu from within a new mail message and choose to encrypt the message or digitally sign it. Remember that you must have a digital certificate to use this feature.

I can't read or send a message in a different language.

Operating Systems Affected   Windows XP Professional and Home Editions are affected.

Cause   E-mail message headers contain encoding information that Outlook Express reads. If a message comes to you in a language other than English but the header information is not present or correct, Outlook Express does not know how to display the message. You can manually select the language, however. In the same manner, it is easy to send encoded messages in other languages by choosing Format | Encoding in the new message you are creating.

The Pain Killer   To read a message in another language, open the message, click View | Encoding, and then choose the correct language.

I can't remove the preview pane.

Operating Systems Affected   Windows XP Professional and Home Editions are affected.

Cause   By default, Outlook Express gives you a multipane interface, as you can see in Figure 11-1. You can see your folders, view their contents in the upper-right

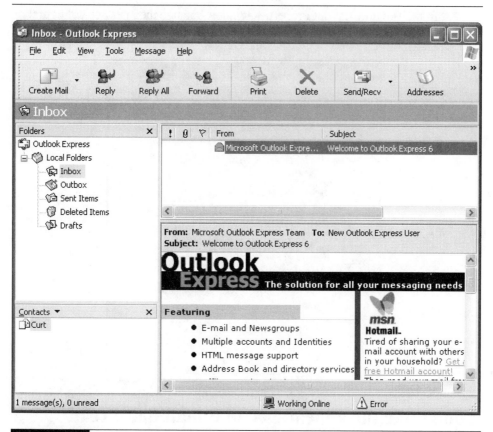

FIGURE 11-1 Outlook Express provides a multipane interface.

pane, and preview messages in the lower-right pane. However, if you wish, most of the panes and the general interface configuration can be changed.

The Pain Killer To change the Outlook Express interface, follow these steps:

1. In Outlook Express, click View | Layout.

2. In the Window Layout Properties window, change the interface configuration as desired, and then click OK.

I don't like the appearance of e-mail that I read/compose.

Operating Systems Affected   Windows XP Professional and Home Editions are affected.

Cause   Outlook Express uses a default configuration and default fonts for e-mail that you type or read. However, if that default setup doesn't work for you, you can easily change it.

The Pain Killer   To change the setup of e-mail fonts and colors, follow these steps:

1. In Outlook Express, click Tools | Options.

2. Click the Read tab, and then click the Fonts button. Make any desired changes, and then click OK. Click the Compose tab and make any desired font setting changes or changes to stationery defaults. Click OK when you are done.

I am afraid to open e-mail attachments because they could contain viruses.

Operating Systems Affected   Windows XP Professional and Home Editions are affected.

Cause   A major way of spreading computer viruses is through e-mail attachments. A user receives an e-mail with an attachment, opens the attachment, and bam— you now have a computer virus. While most e-mail attachments are harmless, some can be very bad and can give your computer nasty viruses.

The Pain Killer   To keep from getting a computer virus from an e-mail attachment, do these three things:

1. First and foremost, you need to install (or update) antivirus software that can detect viruses in e-mail attachments. Most antivirus software, such as Symantec's Norton AntiVirus and McAfee's VirusScan, provides this protection. Invest a little money and use antivirus software!

2. In Outlook Express, click Tools | Options. Click the Security tab. Make sure the two check boxes concerning e-mail from applications and potentially

dangerous attachments are both checked. You can also set Outlook Express to use a restricted zone.

3. Finally, use common sense. If you get an e-mail message with an attachment from someone whom you do not know, don't open it. If things sound fishy, they probably are, so look at attachments with a wary eye. This does not mean attachments you get from friends and family cannot be infected with viruses also; it just means you shouldn't open an attachment from someone you don't know, unless you are 100 percent certain the file is not infected. Play it safe!

My news messages keep disappearing every few days.

Operating Systems Affected   Windows XP Professional and Home Editions are affected.

Cause   News messages are meant to be read and cleaned out quickly due to the volume that you can sometimes receive. By default, Outlook Express automatically deletes new messages after five days, but you can change this behavior if you wish.

The Pain Killer   To change the frequency at which news messages are deleted, follow these steps:

1. In Outlook Express, click Tools | Options.

2. Click the Maintenance tab. In the Delete News Messages scroll box, change the value to the desired number of days. If you don't want Outlook Express to delete your messages at all, just clear the Delete News Messages check box. When you are done, click OK.

My Internet program keeps disconnecting after I send or receive mail.

Operating Systems Affected   Windows XP Professional and Home Editions are affected.

Cause   Outlook Express can be configured to disconnect from the Internet automatically after mail has been sent or received.

The Pain Killer   To stop Outlook Express from disconnecting, follow these steps:

1. In Outlook Express, click Tools | Options.

2. Click the Connection tab. Clear the Hang Up After Sending and Receiving check box, and then click OK.

Solving Problems with Mail Management

One of the most aggravating things about e-mail is getting rid of the mail you don't want, while continuing to receive the mail you do want. Junk mail has been around as long as the postal service, but e-mail junk mail is at an all time high, with millions of pieces of junk mail sent daily, including advertisements for drugs and even pornography. Outlook Express gives you some tools for blocking senders and creating rules to manage e-mail. These rules are somewhat intuitive, but they can cause a few Headaches from time to time. Still, they can be very helpful, and you should try to get all you can out of them. The following Headaches show you how to manage these features.

I can't stop someone from sending me e-mail.

Operating Systems Affected   Windows XP Professional and Home Editions are affected.

Cause   If you want to stop receiving e-mail from a particular person, you can use an Outlook Express option called Block Sender. When you block a sender, any mail received from that sender goes directly into the Deleted Items folder instead of into your Inbox or other folders. Although technically this means you are downloading the mail from the sender, you never have to see it.

The Pain Killer   To block a sender, follow these steps:

1. When you receive an e-mail from the person you want to block, open the message.

2. Click the Message menu, and then click Block Sender.

3. A message appears telling you that the sender has been added to the blocked senders list.

> TIP   *Keep in mind that the blocked senders list blocks a specific e-mail address. If the user begins using a different e-mail address, the mail will show up in your Inbox again. If that happens, you will need to block the new e-mail address as well.*

I accidentally put someone on the blocked senders list.

Operating Systems Affected   Windows XP Professional and Home Editions are affected.

Cause   It is easy to put someone on the blocked senders list by mistake. However, you can edit the blocked senders list and change it as needed—for example, if someone who is blocked should not be blocked any longer.

How Can I Avoid Junk Mail?

Some unpleasant things in life are unavoidable, one of them being junk mail. However, there are some actions you can take that may help minimize junk mail and make your work with e-mail more enjoyable:

- Do not readily give away your e-mail address to web sites. Web sites often sell their contact lists, which causes you to start getting junk mail from sites you have never heard of. Of course, feel free to use your e-mail address when needed, but don't freely give it away. Also, consider using a different e-mail account, such as Hotmail or Yahoo! mail, for communications on the Internet. This will keep more junk mail out of your primary account.

- Use your browser's privacy settings (in Internet Explorer, click Tools | Internet Options, and then click the Privacy tab), which block a site's use of cookies in certain circumstances. This will help control a web site's access to your e-mail address. See Chapter 10 for details.

- Use Outlook Express's blocking and rules features to manage junk mail.

- Don't respond to junk mail. Also, many junk e-mails contain a link saying "If you want to be removed from this list...." Don't click this link! This is actually used to find out if your e-mail address is real, and you will probably end up on more lists if you click the link. Do not respond to junk e-mail in any way.

- Check out some additional tips at www.slipstick.com/rules/junkmail.htm.

The Pain Killer   To manage the blocked senders list, follow these steps:

1. In Outlook Express, click Tools | Message Rules | Blocked Senders List.

2. In the Blocked Senders tab, you can add, remove, or modify a blocked sender by clicking the respective buttons. Click OK when you are done.

| Message Rules | ? X |

Mail Rules | News Rules | Blocked Senders

Messages from senders in the list below will automatically be moved to the Deleted Items folder (for Mail messages) and/or not displayed (for Newsgroup messages).

Mail	News	E-mail Address/Domain Name	
☑	☐	msoe@microsoft.com	Add...
			Modify...
			Remove

OK   Cancel

I can't create a mail/news rule.

Operating Systems Affected   Windows XP Professional and Home Editions are affected.

Cause   Outlook Express provides you the option to create rules that determine how certain e-mail or news messages are handled. You can create rules based on message content, words in the subject heading, and even rules that automatically list certain people in the To field.

The Pain Killer   To create a mail or news rule, follow these steps:

1. In Outlook Express, click Tools | Message Rules. On the Message Rules menu, click Mail or News, depending on whether you want to create a mail rule or a news rule.

2. In the New Mail Rule or New News Rule window, choose the condition, the action, the description, and the name, as shown in the illustration. Be sure to make the rule specific. Click OK when you are done.

New Mail Rule

Select your Conditions and Actions first, then specify the values in the Description.

1. Select the Conditions for your rule:

- [ ] Where the From line contains people
- [x] Where the Subject line contains specific words
- [ ] Where the message body contains specific words
- [ ] Where the To line contains people

2. Select the Actions for your rule:

- [x] Move it to the specified folder
- [ ] Copy it to the specified folder
- [ ] Delete it
- [ ] Forward it to people

3. Rule Description (click on an underlined value to edit it):

Apply this rule after the message arrives
Where the Subject line contains specific words
Move it to the specified folder

4. Name of the rule:

Advertisements

[OK]   [Cancel]

TIP *As you choose the conditions and actions, the rule description will change. Click the underlined hyperlinks to customize the condition.*

3. The new mail or news rule now appears in the mail rules or news rules list, as you can see in the illustration on the following page. You can use this window to create new rules, delete rules, or modify existing rules at any time. Click OK when you are done.

Message Rules   ? ☒

| Mail Rules | News Rules | Blocked Senders |

These rules will be applied to Mail messages.

☑ Advertisements

New...

Modify...

Copy

Remove

Apply Now...

Move Up   Move Down

Rule Description (click on an underlined value to edit it):

Apply this rule after the message arrives
Where the Subject line contains 'sales'
Move it to the Deleted Items folder

OK   Cancel

Chapter 12

Windows XP Networking Headaches

In this chapter, you'll cure…

- Problems with network setup and access

- Difficulties with network shares

- Aggravations with Internet Connection Sharing

- Pains with Remote Desktop and Remote Assistance

Windows XP is the easiest operating system Microsoft has ever produced in terms of networking. There is more wizard help and less configuration for you to do than with any previous version of Windows, and that's great. After all, you want to spend time enjoying your home or small office network, not learning everything under the sun in order to make it actually work.

However, networking is still a complex process, and although Windows XP does a fine job of making your life easier, there are many problems you might run into, no matter whether you have a simple cable connection between two computers or a larger office network with multiple computers and shared printers. Either way, the problems you are likely to experience are about the same.

In this chapter, I assume you have studied a networking book or the Windows XP Help and Support Center and that you already know a thing or two about networking. In fact, I expect that the reason you have turned to this chapter is that you have tried to network computers together and are having problems. In this chapter, I explore the major issues you are likely to have when networking with Windows XP; and I assume those problems relate to your home network or a small office network.

Problems with Network Setup and Access

In order to create a network, you need two primary items:

- **Hardware**   First, your computers must have the necessary hardware that enables them to communicate with each other. This hardware, called a *network adapter card,* allows your computer to be connected to a network. There are several different kinds of network adapter cards, and your computer may have been shipped with one. Before you get too involved in network issues, you'll first need to install a network adapter card if your computer does not have one. If your computer does have one, it will automatically appear in the Network Connections folder in Control Panel, as shown in

Figure 12-1. It will be labeled Local Area Connection. If you do not see the connection in the Network Connections folder, then your computer is not outfitted with a network adapter card or the card is not working.

■ **Software** Your computer must have the correct software to allow the computer to operate on the network. Don't worry, though—that software is already included in Windows XP, so there is nothing else to buy.

Once you gather any needed network adapter cards and cables, depending on the type of network you want to install, you should get everything connected according to the manufacturer's setup instructions. Follow the instructions carefully, and if you are not sure what you are doing, you may consider getting extra help from technical support, or even from a friend or relative who has networked computers together before. Once you get all the hardware connected (and have checked it twice), you are ready to set up your computers for networking. See the Windows XP Help and Support Center for instructions, and see the following Headaches and their solutions for more help!

FIGURE 12-1 Network Connections folder

What Kind of Network Should I Use?

You can use any of several different kinds of networks in your home or small office. Your choice depends on your needs and how much you want to spend. If your computers are not already outfitted with a network adapter card, you can make some choices about the kind of network you might want. I'd suggest you do some additional reading in the Windows XP Help and Support Center before making your decision, but here are the major types of networks:

- **Ethernet**   Ethernet is a standard network type that has been in use for a long time. Your computer is outfitted with a standard Ethernet network adapter, and you connect all of your computers to a little device called a *hub*. You use standard Ethernet wiring, which looks like a large telephone line, and your computers all communicate with each other through the hub. I use this kind of network in my home office; it's easy and works great, but it is not the newest technology out there.

- **HomePNA**   HomePNA networks use phone lines in your home to communicate with each other. A HomePNA network adapter card is installed in your computer, which then plugs into your phone jack. Then, other computers in different rooms of your house do the same, and they can communicate with each other that way. The good news about HomePNA is that it is rather inexpensive, it works well, and it uses the existing phone line system without more cables running everywhere. Most computer stores sell HomePNA kits that can help you set everything up. If you want a home network where you have access in practically every room (that is, in every room with a phone jack), this one is for you.

- **Wireless**   Wireless networks, which use infrared and radio technologies, are also available today. Your computer is outfitted with a wireless network adapter card that communicates with a wireless hub, or two wireless adapter cards can communicate with each other with no hub (called an *ad hoc connection*). Although not as popular as Ethernet or Home PNA, wireless networks are on the cutting edge; you can learn more about them in the Windows XP Help and Support Center or at www.microsoft.com.

I can't get my wired network set up.

Operating Systems Affected   Windows XP Professional and Home Editions are affected.

Cause   Network setup in Windows XP is relatively easy if your network adapter card is installed and working. Be sure to open Network Connections in Control Panel to see if your Local Area Connection is available. If you see it there, you know that the network adapter card is installed and functioning, and you are ready to set up the network. If not, check your computer or network adapter card documentation, or the manufacturer's web site, for more information.

The Pain Killer   Once you are certain that the network adapter is installed as it should be, you can use the Network Setup Wizard to help you configure the first computer on your network.

1. Click Start | All Programs | Accessories | Communications | Network Setup Wizard.

2. Click Next on the Welcome screen.

3. Read the instructions on the Before You Continue screen; they tell you to turn on all computers, printers, and so on, before starting. Click Next.

4. In the Select a Connection Method screen, choose an option that describes your computer, and then click Next.

5. If you chose the first option in step 4, the Network Setup Wizard needs to identify your Internet connection. Select it in the provided screen, shown here, and then click Next.

6. In the Name and Description screen, give the computer a description and a network name. The name should be something friendly and easy to remember. If your computer has a cable or a Digital Subscriber Line (DSL) modem, you may be required to use a certain name provided by the Internet service provider (ISP). If this is the case, do not change the name. Check your broadband documentation for details. Click Next.

7. Choose the name of your network. It should be something simple; it is MSHOME by default, but you can call it anything you like.

8. In the next window, a summary of the settings to be applied are listed. Click Next to apply the settings, and follow any additional instructions that might appear.

NOTE

Now that you have set up the first computer on your network, you are ready to begin setting up the additional computers. If you are having trouble with this task, see the next Headache for assistance.

I can't get my wireless network set up.

Operating Systems Affected   Windows XP Professional and Home Editions are affected.

Cause   Windows XP has built-in wireless support. With the popularity of wireless home and small office networks, this is great news. Still, wireless networks can give you some headaches, so it is important that you carefully read the installation and setup instructions provided by the wireless hardware vendor you are using. Wireless networks typically require that wireless clients be configured with a wireless radio card and you must use a wireless access point or base station. If you are using a shared Internet connection, you'll need to configure that too. The good news is that most wireless networking hardware comes with step-by-step instructions that you should follow. Because this is the case, I can't give you specific painkillers, but I can offer some advice.

The Pain Killer   If you are having problems with your wireless network, make sure that you check out these issues:

1. Make sure the hardware is physically set up and connected as it should be. Check your documentation for details.

2. Security is a common problem. Each wireless card for each PC must be configured with the correct wireless security key for your network. You can find out more information about configuring wireless security for your network through your wireless network hardware documentation. Typically, you'll access the properties for each network adapter card on each PC and click the Configure button. This gives you a window where you can enter the correct security key, as shown in the illustration.

3. Try changing channels. Just like a television or radio, wireless networks use channels. If you are having connectivity problems, you may try changing the channel on all wireless devices. This action alone solved a frustrating wireless connection problem on my home network.

> TIP
>
> *The hardware you purchased should provide support information. If you are having problems getting your wireless network up and running, do not hesitate to contact technical support.*

I can't install additional clients on my network.

Operating Systems Affected   Windows XP Professional and Home Editions are affected.

Cause   Once you have set up the first computer on your network, your next task is to set up the other computers on the network. If you want the first computer to share the Internet connection and all other computers to connect to the Internet through that shared connection, you can easily configure the additional client computers using the Network Setup Wizard. If you need a different configuration, you can set up that as well.

The Pain Killer   To set up your client computers, follow these steps:

1. Click Start | All Programs | Accessories | Communications | Network Setup Wizard.

2. Click Next on the Welcome screen.

3. Read the instructions on the Before You Continue screen; they tell you to turn on all computers, printers, and so on, before starting. Click Next.

4. In the Select a Connection Method screen, you can choose the This Computer Connects to the Internet Through Another Computer on My Network or Through a Residential Gateway option. If this does not describe your network or if Internet Connection Sharing will not be used, click the Other radio button and then click Next.

5. In the Other Internet Connection Methods screen, you have the options to connect to the Internet directly or not connect. If you are not sure about your network setup, click the link at the bottom of the window to learn more about home and small office network configurations. Make your selection, and then click Next.

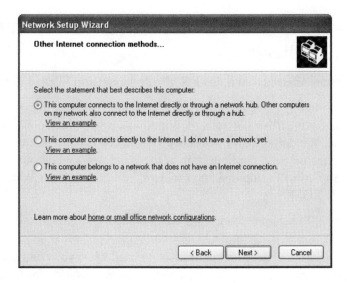

6. Enter a computer description and name. Click Next.

7. Choose the network name. You must use the same network name on all computers. Click Next.

8. Review your settings, and then click Next.

9. Once the settings are applied, you'll see the option to create a network setup disk to use on other computers so that they will be configured in the same way, and another option to use your Windows XP CD. You can also select the Just Finish the Wizard. Make a selection, and then click Next. You may need to follow additional steps, depending on your selection.

I need to set up Windows network clients that are not Windows XP clients.

Operating Systems Affected   Windows XP Professional and Home Editions are affected.

Cause   If you have earlier versions of Windows on your network, such as Windows 2000, Windows Me, or Windows 9x, you can use the setup disk you created during the network configuration of the Windows XP computers. If you did not create a network setup disk, no problem, you can use your Windows XP installation CD-ROM.

The Pain Killer   To set up a down-level client computer, follow these steps:

1. If you have the network setup disk you created when you configured the XP clients, insert the disk and start the Network Setup Wizard from that disk by double-clicking Netsetup. If you do not have a network floppy disk, go to step 2.

2. Insert the Windows XP installation CD-ROM into the down-level computer's CD-ROM drive. On the Welcome screen, click the Perform Additional Tasks option. Then, in the following window, choose the Set Up a Home or Small Office Network option and follow the wizard instructions that appear.

 I can't configure networking with a Linux or Macintosh computer.

Operating Systems Affected   Windows XP Professional and Home Editions are affected.

Cause   Windows XP is able to natively network with other Windows computers (down to systems using Windows 95). However, XP does not provide support for direct networking with Linux or Macintosh. In this case, you need a network server that handles network translation between the two different systems, which of course is not a practical solution for a home or small office network.

The Pain Killer Sorry, there is no workaround for this Headache! (If I were a doctor I might recommend that you try taking two aspirin and e-mailing Microsoft in the morning…, or not.)

My computer does not connect to the network. All other networked computers are functioning correctly.

Operating Systems Affected Windows XP Professional and Home Editions are affected.

Cause If your computer has been set up for the network, but you still cannot access network resources, the problem usually resides with either your network adapter card or your current TCP/IP configuration. Transmission Control Protocol/Internet Protocol (TCP/IP) is a network protocol that your computers use to talk to each other.

The Pain Killer To resolve the problem, follow these steps:

1. First, you should check your network adapter card and make sure that it is working. Click Start | Control Panel. In Control Panel's Classic view, click Network Connections. Right-click your local area connection, and then click Status.

2. In the Connection window, shown here, see if the Status line reads "Connected." If not, click the Support tab.

3. On the Support tab, click the Repair button to attempt to repair the connection. If this does not work, the network adapter card may not be installed correctly or there may be a problem with the card. See the manufacturer's

instructions or web site for more information.

4. If your network adapter card seems to be working, test it one more time with a Ping test. Ping 127.0.0.1 is a command that tests network connectivity against your network adapter card so that you can be sure it is working. To use Ping, click Start | Run. Type Command, and then click OK.

5. In the command window, type **ping 127.0.0.1** and press ENTER.

6. You should see a reply message like the one shown in the illustration. If you do not, there is something wrong with your network adapter card.

```
C:\WINDOWS\System32\command.com

Microsoft(R) Windows DOS
(C)Copyright Microsoft Corp 1990-2001.

C:\DOCUME~1\CURT>ping 127.0.0.1

Pinging 127.0.0.1 with 32 bytes of data:

Reply from 127.0.0.1: bytes=32 time<1ms TTL=128
Reply from 127.0.0.1: bytes=32 time<1ms TTL=128
Reply from 127.0.0.1: bytes=32 time<1ms TTL=128
Reply from 127.0.0.1: bytes=32 time<1ms TTL=128

Ping statistics for 127.0.0.1:
    Packets: Sent = 4, Received = 4, Lost = 0 (0% loss),
Approximate round trip times in milli-seconds:
    Minimum = 0ms, Maximum = 0ms, Average = 0ms

C:\DOCUME~1\CURT>_
```

7. If you do see a reply message, then try to Ping other computers on your network. You can do this using their network name, such as **ping *name***. For example, on my network, I have a computer called "writer," so I would just Ping the computer by typing **ping writer**. If this works, you'll see the same reply message, shown here:

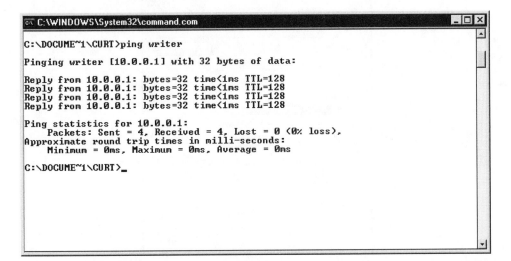

```
C:\WINDOWS\System32\command.com                                    _ □ X

C:\DOCUME~1\CURT>ping writer

Pinging writer [10.0.0.1] with 32 bytes of data:

Reply from 10.0.0.1: bytes=32 time<1ms TTL=128
Reply from 10.0.0.1: bytes=32 time<1ms TTL=128
Reply from 10.0.0.1: bytes=32 time<1ms TTL=128
Reply from 10.0.0.1: bytes=32 time<1ms TTL=128

Ping statistics for 10.0.0.1:
    Packets: Sent = 4, Received = 4, Lost = 0 (0% loss),
Approximate round trip times in milli-seconds:
    Minimum = 0ms, Maximum = 0ms, Average = 0ms

C:\DOCUME~1\CURT>_
```

8. If you cannot Ping other computers using their names, try a few using the IP address. You can find the IP address, such as 192.168.0.190, on the Support tab of the Local Area Connection Status window, (shown previously in step 3). Using the Ping command again, Ping the IP address by typing it, as in **ping 192.168.0.190**.

9. If the Ping command fails again, you'll need to check the IP address of your own computer. The address your computer uses must be in the same family, or more technically, the same subnet. You can easily make sure your computer is using the same IP subnet by clicking Start | Control Panel. Then in Control Panel's Classic view, click Network Connections. Right-click your Local Area Connection, and then click Properties.

10. On the General tab, select Internet Protocol (TCP/IP), and then click the Properties button.

11. In the Internet Protocol (TCP/IP) Properties window, make sure you have selected the Obtain an IP Address Automatically radio button, and click OK. Then use the Repair option found in the Status window, and make sure your computer gets an IP address in the same range and subnet as the other computers on your network. You'll need to check the other computers to see if the IP address is in the same range.

Internet Protocol (TCP/IP) Properties

General | Alternate Configuration

You can get IP settings assigned automatically if your network supports this capability. Otherwise, you need to ask your network administrator for the appropriate IP settings.

◉ Obtain an IP address automatically
○ Use the following IP address:

IP address:

Subnet mask:

Default gateway:

◉ Obtain DNS server address automatically
○ Use the following DNS server addresses:

Preferred DNS server:

Alternate DNS server:

Advanced...

OK   Cancel

I need to use a different IP address configuration on my network.

Operating Systems Affected   Windows XP Professional and Home Editions are affected.

Cause   Windows XP uses TCP/IP to communicate on home and small office networks, as well as on networks that contain thousands of computers. Because TCP/IP is a highly technical and complex subject, Microsoft devised a system known as Automatic Private IP Addressing (APIPA). APIPA allows the computers on your network to automatically assign themselves an IP address so that you don't have to do it—or even know anything about it, for that matter. However, in some cases, such as with cable and DSL modems, you may need to manually assign your network computers an IP address in a particular range for Internet connectivity to work on your network. If this is the case, you need to follow your ISP's instructions carefully, but the Pain Killer gives you the skinny on manual IP address configuration as well.

> NOTE *Unless your ISP has given you instructions to do so, never manually change the IP addresses of your computers. Configuring IP addresses incorrectly will cause your computers to stop communicating with each other.*

The Pain Killer To manually configure an IP address, follow these steps:

1. Click Start | Control Panel. In Control Panel's Classic view, click Network Connections.

2. Right-click the local area connection, and then click Properties.

3. On the General tab, click the Internet Protocol (TCP/IP) option in the dialog box, and then click Properties, as shown in the illustration.

4. In the Internet Protocol Properties window, click the Use the Following IP Address option and enter a valid IP address, subnet mask, and default gateway, as instructed by your ISP. Again, do not change any of these settings unless you have been instructed to do so. Click OK when you are done.

I get an "access denied" message when I try to access another computer on my network.

Operating Systems Affected   Windows XP Professional and Home Editions are affected.

Cause   The computer is using New Technology File System (NTFS) permissions and has not given you access to the computer or the shares on that computer.

The Pain Killer   You, or the administrator of that computer, will need to configure the computer to give you access. See the next section to learn more about share access problems.

Difficulties with Network Shares

Once the network is all connected and working as it should, you can begin sharing folders, printers, drives, just about anything else you might want. After all, that is the purpose of networking to begin with. However, network sharing can be quite complex, especially when you want to finely control permissions, and there are some Headaches you might run into.

> TIP
>
> *The best prevention for network share Headaches is to keep things as simple as possible. Complex shares with complex permissions tend to cause problems, so keep things as simple as you can.*

I want to see all of the shares available on a particular computer or on my network.

Operating Systems Affected   Windows XP Professional and Home Editions are affected.

Cause   You can easily view resources that are available to you, and there are a few different ways to do it.

The Pain Killer   To view resources available on your network, follow these steps:

1. To view resources on a particular computer, click Start | Run. In the Run dialog box, type *computername*. For example, if I wanted to access a computer called "writer," then I would type **writer**.

2. Click OK. A window opens, shown here, and you can see the shared resources available on that computer.

3. You can also view the shared resources available to you on another computer by using the Net View command. Click Start | Run and type **command**. Click OK. At the command prompt, type **net view *computername***, such as **net view \\\\writer**, as shown in the illustration.

```
C:\WINDOWS\System32\command.com

C:\DOCUME~1\CURT>net view \\writer
Shared resources at \\writer

Curt's Writing Machine

Share name            Type    Used as  Comment
-----------------------------------------------------------------
CD Drive (E)          Disk
EPSONSty              Print            EPSON Stylus C40 Series
MCSE XP               Disk
Windows XP Headaches  Disk
The command completed successfully.


C:\DOCUME~1\CURT>
```

4. If you want to see what is available on all of the computers on your network, click Start | My Network Places. A window appears, displaying all of the available shares.

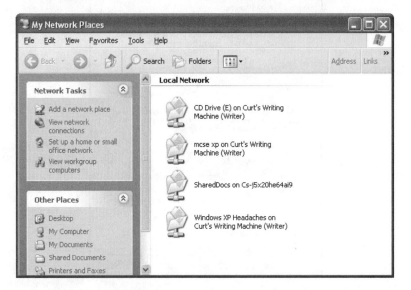

I am having problems sharing a folder (or a printer, a drive, or another device).

Operating Systems Affected   Windows XP Professional and Home Editions are affected.

Cause   Once your computer is configured for networking, you can then begin to share resources, including printers, folders, drives, and just about anything else. You share resources in the same way, by accessing the Sharing tab on the resource's properties sheets. In this case, you access the Sharing tab on the shared folder and configure it for networking.

The Pain Killer   To share a resource, follow these steps:

1. Right-click the folder, drive, or printer, and then click Properties.

2. Click the Sharing tab, shown in the illustration.

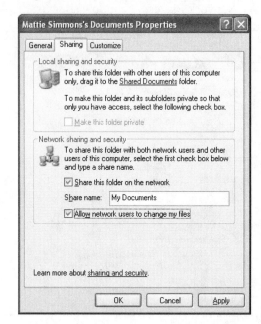

3. You have the option to either share the folder locally, with other users of your computer, by dragging the folder to the Shared Documents folder, or you can click the check box to share the folder on the network. Give the folder a name. (Other users will see this name, so make the name friendly and recognizable.) If you want other network users to be able to change the files in the folder, click the check box option. If you want only to be able to read the files, clear the check box.

The options on the Sharing tab are grayed out.

Operating Systems Affected   Windows XP Professional and Home Editions are affected.

Cause   If you want to share a folder, but the options to share the folder on the Sharing tab are grayed out, then the folder is residing in another folder that has been made private. When a folder is made private, it cannot be shared, and any subfolders in that folder cannot be shared either.

The Pain Killer   Drag the folder out of the private folder to a different location so that it can be shared.

System folders cannot be shared.

NOTE

I can't configure NTFS permissions.

Operating Systems Affected   Windows XP Professional Edition is affected.

Cause   NTFS provides extensive permissions, which you can assign to network resources. However, by default, simple file sharing is enabled in order to make things easier. Simple file sharing allows you to share a resource and give your users full control, or give them just read access by clearing the check box option on the Sharing tab. However, what if you want Bob to have full control to a folder but Susan to have read-only access? You cannot configure this under simple file sharing, so you'll need to turn it off.

> **NOTE**
> *You can turn off simple file sharing and use advanced NTFS permissions on Windows XP Professional only; this option is not available on Windows XP Home Edition.*

The Pain Killer   To turn off simple file sharing, follow these steps:

1. Click Start | Control Panel. In Control Panel's Classic view, click Folder Options.

2. Click the View tab. Scroll to the bottom of the page and clear the Use Simple File Sharing option. Click OK.

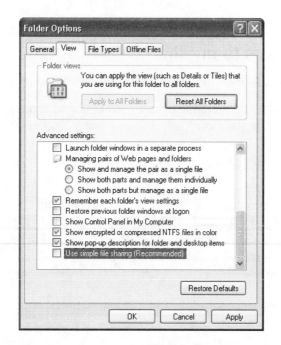

3. Once you clear the option, you will see that the Sharing tab on any resource now allows you to configure permissions (that is, you will see a Permissions button).

I have configured specific permissions, but users still have full access to my share.

Operating Systems Affected   Windows XP Professional Edition is affected.

Cause   Folder and NTFS permissions can be complicated and are beyond the scope of this book. However, the most likely cause of this problem is that you have given the Everyone group full control. Since all users are members of the Everyone group, full control permissions most likely are overriding the permissions you configured for each user.

The Pain Killer   Open the properties pages for the share and click the Security tab. Remove all permissions for the Everyone group by selecting the check boxes and clicking Remove, as shown in Figure 12-2. Keep in mind that this action will stop

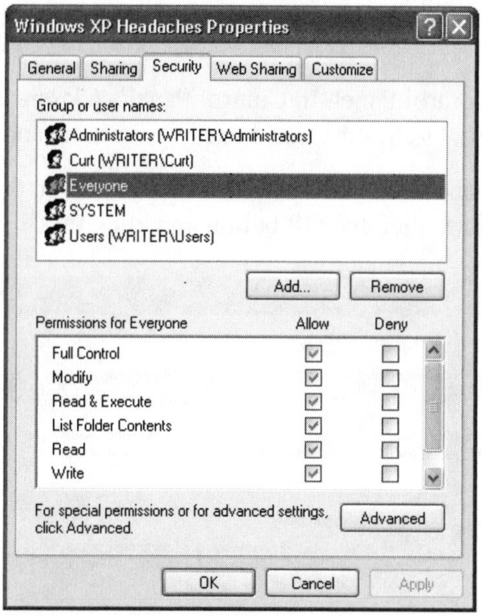

FIGURE 12-2   Remove the Everyone group

everyone from accessing the share, unless you have configured individual permissions for certain users.

I have shared folders on my computer, but no one can access my computer. I can access other computers with no trouble.

Operating Systems Affected   Windows XP Professional and Home Editions are affected.

Cause   If you have shared folders, simple file sharing is in use, and you can access other computers but no one can access yours, the problem is most likely Windows Firewall. WF can be enabled on your Internet connection but never on your network adapter card. If you enable WF on your network adapter card, users on the network will not be able to access your computer.

The Pain Killer   To turn off Windows Firewall on the network adapter card, follow these steps:

1. Click Start | Control Panel. In Control Panel's Classic view, click Network Connections. Right-click the Local Area Connection, and then click Properties.

2. Click the Advanced tab, click the Settings button. In the Windows Firewall Settings window, click the Off button and click OK.

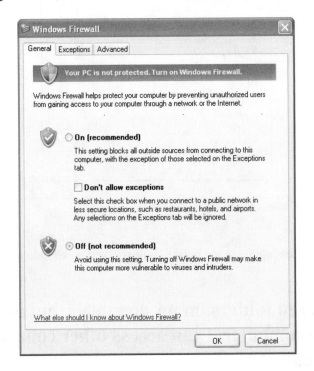

Aggravations with Internet Connection Sharing

Internet Connection Sharing (ICS) is a cool feature that allows you to share an Internet connection with other computers on your network. For example, you may have one computer that is outfitted with a DSL modem. You can share this connection so that other computers on your network can use the DSL connection.

When you used the Network Setup Wizard to configure your Internet connection, you had the option to share the Internet connection with other users on your network. If you chose this option in the wizard, the other computers on your network were configured with the IP address of the main computer's connection so that Internet Explorer and mail programs could access the Internet through that shared connection.

Overall, ICS works great once you have it configured; and you are likely to run into only a few problems, which I'll explore in this section.

I did not set up ICS when I first configured my network, but I want to use it now. How can I configure it?

Operating Systems Affected   Windows XP Professional and Home Editions are affected.

Cause   If you did not configure ICS when you first used the Network Setup Wizard, you can enable it and use it later. See the Pain Killer for instructions.

The Pain Killer   To configure ICS after the network is already configured, follow these steps:

1. Click Start | Control Panel. In Control Panel's Classic view, click Network Connections. Right-click the Internet connection, and then click Properties.

2. Click the Advanced tab. Enable all three of the ICS check boxes, as shown in the illustration, and click OK.

```
┌─────────────────────────────────────────────────┐
│  My Connection Properties                  [?][X] │
├─────────────────────────────────────────────────┤
│ General │ Options │ Security │ Networking │ Advanced │
│  ┌─Internet Connection Firewall──────────────┐   │
│  │ [✓] Protect my computer and network by     │   │
│  │     limiting or preventing access to this  │   │
│  │     computer from the Internet             │   │
│  │                                            │   │
│  │ Learn more about Internet Connection Firewall. │
│  └────────────────────────────────────────────┘   │
│  ┌─Internet Connection Sharing───────────────┐   │
│  │ [✓] Allow other network users to connect   │   │
│  │     through this computer's Internet       │   │
│  │     connection                             │   │
│  │                                            │   │
│  │ [✓] Establish a dial-up connection whenever│   │
│  │     a computer on my network attempts to   │   │
│  │     access the Internet                    │   │
│  │ [✓] Allow other network users to control or│   │
│  │     disable the shared Internet connection │   │
│  │                                            │   │
│  │ Learn more about Internet Connection Sharing. │
│  └────────────────────────────────────────────┘   │
│  If you're not sure how to set these properties,  │
│  use the Network Setup Wizard instead.  [Settings...] │
│                                                   │
│                         [   OK   ] [  Cancel  ]   │
└─────────────────────────────────────────────────┘
```

3. On the client computers, run the Network Setup Wizard again. You'll see a new screen that detects the shared connection and asks if you want to use

it. Choose the Yes option, and complete the wizard. Now ICS will work on your network.

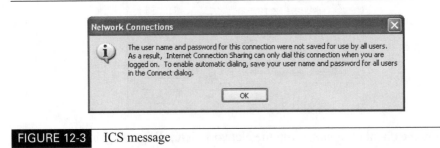

When I try to enable ICS, a message appears telling me that my user name and password are not saved for all users.

Operating Systems Affected   Windows XP Professional and Home Editions are affected.

Cause   When you first configured the Internet connection, you had the option to make your user name and password for the ISP "public" for the other users on your computer. If you chose to keep it private, ICS will not work because no other users can access the connection. If you see the message shown in Figure 12-3, you need to change the connection's user name and password so that it is saved for all users.

FIGURE 12-3   ICS message

The Pain Killer   To save your user name and password for use by all users, follow these steps:

1. Click Start | Control Panel. In Control Panel's Classic view, click Network Connections. Right-click the Internet connection, and then click Connect.

2. In the Connection window that appears, choose the Anyone Who Uses This Computer radio button. Click the Dial button to activate the option.

When I try to configure a computer for Internet Connection Sharing, I receive a message telling me there is an IP address conflict.

Operating Systems Affected   Windows XP Professional and Home Editions are affected.

Cause   If you try to turn on ICS for a computer and you receive the message shown in Figure 12-4, then another computer on your network is configured for ICS. Only one computer on the network can be an ICS host; in other words, only one computer can share its Internet connection.

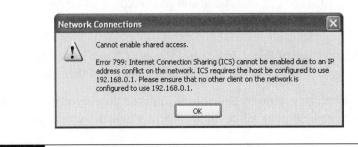

FIGURE 12-4 ICS host message

The Pain Killer To resolve the problem, locate the other shared ICS computer and clear the ICS sharing options on the Advanced tab of the Internet connection's properties sheets.

Users can disconnect the ICS Internet connection, and I don't want them to be able to control the connection.

Operating Systems Affected Windows XP Professional and Home Editions are affected.

Cause By default, users can disconnect and control the ICS Internet connection. However, if you do not want users to be able to access the ICS connection and manage it, you can disable the option.

The Pain Killer To stop users from controlling the Internet connection, follow these steps:

1. Click Start | Control Panel. In Control Panel's Classic view, click Network Connections. Right-click the Internet connection, and then click Properties.

2. Click the Advanced tab. Clear the Allow Other Network Users to Control or Disable the Shared Internet Connection check box, and click OK.

The ICS computer does not dial a connection when a network user needs it.

Operating Systems Affected Windows XP Professional and Home Editions are affected.

Cause   By default, ICS will dial a connection (if dialing is required) when a network user needs the connection. However, if the setting is turned off, the ICS host will not dial.

The Pain Killer   To make sure the ICS host dials the connection, follow these steps:

1. Click Start | Control Panel. In Control Panel's Classic view, click Network Connections. Right-click the Internet connection, and then click Properties.

2. Click the Advanced tab. Enable the Establish a Dial-Up Connection Whenever a Computer on My Network Attempts to Access the Internet check box and click OK.

ICS dial-up connections are slow.

Operating Systems Affected   Windows XP Professional and Home Editions are affected.

Cause   ICS enables you to share an Internet connection among several computers. However, if several people are using the Internet connection at the same time, access will seem slow over dial-up connections due to traffic.

The Pain Killer   The only workaround is to upgrade to a broadband connection, such as DSL or cable, keep users from accessing the shared connection at the same time, or make sure that no large file downloads are performed while two or more people are using the connection.

My e-mail does not work with ICS.

Operating Systems Affected   Windows XP Professional and Home Editions are affected.

Cause   Assuming you are using Outlook or Outlook Express, you must configure the mail client to get e-mail using a Local Area Connection rather than a direct Internet connection.

The Pain Killer   See the mail client's documentation for information about setting up the mail client to access mail through a Local Area Connection.

No clients can use the ICS computer.

Operating Systems Affected   Windows XP Professional and Home Editions are affected.

Cause   If ICS is configured but clients cannot access the Internet, it is usually one of two possible problems:

- The ICS computer is not turned on or the Internet connection is not working. Check the ICS computer and make sure it is operational and that the connection is working.

- If the connection is working and your clients are configured correctly, the default gateway address of the ICS computer may be incorrect if you have manually configured your IP addresses.

If neither of these options is true, try rebooting the computer to clear out any software or Internet access glitches.

The Pain Killer   If you have manually configured or changed the IP addressing information on the ICS computer, check the IP address properties. The default gateway should be 192.168.0.1.

Pains with Remote Desktop and Remote Assistance

Remote Desktop and Remote Assistance are two new features in Windows XP. Remote Desktop enables you to connect to a remote computer over the Internet and use the computer as though you are actually sitting at it. Remote Assistance is similar, but it is used to support other people and help them solve problems. See the Windows XP Help and Support Center for setup and configuration information; and if you are having problems, the following sections explore the issues you are likely to run into.

Remote Desktop

The following Headaches and solutions pertain to Remote Desktop. Remote Desktop is designed to be an office solution to enable remote users to connect to the LAN and access a computer that allows remote desktop connections. In addition, it can be used by several users for collaborative purposes within the network.

NOTE   *Remote Desktop is only available for the Windows XP Professional Edition.*

I can't use Remote Desktop.

Operating Systems Affected   Windows XP Professional Edition is affected.

Cause   In order to remotely connect to a Windows XP Professional computer, you have to configure the computer to allow a Remote Desktop connection and indicate what users are allowed to connect to it remotely.

The Pain Killer   To configure Remote Desktop, follow these steps:

1. Click Start | Control Panel. In Control Panel's Classic view, click System.

2. Click the Advanced tab and click the Remote Desktop option to enable the feature, as shown here.

3. Click the Select Remote Users button. In the dialog box that appears, click the Add button and select the users that you want to allow to connect from a remote location. If the user you want is not available, use the Users option in Control Panel to configure an account for the user. Every user that connects to your computer via Remote Desktop must have a valid user account configured on your computer in order to gain access.

NOTE   *It is important to keep in mind that a Remote Desktop computer must have an Internet connection that is "always on" and is designed for corporate computers where you access the corporate computer over the Internet from a home computer.*

Remote Desktop does not work with Windows Firewall.

Operating Systems Affected   Windows XP Professional Edition is affected.

Cause   Windows Firewall does not allow incoming traffic that is not explicitly requested by a local user, so Remote Desktop traffic is dropped by default. However, you can configure Windows Firewall to allow Remote Desktop traffic.

The Pain Killer   To configure Windows Firewall to allow Remote Desktop traffic, follow these steps:

1. Click Start | Control Panel. In Control Panel's Classic view, click Network Connections. Right-click the Internet connection, and then click Properties.

2. Click the Advanced tab and click the Settings button.

3. In the Advanced Settings window, click the Remote Desktop check box on the Services tab and click OK. Click OK again.

Advanced Settings   [?][X]

Services | Security Logging | ICMP

Select the services running on your network that Internet users can access.

Services

- [ ] FTP Server
- [ ] Internet Mail Access Protocol Version 3 (IMAP3)
- [ ] Internet Mail Access Protocol Version 4 (IMAP4)
- [ ] Internet Mail Server (SMTP)
- [ ] Post-Office Protocol Version 3 (POP3)
- [x] Remote Desktop
- [ ] Secure Web Server (HTTPS)
- [ ] Telnet Server
- [ ] Web Server (HTTP)

[Add...]   [Edit...]   [Delete]

[OK]   [Cancel]

I need to connect to a Remote Desktop computer from a Windows computer that does not use Windows XP Professional Edition.

Operating Systems Affected   Windows XP Professional Edition are affected.

Cause   Only Windows XP Professional Edition computers can be configured to provide Remote Desktop, but any Windows client can be configured to access the Remote Desktop computer by installing a program available on the Windows XP Professional Edition CD-ROM.

> **NOTE** *Although Windows XP Home Edition cannot host a Remote Desktop configuration, it can connect to one by using the Remote Desktop connection option found in Start | All Programs | Accessories | Communications | Remote Desktop Connection. The installation option presented in the following Pain Killer, however, is needed for down-level clients, such as Windows 2000, Windows Me, Windows NT, and Windows 9x.*

The Pain Killer   To configure a client to access a Remote Desktop computer, follow these steps:

1. Insert the Windows XP Professional CD-ROM into the CD-ROM drive.

2. On the Welcome screen, choose Perform Additional Tasks, and then choose the Set Up a Remote Desktop Connection option.

3. Click Next on the Welcome screen that appears.

4. Read and accept the licensing agreement, and then click Next.

5. Enter your name, and choose the option to allow the software to be used only by you or someone who accesses the computer. Click Next.

6. Click the Install button.

Remote Desktop is slow.

Operating Systems Affected   Windows XP Professional is affected.

Cause   Depending on your Internet or network connection, Remote Desktop may respond slowly, considering the amount of information and graphics that must be downloaded to your computer. However, you can configure Remote Desktop to work more quickly over slow connections.

The Pain Killer   To configure Remote Desktop to work more quickly over slow connections, follow these steps:

1. Click Start | All Programs | Accessories | Remote Desktop Connection.

2. Click the Options button, and then click the Experience tab that appears.

3. On the Experience tab, click the drop-down menu and choose the connection speed. Then, clear any desired check boxes concerning desktop background settings, themes, and so on. The more options you clear here, the faster the connection is likely to work. When you are done, click OK. Click OK again.

Remote Assistance

Remote Assistance is similar to Remote Desktop, but the difference is that a user sends an invitation to another user with Windows Messenger, Microsoft Outlook, or Outlook Express so that a user on the Internet may connect to and configure the computer system. Again, make sure you check Windows XP Help and Support Center to learn how to use Remote Assistance.

NOTE *Remote Assistance works on both Windows XP Professional and Home Editions.*

I can't create a Remote Assistance invitation.

Operating Systems Affected   Windows XP Professional and Home Editions are affected.

Cause   Make sure you have enabled Remote Assistance on the Remote tab of System Properties. Once you have enabled it, follow the steps in the Pain Killer.

The Pain Killer   To create a Remote Assistance invitation, follow these steps:

1. Click Start | Help and Support.

2. Click the link in the right side of the window that allows you to get help and support using Remote Assistance.

3. In the Remote Assistance window, click the Invite Someone to Help You link.

4. As you can see here, you have the option to contact the user via Windows Messenger or by sending an e-mail message. Make your selection and follow the rest of the steps that appear.

I want to use Remote Assistance, but I don't want the user to be able to control my computer.

Operating Systems Affected   Windows XP Professional and Home Editions are affected.

Cause   With Remote Assistance, you can simply talk to someone using Windows Messenger, or you can allow that user to remotely control your computer and make configuration changes. If you do not want the user making changes to your computer, see the Pain Killer.

The Pain Killer   To stop remote control, follow these steps:

1. Click Start | Control Panel. In Control Panel's Classic view, click System.

2. On the Remote tab, click the Advanced button. Clear the check box that allows the computer to be controlled remotely, as shown in the illustration.

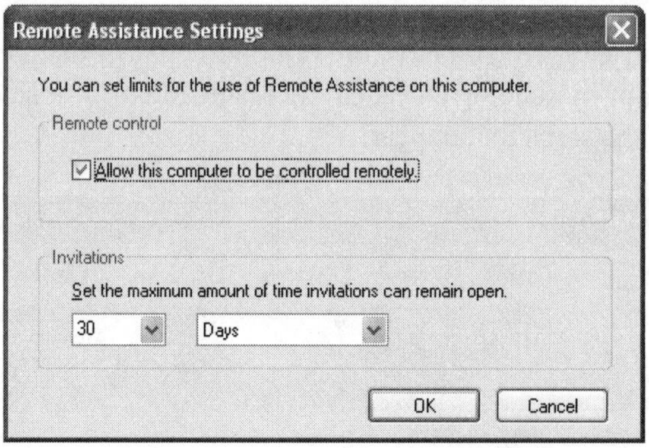

![Remote Assistance Settings dialog box. Title bar reads "Remote Assistance Settings" with a close button. Text: "You can set limits for the use of Remote Assistance on this computer." Under "Remote control" section, a checked checkbox labeled "Allow this computer to be controlled remotely." Under "Invitations" section: "Set the maximum amount of time invitations can remain open." with dropdowns showing "30" and "Days". OK and Cancel buttons at bottom.]

Chapter 13

Media Player Headaches

In this chapter, you'll cure...

- Problems with the interface

- Difficulties with music and movie clips

- Aggravations with Media Library

- Problems ripping music

Windows Media Player 10 is the new version of Media Player that you can freely download from Microsoft. In the past, Windows Media Player did little more than provide audio CD playback features; but today, it is a complex program that does all kinds of things. Because of the multimedia nature of the Internet today, and our computing experiences in general, you will probably use Windows Media Player a lot.

First of all, let me note that you can avoid a number of Headaches just by getting familiar with Windows Media Player and how it works. See Windows XP's Help and Support Center and a general user book, such as *How to Do Everything with Windows XP, 3rd Edition* (Berkeley, CA: McGraw-Hill/Osborne, 2004), to find out how to use the software. For Headaches and problem solving, read on.

Configuring the Interface

Windows Media Player provides a default interface, as you can see in Figure 13-1. The default interface contains the look and features that most people need. However, you can change the interface in a number of different ways, all of which can be both cool and Headache provoking, depending on your perspective. No worries, though; in this section, we'll take a look at common interface Headaches you are likely to run into.

 ## The menu bar keeps disappearing.

Operating Systems Affected   Windows XP Professional and Home Editions are affected.

Cause   Windows Media Player has a menu bar that contains the File, View, Play, Tools, and Help menus, as you see in any typical window. However, by default, the media bar disappears if you are not using it, which gives Windows Media Player a sleeker appearance than previous versions of the product. Just point to the area

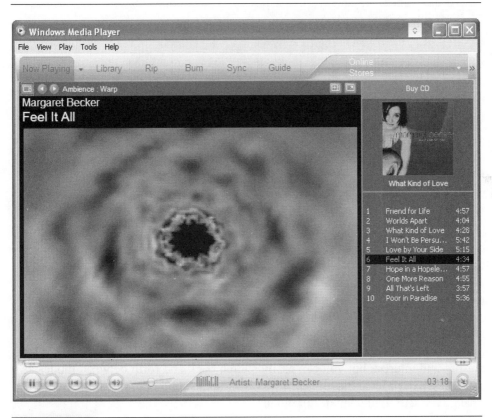

FIGURE 13-1   Windows Media Player 10

where the menu bar should be, and it will reappear. However, if you do not like the disappearing behavior, you can change it.

The Pain Killer   To make the menu bar appear at all times, follow these steps:

1. Open Windows Media Player.

2. Click View | Full Mode Options, and then choose Show Menu Bar.

Windows Media Player always opens in skin mode.

Operating Systems Affected   Windows XP Professional and Home Editions are affected.

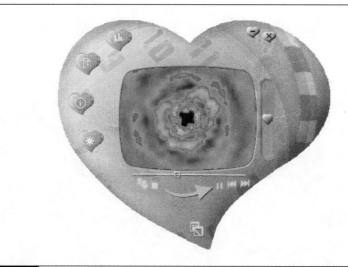

FIGURE 13-2   Skin mode

Cause   Windows Media Player has two appearance modes—full mode and skin mode. Full mode gives you the full interface (Figure 13-1), while skin mode gives you a different, more compact look, as you can see in Figure 13-2. Skins are provided for fun and interest, but you can easily switch back and forth between modes as needed. If your Media Player is always opening in skin mode, you simply need to change the setting to open in full mode.

The Pain Killer   To switch from skin mode to full mode and vice versa, do the following:

- In skin mode, you see a Return to Full Mode button (looks like two boxes with an arrow). Click it to return to full mode.

- If you're in full mode, click View | Skin Mode, or click the Switch to Skin Mode button (the arrow button that appears on the lower-left side of the interface) to switch to skin mode.

I can't use the More Skins option.

Operating Systems Affected   Windows XP Professional and Home Editions are affected.

Cause   Windows Media Player provides you with a number of skins to choose from and apply, as you can see in Figure 13-3. You can access the skin options by clicking

View | Go To | Skin Chooser. Notice the More Skins button. This feature opens Internet Explorer and enables you to check for and download more skins from Microsoft.com. You may find, however, that the More Skins button doesn't take you to Microsoft.com, or that you have difficulty downloading skins from the site.

The Pain Killer If you are having problems getting connected to the web site, connect to the Internet first, and then try the More Skins option. If you are having trouble downloading the skins, the problem is most likely due to the quality of your current connection. You may have success downloading the skin you want at a later time.

NOTE   *Downloads can range in size from 200KB to over a megabyte. Downloading with a modem will take several minutes or even longer. Always try to download at off-peak usage times, such as very late at night or early in the morning; you'll tend to have better results then.*

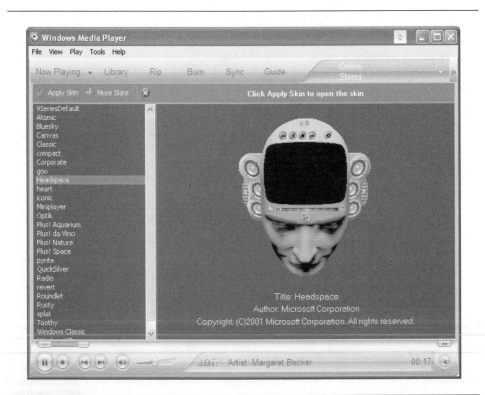

FIGURE 13-3   Skin Chooser

I don't know how to manage visualizations.

Operating Systems Affected   Windows XP Professional and Home Editions are affected.

Cause   Windows Media Player provides *visualizations,* little programs that give you visual stimulation while you are playing CD music. In non-techno terms, they are cool to look at when you listen to music. You can select different visualizations, and you can even download them from the Internet. However, how to use visualizations may not be readily apparent in the Media Player interface.

The Pain Killer   Here's how to manage visualizations:

- You can choose a different visualization at any time by clicking View | Visualizations and then choosing the visualization you want from one of the subcategories that appears.

- You can also download visualizations from Microsoft's web site. To do this, your computer must be configured to use an Internet connection (see Chapter 9). To download visualizations, follow these steps:

    1. Click Tools | Download | Visualizations.

    2. Click Tools | Options, and then click the Plug-ins tab. You can select the Visualization category, and then click the Add button to add the visualizations you have downloaded. Note that you can only remove visualizations that you have added—not the default visualizations provided by Windows Media Player.

    3. If you are having problems with the display of a visualization, select the category from the visualization list and click Properties. The Properties window enables you to select the screen size and

the buffer size. Under most circumstances, the default setting is what you need, but if you are having problems, try using alternate settings.

You can also download visualizations for Windows Media Player from third-party web sites. For example, check out www.skinz.org.

I don't want to see the anchor window when I'm in skin mode.

Operating Systems Affected   Windows XP Professional and Home Editions are affected.

Cause   When you are in skin mode, Windows Media Player displays an anchor window in the lower-right corner of your screen. However, this anchor window may get on your nerves, so if you want to remove it, you can.

The Pain Killer   To remove the anchor window, follow these steps:

1. Click Tools | Options.

2. On the Player tab, clear the Display Anchor Window When in Skin Mode check box, and then click OK.

TIP   *Take note of the other Player settings here as well; you may find others you want to change.*

Music and Movie Difficulties

One of the main purposes of Windows Media Player is to play audio music, as well as movie and Digital Video Disc (DVD) clips. Under most circumstances, you don't need to configure anything. You can insert a music CD into your CD-ROM drive, and Windows Media Player automatically opens and begins playing the CD. The same is true when you open a movie clip or start a DVD. However, things do not always work perfectly, so this section helps you with issues you might face with music and movie playback.

XP HEADACHE

My CD player will not play CD music.

Operating Systems Affected   Windows XP Professional and Home Editions are affected.

Cause   Most of the time, CD-ROM drives play CD music without any difficulties. However, there are a few settings that can prevent CD-ROMs from playing CD music. Before troubleshooting these problems, however, you need to make sure the CD-ROM drive is working. Try a different CD or an application CD to see if you can open and read the CD-ROM drive's contents. If the drive seems to be working as it should, except for CD music playback, then follow the steps in the Pain Killer.

The Pain Killer   To get your CD-ROM drive to play CD music, follow these steps:

1. Click Start | My Computer.

2. In the My Computer window, right-click your CD-ROM drive, and then click Properties.

3. Click the AutoPlay tab. Under Actions, choose the Select an Action to Perform button. Choose the Play Using Windows Media Player action, as shown in the illustration, and then click OK.

4. Next, make sure the device is configured to play CD music. To do this, click Start | Control Panel. In Control Panel's Classic view, click System.

5. Click the Hardware tab, and then click the Device Manager button.

6. Expand the DVD/CD-ROM Drives category, then right-click the CD-ROM and click Properties.

7. Click the Properties tab. Move the slider to the right to set the CD Player Volume to High. If the Enable Digital CD Audio for This CD-ROM Device is selected, leave it selected. If not, select the check box and click OK. Close Device Manager.

8. Now open Windows Media Player. Click Tools | Options.

9. Click the Devices tab. Make sure that your Audio CD drive appears in this window. If it does not, try clicking the Refresh button.

10. If the CD-ROM drive still will not play CDs, go back to the Device Manager CD-ROM Properties window (see steps 4, 5, and 6) and click the Properties tab. Clear the Enable Digital CD Audio for This CD-ROM Device check box and click OK.

11. If the CD-ROM drive still will not play music, make sure you have tried several CDs. When you are sure you have tried all of these steps, it's time to get some help from technical support. Consult your computer documentation for support contact information.

My system's CD playback does not sound good.

Operating Systems Affected   Windows XP Professional and Home Editions are affected.

Cause   Windows Media Player uses some automatic settings for playing CD music, which some users may not like. However, you can change those settings so that the music quality is set the way you like it. You can do this with a graphic equalizer, just as you would set on a physical stereo.

The Pain Killer   To adjust graphic equalizer settings, follow these steps:

1. Open Windows Media Player and click Now Playing.

2. Click View | Enhancements | Graphic Equalizer.

3. The equalizer appears in the Now Playing area, as you can see in Figure 13-4. Adjust the settings as desired using the slider bars.

You can also click the Select View button to view additional settings, such as SRS Wow Effects (for surround-sound settings), Media Information, and other features.

The quality of a video clip I'm playing is poor.

Operating Systems Affected   Windows XP Professional and Home Editions are affected.

Cause   Windows Media Player uses default settings to govern video playback. If you are playing a video clip that is stored on your computer, you are likely to see better quality playback than if you are playing one being downloaded from the Internet. Online video clips come to your computer in a *streaming* format. This means bits and pieces of the video are sent over the Internet to your computer and assembled by your computer. Glitches in transmission often interrupt quality, even with broadband connections. While there's not much you can do about that, you can check Windows Media Player's settings to verify that they are configured for optimal performance.

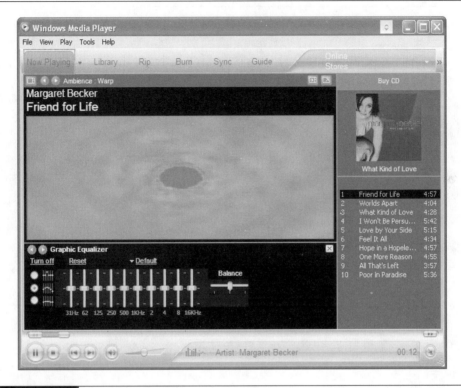

FIGURE 13-4   Graphic Equalizer

The Pain Killer   To adjust video playback performance, follow these steps:

1. Open Windows Media Player and start the video clip. Click Now Playing.

2. Click the Graphic Equalizer button and choose Video Settings from the drop-down menu that appears. Alternatively, you can click View | Enhancements Video Settings.

3. The Video Settings options appear, as shown in Figure 13-5. Make any desired adjustments using the slider bar options.

FIGURE 13-5   Adjust the Video Settings for better playback.

I am having performance problems with streaming media.

Operating Systems Affected   Windows XP Professional and Home Editions are affected.

Cause   Streaming media, such as video clips, arrive over the Internet to your computer in a streaming fashion. This means that your computer assembles bits and pieces of the video and plays it back to you. Distortion and disruption of video playback can occur for three main reasons:

■ **Slow connection speed**   If you are using a modem, media streaming will not work well. There simply is too much data in a media stream for a modem connection to keep up with. For this reason, the video will play a few seconds and stop for a few seconds (or even minutes) before continuing. A modem connection cannot download the data fast enough to keep one continual stream going. There is no workaround for this problem other than to upgrade to a broadband connection—that is, Digital Subscriber Line (DSL), cable, and so on.

■ **Traffic and web site problems** If you have a broadband connection, you still may experience problems with streaming media if there is a lot of traffic or if the web site to which you are connected is working slowly.

■ **Windows Media Player settings** On rare occasions, some Windows Media Player settings can keep you from getting the best media stream, and the following Pain Killer shows you how to check those out.

The Pain Killer To check your video stream settings, follow these steps:

1. In Windows Media Player, click Tools | Options.

2. Click the Performance tab.

3. Under Connection Speed, make sure the Detect Connection Speed option is selected, as shown here. Under Network Buffering, make sure the Use Default Buffering option is selected. In addition, you should make sure the Video Acceleration slider is set to Full. Click OK.

I can't play a DVD with Windows Media Player because of a decoder problem.

Operating Systems Affected Windows XP Professional and Home Editions are affected.

Cause DVDs have to have the correct decoder in order to be able to work with Windows XP, and if you don't have the decoder the DVD needs, you'll need to get it to use the DVD.

The Pain Killer   This is a bother, but you'll need to download the correct decoder from the DVD manufacturer's web site if it is not available on your computer. Check the DVD instructions that came with the disk for details.

Media Library Aggravations

Windows Media Player contains something called Media Library that holds audio and video media. This feature enables you to add music and video clips that you want to keep and view in the library so that they are available anytime you want to hear or see them. You can copy CD music and video clips to your computer's hard drive and then place them in the Media Library. Then, you simply click on the item in Windows Media Player to play it, instead of having to have the actual CD handy.

Media Library, as you can see in Figure 13-6, contains an expandable list of categories in the left pane, and the contents of the selected category in the right pane. You can add and remove content at any time, and you can also create customized lists of music, called *playlists*. You should spend some time working with the Media Library to learn how to use it, and Windows Media Player Help can be of assistance as well. For particular problems, read on.

NOTE   *Although Media Library is great, you should have good housekeeping skills. Because audio and video media consume a lot of disk space on your computer, make sure you regularly delete old items to avoid wasting storage space on your computer.*

 ## I can't add CD music to Media Library.

Operating Systems Affected   Windows XP Professional and Home Editions are affected.

Cause   In order to add music or video to the library, that music must be stored on your hard drive. In other words, you cannot play a CD and add it to your library without first copying the CD to your hard drive. Then, you can add it, as explained in the following Pain Killer.

The Pain Killer   To add a CD to Media Library, follow these steps:

1. Use the Rip feature to copy the CD to your hard drive. See the next section if you are having problems copying from CDs.

Windows Media Player

File   View   Play   Tools   Help

Now Playing   Library   Rip   Burn   Sync   Guide   Online Stores

Search   More Info   Add to Now Playing List   New

What Kind of Love		Title	Artist	Album	Rating	Genre
All Music	1	Friend for Life	Margaret Becker	What Kind of Love	★★★★	Religiou
Album Artist	2	Worlds Apart	Margaret Becker	What Kind of Love	★★★★	Religiou
Contributing Artist	3	What Kind of Love	Margaret Becker	What Kind of Love	★★★★	Religiou
Composer	4	I Won't Be Persuaded	Margaret Becker	What Kind of Love	★★★★	Religiou
Album	5	Love by Your Side	Margaret Becker	What Kind of Love	★★★★	Religiou
Unknown	6	Feel It All	Margaret Becker	What Kind of Love	★★★★	Religiou
I Hope You Dance	7	Hope in a Hopeless World	Margaret Becker	What Kind of Love	★★★	Religiou
What Kind of Love	8	One More Reason	Margaret Becker	What Kind of Love	★★★	Religiou
Genre	9	All That's Left	Margaret Becker	What Kind of Love	★★★	Religiou
Year Released	10	Poor In Paradise	Margaret Becker	What Kind of Love	★★★	Religiou
Rated Songs						
Purchased Music						
All TV						
All Video						
Other Media						
My Playlists						
Curt						
Like Humans Do (radio						
Sample Playlist						
Auto Playlists						
Now Playing						

P1010083

Press Previous to resume
playing "All Video".

Add to Library   10 Item(s)   Total Time: 48:28 / 44.70MB   Start Sync   Start Burn

FIGURE 13-6   Media Library

2. In Media Library, expand the All Music category and select Album. Then,
click the Add to Library button, which looks like a plus sign (+), located at
the bottom of the Media Player window. From the pop-up menu that appears,
select Add File or Playlist. In the Shared Music folder that appears, select
the desired album or browse to the location of the copied CD. When you
find the file you are looking for, select it and click Open. The new album
now appears in the Media Library.

NOTE   *When you click the Add to Library button, you also see the Add Currently
Playing Item option. You can use this option only if the currently playing
track is stored on your hard drive. If you are playing an actual CD in the
CD-ROM drive, this will be grayed out until you save the music to your
hard drive.*

I can't figure out how to create a playlist.

Operating Systems Affected   Windows XP Professional and Home Editions are affected.

Cause   Media Library allows you to create playlists, which are groups of songs, albums, or even video clips that you can hear or watch as one unit. It's sort of like creating an album of your favorite songs or a videotape of your favorite video clips. However, the process can be a little confusing.

The Pain Killer   To create a playlist, you must first have media in your library from which create the list. Once you have added media to Media Library, follow these steps:

1. In Media Library, click the New button (you'll find it on the right side of the interface) and then click the Playlist button.

2. In Media Library, select the desired songs, albums, or videos in the right pane after expanding the appropriate category. Click the Add to New Playlist button, or you can simply drag songs to the playlist pane, as shown in the illustration.

3. Repeat step 2 for each category, as necessary, until you have added all of the desired media.

4. When you are done, you can simply right-click the new playlist and click Play to hear it.

I can't import/export a playlist from another Windows Media Player.

Operating Systems Affected   Windows XP Professional and Home Editions are affected.

Cause   Using the File menu, you can export existing playlists for use on different computers or import playlists from other computers. To perform this action, you use the Save Playlist As option.

The Pain Killer   To export a playlist, follow these steps:

1. In Media Library, select the desired playlist from the left pane.

2. Click File | Save Playlist As.

3. In the Save As window, give the playlist a filename. Note that the playlist is exported as a Media Playlist file (that is, a file with a .asx, .wax, or .wvx extension). The playlist is saved, along with all of the media in the list. You can now use the playlist on Windows Media Player on another computer, or you can send it to someone else by e-mail.

NOTE   *When you export a playlist, keep in mind that the media is not included. In other words, in order to hear the songs or see the video on the computer where the list is imported, the media will have to be copied to the library on that computer. The playlist is just a list—it does not provide the actual media.*

To import a playlist, follow these steps:

1. Open the File menu and choose Open.

2. Select the playlist you want to import, and then click Open again.

Problems Ripping Music

Windows Media Player allows you to rip music from a CD to a writeable CD or to the computer's hard disk (or even another device). This feature allows music or video to be stored locally on your computer's hard drive and in Media Library so that you can play the media whenever you want without having to look for the music on a CD or disk. It's a great feature, and for the most part trouble free. However, you might run into a few snags, which you'll read about in this section.

The defaults for the Rip feature do not work the way I want them to.

Operating Systems Affected   Windows XP Professional and Home Editions are affected.

Cause   Windows Media Player sets default behavior for the Rip music feature. You can change a number of default settings by accessing the Rip tab in Media Player's default window.

The Pain Killer   To change the default Rip options, follow these steps:

1. In Windows Media Player, click Tools | Options.

2. Click the Rip Music tab. You can change the default location where copied music is stored (the My Music folder), as well as other copy settings in the second half of the window. Note the Protect Content check box. Selecting this box enables Windows Media Player to track copied music in order to ensure that it is used in a way that does not violate copyright law.

The View Album Info feature of Copy Music does not work.

Operating Systems Affected   Windows XP Professional and Home Editions are affected.

Cause   If you click the View Album Info button on the Rip music window, you can get the names of the songs, album name, artist name, and such downloaded to your computer. However, in order to get the names of the tracks, you must have an Internet connection; otherwise, you will see an Internet Connection message, as shown in Figure 13-7.

The Pain Killer   To solve the problem, launch an Internet connection and try the option again.

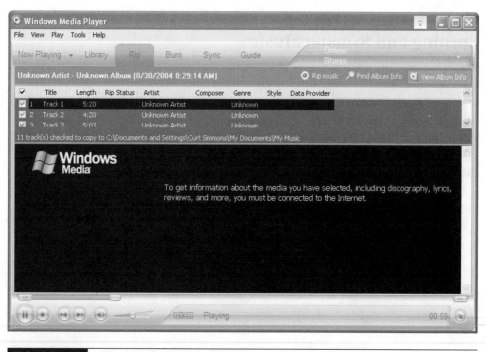

FIGURE 13-7   You must have an Internet Connection.

The music ripping process takes too long or takes up too much disk space.

Operating Systems Affected   Windows XP Professional and Home Editions are affected.

Cause   The Rip music feature does take a little time, and audio CD files take up disk space. Fortunately, you can manage the amount of disk space that is consumed by adjusting the slider bar on the Rip Music tab to a lower value. However, this will also reduce the quality of the copied music.

NOTE   *In most cases, the quality of copied music and video comes down to how much disk space you are willing to sacrifice. You'll have to strike a balance between your need for storage and your desire for music quality.*

The Pain Killer   Click Tools | Options, and then click the Rip Music tab to adjust the slider bar.

Burning and Syncing Music

You'll notice a Burn tab and a Sync tab in Media Player. As you are aware, you can also burn music to a CD directly from the Media Player library, and you can also synchronize items in your library with another device, such as a PDA. Each of these tab options is ease to use. Simply connect your device or put a burnable CD in the CD drive, and then click either the Burn or Sync tab. You then select the music you want to burn or sync and start the process. It's a quick and easy way to use your music and other media files when you're on the move!

Chapter 14

Movie Maker 2 Headaches

In this chapter, you'll cure...

- ■ Difficulties with video
- ■ Problems editing video
- ■ Annoyances with audio
- ■ Aggravations with file types

Windows XP provides you with Windows Movie Maker, a free program included with Windows XP that enables you to edit and digitize analog movies from your camcorder or edit movies from your digital camera. Movie Maker is a fun and cool tool, especially considering the fact that it is free, and it provides you with an easy way to create video clips that you can e-mail to friends. Or, you can burn movies onto a CD for safe storage—which is one of my favorite features of the product.

However, I do not live in Movie Maker lala land, and let me be the first to tell you that Movie Maker is not perfect. It has some difficult annoyances, and the simple truth is that there are other video editing software packages on the market that are better and easier to use. The downside of that is they can be expensive. So, use Movie Maker, explore it, have fun—but remember, if you want to get serious about movie editing, you'll probably outgrow Movie Maker fairly quickly. In this chapter, you can explore the Movie Maker Headaches you are most likely to experience and learn how to solve them—or at least how to get around them!

NOTE *As in all chapters in this book, I assume you are already working with Movie Maker and need some extra help. Since this is the case, this chapter does not function as a tutorial. If you need to learn more about Movie Maker, read a good Windows XP book and check the Windows XP Help and Support Center files. Also, this chapter only applies to Movie Maker 2, not Movie Maker 1. Visit www.microsoft.com/moviemaker to download the latest version if you are still using version 1.*

Difficulties with Video

Windows Movie Maker is a video editing tool, so in order to actually use the software, you have to provide it with some video. Sounds easy enough, but the process can be difficult. Movie Maker can work with either digital video that comes from a digital camera connected to your computer or with analog video from a camcorder that you can connect to your computer, typically with a special video card that allows analog audio and video input—otherwise known as a capture device. The following Headache sections explore the problems you are likely to experience.

Movie Maker doesn't recognize my capture device.

Operating Systems Affected   Windows XP Professional and Home Editions are affected.

Cause   Windows Movie Maker automatically recognizes most capture devices. When you start playing a movie, you can open Movie Maker and see the movie appear in the monitor area, as you can see in Figure 14-1. However, Windows

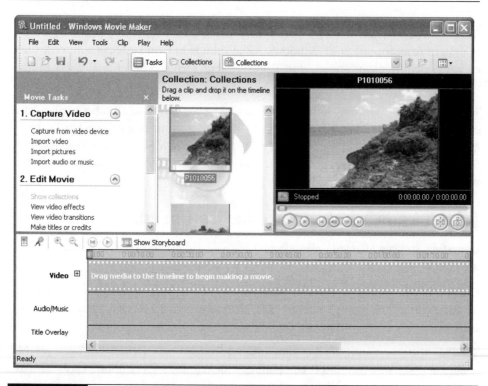

FIGURE 14-1   Windows Movie Maker

Movie Maker may have trouble with some devices and no matter how much you cry and scream, Movie Maker will not see the video playing.

The Pain Killer   In these cases, the best way to solve the problem is to use the capture device's software that came with the capture device. Capture the movie that you want and save it in a file type that is supported by Movie Maker, then (in Movie Maker) click File | Import into Collections and import the movie.

NOTE   *Movie Maker can read most all movie, video, and picture file formats, including MPEG, MPG, MIV, MPA, AVI, WMV, WAV, SND, AU, MP3, BMP, JPEG, GIF, and several others.*

Movie Maker works very slowly.

Operating Systems Affected   Windows XP Professional and Home Editions are affected.

Cause   Movie Maker works with graphics and sound files, which consume a lot of system resources. If your Windows XP system is low on system resources, such as RAM or processor speed, you'll notice that Movie Maker will work more slowly.

The Pain Killer   The only solutions are to make sure you have all other applications closed when Movie Maker is running and to upgrade your computer's hardware if necessary. Movie Maker's minimum requirements are a 300 MHz processor and 64MB of RAM. Of course, systems that have better processor speed and more RAM will perform much better.

I don't know what capture device I need.

Operating Systems Affected   Windows XP Professional and Home Editions are affected.

Cause   If you want to use analog data on your computer, such as movies from a VCR tape or a camcorder, you must have a capture device, which is typically a video card with RCA ports so that you can connect a VCR/camcorder to it.

The Pain Killer   You'll need to shop around for the kind of video card you might want, but make sure the card is compatible with Windows XP. Capture cards tend to be expensive, and you might expect to pay anywhere from $100–$300 for the card.

I upgraded to Windows XP and now my capture device does not work.

Operating Systems Affected   Windows XP Professional and Home Editions are affected.

Cause   If you upgraded from a previous version of Windows, particularly 9*x* or Me, your capture device may not work the way it used to under the old operating system. Typically, all you need is an updated driver for the card.

The Pain Killer   In order to obtain an updated driver for the capture device, you'll need to visit the manufacturer's web site to see if a driver for Windows XP is available. If so, you can download the driver and install it on your system. See Chapter 5 to learn more about driver installation.

I can't copy or record a commercial movie.

Operating Systems Affected   Windows XP Professional and Home Editions are affected.

Cause   Commercial movies found on VHS or DVDs have a copy protection feature that prevents you from copying them. It is not legal to copy a commercial movie into Movie Maker.

When I record, I cannot hear the audio.

Operating Systems Affected   Windows XP Professional and Home Editions are affected.

Cause   During the recording process, Windows Movie Maker does not provide you with the ability to hear the movie. This is a not a problem, but rather just the way the program works. Once recording is completed, you play back the movie and hear it. However, in most cases, you can still hear the movie during recording by listening to your computer's speakers, since the sound card can still provide output.

I'm having problems with my video capture device, or I receive a message telling me that the device is already in use.

Operating Systems Affected   Windows XP Professional and Home Editions are affected.

Cause   This problem can occur when another program is using the video capture device, or when the movie is not recognized by Windows Movie Maker.

The Pain Killer   First, make sure that no other programs are using the capture device. Then, click File | Capture Video. In the Capture Video window, check the drop-down menus to make sure that the correct device is selected and the recording options are correct. You can adjust these settings as needed, then click Record and try again. If you continue to have problems, check the camera manufacturer's web site for information about interoperability with Movie Maker.

Problems Editing Video

Once you get your movie recorded or imported, you can then use Movie Maker to edit the video. Once you get the hang of how Movie Maker works, editing movies is not too difficult. However, there are certainly some problems, or at least aggravations, you may run into. Check out the following sections for help.

I can't create a trim point.

Operating Systems Affected   Windows XP Professional and Home Editions are affected.

Cause   Movie Maker enables you to trim clips so that you can remove dead spots or portions of the movie that are boring. You can create and end a trim point by clicking the Clip menu and selecting Set Start Trim Point. However, if the options here are grayed out, then you need to add the clip to the storyboard/timeline before you can trim it.

The Truth about Capture Devices

I've used Movie Maker with a number of different devices since it first appeared in Windows Me, and I'll be perfectly honest with you—I've had a lot of problems with interoperability between capture devices and Movie Maker. Sometimes it seems to work, and sometimes not. The easiest work-around is to use the software that comes with your capture device. You can capture the video, save it to a common file format, such as AVI, and then use the File | Import into Collections feature to import the movie into Movie Maker. You can then edit and create your movie from there.

The Pain Killer   To add a clip to the storyboard/timeline, follow these steps:

1. In the Preview area, select the clip that you want to trim and click Clip | Add to Storyboard/Timeline. Or, you can just drag the clip to the storyboard/ timeline, as you can see in the illustration.

2. Click the Clip | Set Start Trim Point to start the trim point and use the same menu to set the end trim point as needed.

Trimming seems to throw away the pieces of the movie I want.

Operating Systems Affected   Windows XP Professional and Home Editions are affected.

Cause   Trimming can be a little confusing, and if Movie Maker seems to be throwing away the trimmed portions that you want, you are probably setting your beginning and ending trim points incorrectly.

The Pain Killer   When you set the beginning and ending trim points, everything *outside* of this area is discarded. In other words, the beginning and ending trim points *keep* the video inside of them and discard the rest. If you are having problems trimming clips, consider using a practice clip until you get the hang of the process.

I can't split a clip.

Operating Systems Affected   Windows XP Professional and Home Editions are affected.

Cause   Clips can be split in two at the desired split point in order to make the clips easier to work with. To split the clip, however, you have to play the clip in the monitor window and choose the point at which you want to split the clip.

The Pain Killer   To split the clip, select the clip that you want to split and press the Play button in the monitor. When the clip reaches the point where you want to split it, press the Split Clip button, or you can press CTRL+SHIFT+S on your keyboard. The clip is split and the new clip now appears in the window.

I can't combine two clips.

Operating Systems Affected   Windows XP Professional and Home Editions are affected.

Cause   Just as you can split a clip, you can also combine clips so that they function as one clip.

The Pain Killer   In the Collections area, select the first clip and hold down the SHIFT key on your keyboard, and then select the second clip. Click Clip | Combine to combine the two clips.

I can't create a transition.

Operating Systems Affected   Windows XP Professional and Home Editions are affected.

Cause   When you place clips on the storyboard/timeline, you can create transitions between the clips so that the clips fade into each other instead of looking choppy when you play the movie. To create the transitions, you use the storyboard/timeline area.

The Pain Killer   To create a transition, follow these steps:

1. In the film workspace at the bottom of the window, click the Timeline view.

2. In the Movie Tasks pane, click the View Video transitions link under Edit Movie.

3. Locate the transition you want to use in the Video Transitions pane, and then simply drag the desired transition between the two clips where you want to make the transition. You can see the transition appear on the Timeline, as shown in the illustration.

Annoyances with Audio

Windows Movie Maker allows you to mix audio with your video. For example, let's say that you shoot some video of a family reunion. You can mix a song into the background when you create the movie, or you can even create narration if you like. To include audio in your video, you must use the File | Import into Collections feature to import the audio that you want to use. If you want to record narration, you can do that directly from the Move Maker interface, assuming your computer is outfitted with a sound card and microphone. Overall, using audio is easy, but the next three Headaches point out the trouble you might run into.

I can't import an audio file.

Operating Systems Affected   Windows XP Professional and Home Editions are affected.

Cause   In order to import a sound file, the file has to be stored in a supported audio file format.

The Pain Killer   Use a supported sound file, such as WAV, SND, AU, AIF, AIFC, AIFF, WMA, or MP3.

I can't record narration.

Operating Systems Affected   Windows XP Professional and Home Editions are affected.

Cause   To record narration, make sure your sound card and microphone are working, and then follow the steps in the Pain Killer.

The Pain Killer   Follow these steps to record narration:

1. In the workspace area, click the Microphone icon.

2. In the Narrate Timeline pane, you see Start Narration and Stop Narration buttons. You can also adjust the volume of the input.

Narrate Timeline
Drag the playback indicator on the timeline to an empty point on the Audio/Music track, click Start Narration, and begin your narration.

Steps: Input level
1. [Start Narration]
2. [Stop Narration]
Done
Show more options   Mic Volume

Learn more about narrating the timeline

3. As you are recording, you will see the movie playing in the monitor area so that you can synchronize your narration with the movie events.

Audio levels on the movie track and my narration are not good.

Operating Systems Affected   Windows XP Professional and Home Editions are affected.

Cause   Once you record a narration track, you may need to adjust the levels in the movie soundtrack and your narration so that the mix sounds good.

The Pain Killer   You can use the Timeline view to adjust the levels of the audio tracks and music tracks. Simply right-click each audio track and click Properties, and then adjust the Volume for each track as needed.

Aggravations with File Types

When you get ready to save your movie, you can click the File | Save As, or File | Save Movie. You'll quickly see that you can only save your movie as a Windows Media Video (WMV) file. This means that applications must be able to read WMV files in order to play them. This is a serious aggravation, because only Windows computers will be able to play your movies. In many cases, this might not be a big deal, but if you want to trade video files with someone using an Apple Macintosh computer, you might have problems. I have found this to be an aggravation since it is easier to use movie files that are saved in a more universal file format, such as an AVI. However, there isn't anything you can do about this issue. Not very comforting, I know, but I thought I would point this aggravation out.

Chapter 15

Tools and Utility Headaches

In this chapter, you'll cure...

- ■ Problems with Windows XP tools
- ■ Aggravations with utilities

Windows XP contains a number of helpful tools and utilities that configure all kinds of operating system features and even help you solve problems. The problem is, those tools and utilities can sometimes be as much of a headache as the issue you are trying to resolve. The tools and utilities in Windows XP all have very specific functions and purposes, and using them can even require a little help from the Windows XP Help and Support Center. Overall, the tools and utilities are easy to use, but you may run into some specific snags along the way. So, in this chapter I've included an assortment of Headaches and Pain Killers on a number of different Windows XP tools and utilities. This chapter serves as a "catchall" for issues that do not naturally fit into other chapters, so you can expect the Headaches and Pain Killers you see here to vary a lot. Okay—ready to solve those nagging problems? Then let's get started!

I can't get my computer to play any sound.

Operating Systems Affected   Windows XP Professional and Home Editions are affected.

Cause   In order for your computer to play any sound, including CD music or Windows event noises, your computer must have a sound card that is installed and working. If your computer has a sound card installed but it does not seem to work, you probably need an updated driver. See Chapter 5 for more information about driver installation and management. If the driver is new or you know the sound card once worked on the same computer, you probably need to check your volume controls—the sound may have been muted somehow.

The Pain Killer   To check the volume controls, follow these steps:

> NOTE   *The following steps assume you are using the Classic view of Control Panel. If you are not sure if you are using the Classic view of Control Panel, click Start | Control Panel. In the left window pane, click the Switch to Classic View option.*

1. Click Start | Control Panel | Sounds and Audio Devices.

2. On the Volume tab, make sure the volume is turned up and the Mute option is not checked. You can also check your speaker volume by clicking the Speaker Volume button. Click OK when you are done.

TIP

You may find it helpful to have a Volume Control icon in your notification area so you can easily adjust the sound volume. Just click the Place Volume Icon In the Taskbar check box on the Volume tab and click OK. Also, click the Advanced button to check the mixer settings.

My microphone does not work.

Operating Systems Affected Windows XP Professional and Home Editions are affected.

Cause Microphones work with the sound card on your computer and plug into a microphone jack on that sound card. Before your microphone can work, you must ensure that the sound card itself is working (see the first Headache in this chapter). If the sound card is working but the microphone does not work, make sure the microphone is plugged into the correct port. When you are sure it is, you may just need to adjust the microphone volume.

The Pain Killer To check the microphone volume configuration, follow these steps:

1. Click Start | Control Panel | Sounds and Audio Devices.

2. Click the Audio tab. Make sure the sound card is listed under Default Device in the Sound Recording section.

3. Click the Volume button. Make sure the Mic Volume is turned up and the Select box is clicked, as shown here. If there is no Mic section, click Options | Properties to show it.

 If you are still having problems, make sure to check your computer's documentation. If you bought the sound card/microphone separately from the computer, check the info that came with the hardware. You usually find additional troubleshooting help on the manufacturer's web site as well.

My computer plays sound, but works erratically or the computer locks up.

Operating Systems Affected   Windows XP Professional and Home Editions are affected.

Cause   If you hear some sounds from time to time, or the sound works erratically or Windows XP locks up, you have a driver problem or a hardware conflict with another device.

The Pain Killer   The odds are good that you have a driver problem. It is also possible that the sound card is conflicting with another device, although this is less likely. To check the problems, you can open Device Manager and see if there are any clicks on the Resources tab. You need to also check the manufacturer's web site for more information about updated drivers that you can use, or for other troubleshooting steps. See Chapter 5 to learn more about troubleshooting hardware.

I use the Volume Control feature in my notification area, but the microphone volume does not appear.

Operating Systems Affected   Windows XP Professional and Home Editions are affected.

Cause   The Volume Control window provides you standard volume control slider bars for playback volume. By default, it does not include microphone volume or a number of other volume features. Fortunately, you can add microphone volume to the window; however, you don't really need to unless you just want to hear the microphone volume of your speakers.

The Pain Killer   To add microphone volume to the window, follow these steps:

1. Right-click the Volume icon in your notification area and click Open Volume Control.

2. In the Volume Control window, click Options | Properties.

3. In the Properties window, click the Mic Volume check box (as well as any others that you want) and click OK. The additional volume controls you select appear in the Volume Control window.

My computer shows the wrong date/time.

Operating Systems Affected   Windows XP Professional and Home Editions are affected.

Cause   Windows XP keeps track of the date and time, even when the computer is not turned on (through a small battery). If the date and time that appear in your notification area are not correct, you can easily adjust them.

The Pain Killer   To change the date and/or time, follow these steps:

1. Right-click the time in your notification area and click Adjust Date/Time, or click Start | Control Panel, Date and Time.

2. On the Date and Time tab, adjust the date and time as necessary, and verify that the time zone is correct. Click OK.

My computer does not automatically adjust for daylight savings time.

Operating Systems Affected   Windows XP Professional and Home Editions are affected.

Cause   If you live in an area where daylight savings time is in use, you can configure Windows XP to automatically adjust the time when daylight savings time is in use.

The Pain Killer   To automatically adjust for daylight savings time, follow these steps:

1. Right-click the time in your notification area and click Adjust Date/Time, or click Start | Control Panel, Date and Time.

2. On the Time Zone tab, click the Automatically Adjust Clock for Daylight Savings Changes check box, as shown in the illustration.

I want my computer to automatically run Disk Cleanup, or automatically run another utility.

Operating Systems Affected   Windows XP Professional and Home Editions are affected.

Cause   Windows XP contains a Scheduled Task feature where you can configure utilities or even programs to run at a certain time. For example, you can configure utilities like Disk Cleanup to run every week or so in the middle of the night. This keeps your computer clean but does not waste your time doing so. You can configure a Scheduled Task with the help of a wizard.

The Pain Killer   To configure a scheduled task, follow these steps:

1. Click Start | Control Panel | Scheduled Tasks.

2. In the Scheduled Tasks folder, click the Add Scheduled Task option. The wizard's Welcome screen appears. Click Next.

3. In the Program window, choose the program that you want to automatically schedule, as shown in the illustration, and click Next.

4. In the Perform Task window, you can choose to perform the task daily, weekly, monthly, one time only, when the computer starts, or when you log on. Make a selection by clicking the appropriate radio button and click Next.

5. In the Time and Day window, configure the Start time and day that you want the task to run and then click Next.

6. Enter your user name and password and click Next.

7. Click Finish. The new task now appears in the Scheduled Tasks window. You can add more tasks by repeating these steps.

 If you want to stop using a scheduled task, just right-click it in the Scheduled Tasks folder and click Delete. You can also override the schedule at any time by right-clicking the task and clicking Run.

 # A scheduled task does not run.

Operating Systems Affected   Windows XP Professional and Home Editions are affected.

Cause   If a scheduled task does not run when it is supposed to, there are a few things you need to check.

The Pain Killer   Check these items:

1. Was the computer turned on when the task was supposed to run? Will the task run at all? Try running the task and see if it will work.

2. Open the Scheduled Tasks folder and right-click the scheduled task that did not run. Click Properties.

3. On the Task tab, make sure the Enabled check box is selected.

4. On the Schedule tab, make sure that the time and date are correct.

5. Click the Settings tab. Make sure that none of these settings are overriding the way you want the scheduled task to behave (such as the Idle Time requirement or battery power option). When you are done, click OK.

6. Make sure that you do not have multiple tasks scheduled to run at the same time. Some tasks, such as Disk Cleanup and Disk Defragmenter, will not run correctly if they do not have exclusive drive access. Schedule the tasks to run at different times.

7. If you are connected to a Windows 2000/.NET domain (a large Windows network), your network administrators may have policies in place that prevent your computer

from running scheduled tasks. Check with a network administrator for details.

8. Finally, if you are not logged on at the time a scheduled task is supposed to run, the task will still run but simply not be visible (since you are not the logged-on user). Check the Status column in the Scheduled Tasks window to see if the task actually ran. The Status column will tell you if the task ran, or give you some indicator as to why not if it didn't.

Disk Defragmenter does not completely defragment my hard drive.

Operating Systems Affected Windows XP Professional and Home Editions are affected.

Cause Disk Defragmenter is a great tool that defragments your hard disk and helps Windows XP run faster. However, Disk Defragmenter cannot defragment your drive completely. Some fragmentation is normal and you should not see it as a problem.

The Pain Killer First of all, do not worry if disk defragmenter leaves some fragmented files. This is normal. As you can see in Figure 15-1, a newly defragmented disk on my computer still has fragmented files. If you think there are too many files still fragmented, run Disk Defragmenter several times in a row, which sometimes further reduces fragmentation.

Disk Defragmenter stops working before it is finished.

Operating Systems Affected Windows XP Professional and Home Editions are affected.

Cause In order for Disk Defragmenter to work, it must have exclusive access to your disk. This means no other programs should be running when Disk Defragmenter is trying to work.

The Pain Killer Close all programs and close all items in your notification area (antivirus programs too). Turn off your Screen Saver. Then, allow Disk Defragmenter to run with no interruptions.

Error-checking stops working.

Operating Systems Affected Windows XP Professional and Home Editions are affected.

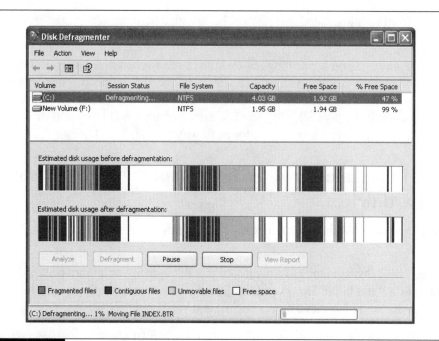

FIGURE 15-1   Disk Defragmenter

Cause   The Error-checking tool, which you can find on the Tools tab of the hard disk's properties sheets, checks your computer's hard disk for file system errors and surface sector problems. The Error-checking tool takes some time to run, depending on the size of your computer's hard disk, and must have exclusive access to the disk in order to work.

The Pain Killer   To get error-checking to work as it should, you need to close all programs and close all items in your notification area. Make sure you have closed any antivirus or third-party disk management tools before running error-checking.

I need to easily move files and/or settings from one computer to my XP computer.

Operating Systems Affected   Windows XP Professional and Home Editions are affected.

Cause   Getting a new computer can be a really exciting time, but the problem is moving all your files and trying to get the new computer to work the way your old one did. With this thought in mind, Windows XP provides a Files and Settings Transfer Wizard, which is an easy way to move files from one Windows computer to your new Windows XP computer.

The Pain Killer   To use the Files and Settings Transfer Wizard, follow these steps:

1. On the computer that you want to move the files and/or settings from, click Start | All Programs | Accessories | Files and Settings Transfer Wizard if the computer is a Windows XP computer. If it is not, insert your Windows XP CD-ROM into the computer's CD-ROM drive and click Perform Additional Tasks, then click Transfer Files and Settings.

> TIP   *You can transfer settings from Windows 9x, Me, NT, and 2000 computers using the wizard on the Windows XP CD-ROM.*

2. The wizard appears. Click Next on the Welcome screen.

3. In the Which Computer Is This window, click the Old Computer radio button, shown in the illustration, and click Next.

4. The wizard prepares for the next step. In the Select a Transfer Method window, you can transfer the files and settings using a direct cable connection or a removable disk (floppy, zip, and so forth), or use another method such as a network share. Make a selection and click Next.

5. In the What Do You Want to Transfer window, you can choose to transfer settings only, files only, or both files and settings. If you want to select custom options, click the Let Me Select a Custom List check box and click Next.

CAUTION   *Do not move your Windows folder using this process! This will move all of your data and applications to the new system, which is not what you want! Use this wizard to move files and settings only.*

6. If you chose the Custom option, shown here, you can use this window to add settings, folders, and files to the list that you want to transfer. When you are done, click Next.

7. The files and settings are collected and transferred according to the method that you selected. Click Finish.

8. Now that you have created the transfer file, your next step is to run the wizard on the Windows XP computer where you are transferring the files and settings. Click Start | All Programs | Accessories | System Tools | Files and Settings Transfer Wizard.

9. Click Next on the Welcome screen.

10. On the Computer screen, click New Computer.

11. In the Windows XP CD window, you can click the I Don't Need a Wizard Disk option, since you have already collected your settings from the old computer. However, if you had trouble using the Windows XP CD on the old computer, note here that you can create a wizard floppy disk to use instead, as you can see in the illustration.

Files and Settings Transfer Wizard

Do you have a Windows XP CD?

You will also need to run this wizard on your old computer. You can either create a wizard disk to use on your old computer, or use the wizard from the Windows XP CD.

To create a Wizard Disk, insert a blank, formatted disk into this computer's disk drive. Make sure the old computer has the same type of drive.

○ I want to create a Wizard Disk in the following drive:

　　🖫 3½ Floppy (A.)

○ I already have a Wizard Disk

○ I will use the wizard from the Windows XP CD

◉ I don't need the Wizard Disk. I have already collected my files and settings from my old computer.

　　< Back　　Next >　　Cancel

12. In the next window, choose the location of the files you are importing (disk, direct cable, network share, and so forth). Click Next.

13. The transfer takes place. Click Finish when the wizard is done.

I think I may have unsigned digital files on my computer.

Operating Systems Affected　Windows XP Professional and Home Editions are affected.

Cause　In order to make sure the files on your computer are safe and are from appropriate sources, Windows XP keeps track of the digital signature on the files. If you think you may have some unsigned files, or if you just want to check them to make sure they are signed, you can use the File Signature Verification utility.

The Pain Killer　To run the File Signature Verification utility, follow these steps:

1. Click Start | All Programs | Accessories | System Tools | System Information.

> NOTE　*You can also access System Information by clicking Start | Run, typing **Msinfo32**, and clicking OK.*

2. In the System Information window, click Tools | File Signature Verification Utility.

3. Click the Start button to run the utility.

> TIP
>
> *You can also click the Advanced button in order to scan a specific folder or configure logging options. You can explore these settings and see if you want to try them out.*

I am having problems with DirectX.

Operating Systems Affected   Windows XP Professional and Home Editions are affected.

Cause   DirectX is a technology that governs how video and sound function on your computer with games and other multimedia applications. If you are having problems with DirectX functionality, you will need to check your Windows XP documentation to learn more about DirectX versions and possible troubleshooting information. However, there is also a DirectX Diagnostic tool that can be very helpful in diagnosing the problem.

The Pain Killer   To use the DirectX Diagnostic tool, follow these steps:

1. Click Start | All Programs | Accessories | System Tools | System Information.

2. In the System Information window, click Tools | DirectX Diagnostic Tool.

3. The tool runs a check on your system, and then gives you a number of tabs that contain information and options about DirectX, as you can see here. Browse through the tabs and look for any problems or suggestions in the Notes section of each one.

System Restore does not work.

Operating Systems Affected   Windows XP Professional and Home Editions are affected.

Cause   System Restore is a feature that enables you to return your computer to an earlier time in the event that something goes wrong and a new configuration causes a bunch of problems. System Restore periodically creates a system checkpoint. In the event that you need to restore your computer to an earlier time, the checkpoint is used to reconfigure your system and return it to a normal operating state. It is a very handy tool that should be available to you at all times.

If System Restore does not seem to be working, you need to turn it on.

The Pain Killer   To turn on System Restore, follow these steps:

1. Click Start | Control Panel | System.

2. Click the System Restore tab. Make sure the Turn Off check box is not selected.

3. Click the Settings button for the desired drive. In the Settings window, make sure you are allowing plenty of disk space for System Restore to

work. By default, the Maximum setting uses 12 percent of your disk space to store checkpoint information, as shown in the illustration. I recommend leaving the setting at Maximum.

Drive (C:) Settings   `?` `X`

     (C:) Monitoring

(C:) is the system drive. You cannot turn off System Restore on this drive without turning it off on all drives. To do this, click OK or Cancel to return to the System Restore tab.

Disk space usage

Move the slider to the right to increase or to the left to decrease the amount of disk space for System Restore. Decreasing the disk space may reduce the number of available restore points.

D̲isk space to use:

Min   Max

12% (495 MB)

OK   Cancel

I can't back up data.

Operating Systems Affected   Windows XP Professional is affected.

Cause   Windows XP Professional includes a Backup utility that can help you back up information on your computer. You can store the backup job in a safe location, such as on a CD or network share. In the event of a failure, you can use the backup job to restore data when the computer is functional again.

The Backup feature is not available on Windows XP Home Edition, but it is found in System Tools in Windows XP Professional. The Pain Killer gives you a walkthrough of the utility.

The Pain Killer   To use the Backup utility, follow these steps:

1. Log on with an administrator account and click Start | All Programs | Accessories | System Tools | Backup.

2. The Backup Wizard appears. Click Next on the Welcome screen.

3. Choose to back up files and settings and click Next.

4. In the What to Back Up window, you can choose to back up different items, as shown here, or you can have the wizard let you specifically choose what to back up. Make a selection and click Next.

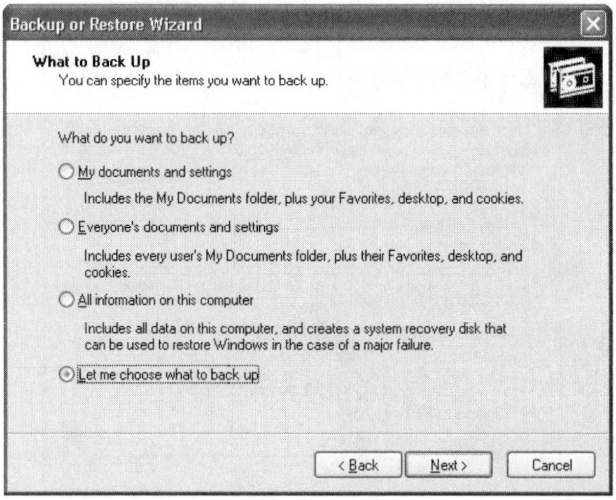

5. If you chose the option in step 4 to select what you want to back up, a selection window appears. Make your selection and click Next.

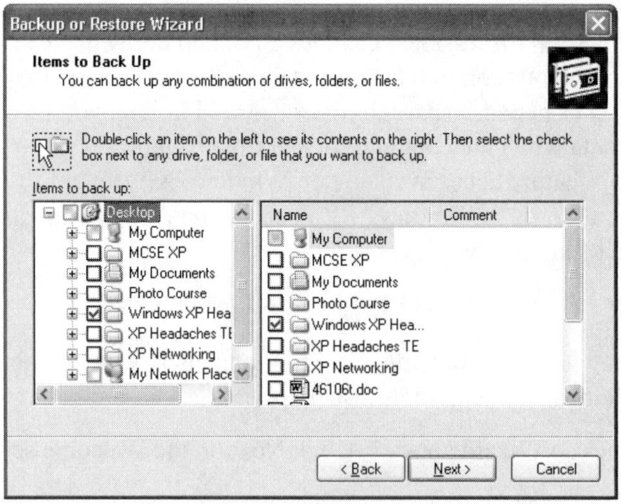

6. Choose a location and name for your backup job (such as a CD-RW drive or a network location). Click Next.

7. Click Finish. The Backup Progress window appears. When the backup is complete, click Close.

Backup Progress		? ✕
Drive:	C:	
Label:	Backup.bkf created 2/14/2002 at 10:42 AM	
Status:	Backing up files from your computer...	
Progress:	▮▮▮▮▮▮▮▮▮▮▮▮	
	Elapsed:	Estimated remaining:
Time:	14 sec.	16 sec.
Processing:	C:\...adaches\XP Headaches CH 13\I1301.TIF	
	Processed:	Estimated:
Files:	97	242
Bytes:	10,636,053	22,721,193

Chapter 16

Performance Headaches

In this chapter, you'll cure...

- Problems with Windows XP performance

- Issues with application performance

- Aggravations with printing performance

- Difficulties with laptops and Windows XP

Windows XP, like all computer systems, can be affected by performance problems. In broad terms, "performance problems" simply means that Windows XP or some application or process does not work fast enough or does not work very well. As a general rule, if your computer exceeds the Windows XP installation requirements, you will probably not have too many performance problems. However, depending on the kinds of applications you run and things you want to do with Windows XP, you may run into a number of the Headaches presented in this chapter.

TIP   *Keep in mind that there are a number of third-party programs that can help your computer run more efficiently, such as Norton Utilities. You might consider investing in one of these programs to help you optimize your computer.*

Windows XP Performance Problems

In this section you'll take a look at the performance problems you are most likely to experience with Windows XP. As you'll soon see, many of the issues have to do with the amount of RAM and processor speed available on the computer. If you purchased your Windows XP computer directly from the computer manufacturer, your computer most likely exceeds the installation requirements of Windows XP. If you upgraded to Windows XP from Windows 2000, Me, or 98, you are much more likely to experience performance problems. Check out the following Headaches to learn more!

My computer runs too slowly.

Operating Systems Affected   Windows XP Professional and Home Editions are affected.

Cause   A slow-running computer is usually caused by one or two things—a processor that cannot keep up with the demands of the operating system or not enough RAM. According to Microsoft, your computer should have at least a 233 MHz processor and at least 64MB of RAM to run Windows XP. But I don't mind telling you, that is the bare-bones minimum. Your computer will limp along using Windows XP with this processor and amount of RAM. As a point of recommendation, you really should have at least a 300 MHz processor and 128MB of RAM for better performance. For the best performance, have more. I have written this book on a Windows XP Professional computer that has a 1.6 GHz processor and 256MB of RAM—and it jams! I also use another computer with Windows XP Home Edition that has a 400 MHz processor with 256MB of RAM, and there is a noticeable performance difference between the two systems—so, the more the better.

The point is simply this: You must have enough RAM and a processor that can keep up. If you barely meet the requirements, there are things you can do to help Windows XP, but you should consider some hardware upgrades if you want things to work really well.

The Pain Killer   To check out your processor and amount of RAM, follow these steps:

> NOTE   *The following steps assume you are using the Classic view of Control Panel. If you are not sure if you are using the Classic view of Control Panel, click Start | Control Panel. In the left window pane, click the Switch to Classic View option.*

1. Click Start | Control Panel | System.

2. On the General tab, you'll see the processor speed and amount of RAM towards the bottom of the tab.

> NOTE   *If you are thinking about upgrading your RAM and processor, you'll need to get in touch with a quality computer service center or store in your area. Check your local yellow pages to find a location and ask around for advice. But beware—it is often less expensive to simply buy a new computer than to completely upgrade your RAM and processor!*

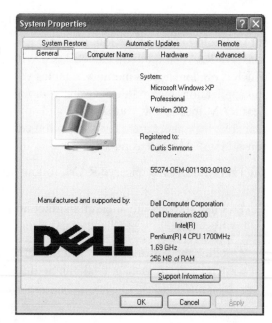

My computer once worked great, but opening and closing files now takes a long time.

Operating Systems Affected   Windows XP Professional and Home Editions are affected.

Cause   If your computer takes a long time to open or close files, your hard disk is probably fragmented. Fragmentation is a normal process that occurs over time as files are saved, resaved, opened, and deleted. Fragmentation causes different portions of the file to be stored in different places on the hard drive, which makes the opening and closing of the file take longer.

The Pain Killer   Run the Disk Defragmenter utility, found in Start | All Programs | Accessories | System Tools | Disk Defragmenter. See Chapter 6 to learn more about hard disk problems.

My computer barely has enough RAM, but I cannot upgrade.

Operating Systems Affected   Windows XP Professional and Home Editions are affected.

Cause   If you know that your computer really does not have enough RAM, but upgrading is not an option, there are a few things you can do that can help conserve RAM so that you can still use Windows XP. Keep in mind that RAM, which is random access memory, enables your computer to run internal processes and applications. More RAM means your computer can do more in a faster way. Less RAM means that your system and applications must fight over what is available. Still, there are a few things you can do to make sure Windows XP is conserving RAM and using what it has in the best possible way.

The Pain Killer   To conserve RAM, follow these steps:

1. First, log on with an administrator account, then click Start | Control Panel | System.

2. Click the Advanced tab. You see three sections, shown in the illustration. Under Performance, click the Settings button.

3. On the Visual Effects tab in the Performance Options window, click the Adjust for Best Appearance radio button. This will cause Windows XP to lose most of its cool, new look, but it will save RAM and processor cycles because Windows XP will not have to generate all of those visual effects for you. On a system that is limping along, though, this setting will help you.

4. Click the Advanced tab. Make sure that the Programs button is selected for both Processor Scheduling and Memory Usage.

Performance Options

Visual Effects | Advanced

Processor scheduling

By default, the computer is set to use a greater share of processor time to run your programs.

Adjust for best performance of:

◉ Programs   ○ Background services

Memory usage

By default, the computer is set to use a greater share of memory to run your programs.

Adjust for best performance of:

◉ Programs   ○ System cache

Virtual memory

A paging file is an area on the hard disk that Windows uses as if it were RAM.

Total paging file size for all drives: 384 MB

Change

OK | Cancel | Apply

5. Under Virtual Memory on the Advanced tab, click the Change button. You see the Virtual Memory tab, shown in the illustration. Virtual memory allows Windows XP to use a portion of your computer's hard disk to store memory data when RAM is running low. You should let Windows XP manage these settings, so make sure that the System Managed Size radio button is selected. Click OK twice to save any changes you have made.

Virtual Memory

Drive [Volume Label]   Paging File Size (MB)

C: 384 - 768
D: [ZIP-100]
F: [New Volume]

Paging file size for selected drive

Drive: C:
Space available: 2336 MB

○ Custom size:
   Initial size (MB):   384   3096
   Maximum size (MB):   768   4092

◉ System managed size
○ No paging file   Set

Total paging file size for all drives

Minimum allowed: 2 MB
Recommended: 382 MB
Currently allocated: 384 MB

OK | Cancel

TIP

Windows XP does a good job of managing its virtual memory settings. If you change them yourself, you may experience performance problems—it is always best to leave these settings alone!

XP HEADACHE

Sometimes my computer works well and other times it seems very slow.

Operating Systems Affected   Windows XP Professional and Home Editions are affected.

Cause   If Windows XP seems to work well at times and is sluggish at other times, there is probably some program that is taking up too much RAM or processor cycles, slowing everything down. Have you installed a new program? Has anything changed? These are important questions to ask yourself. In the meantime, you can also use a handy tool called Windows Task Manager to see if you can figure out what is going on.

The Pain Killer   To use Windows Task Manager, follow these steps:

1. On your keyboard, press CTRL+ALT+DEL. This means to press the CTRL key, the ALT key, and the DEL key at the same time.

2. The Windows Task Manager appears. Click the Performance tab. The Performance tab tells you how much of the CPU is in use (percentage) as well as the amount of RAM. If the computer is running slowly, this can quickly tell you if the problem is a RAM problem or a CPU problem.

3. Click the Processes tab. As you can see in the illustration, the Processes tab shows what programs are using how much of the CPU and the memory. You can inspect this list and look for anything that seems much higher than the others. This may alert you to the program that is causing the problems. If you find the program, you may have to do a little homework to decipher its name under Image Name. Once you do, though, you can stop using that program if necessary.

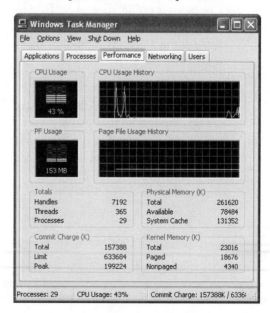

Also, you can select the program in the Processes tab and click the End Process button to make it stop working immediately.

NOTE
The End Process option can be helpful, but it should be used judiciously. Programs should always be shut down in the correct way if possible. Internal programs and processes are also listed here (such as explorer.exe). If you stop one of them from working, you may have to reboot your computer. If it seems that one of Windows XP's internal processes is eating up the processor time, you may need to call your technical support personnel for troubleshooting help.

4. Check your notification area. Do you have a lot of icons there? If so, there are probably a number of background programs running. You can disable these one at a time by right-clicking them and see if this makes any difference on performance.

5. There is also an advanced tool called Performance, which you can find in Start | Control Panel | Administrative Tools. This program, allows you to set up counters so that you can view the performance of various system processes. You can learn more about using the Performance tool from the Windows XP Help and Support Center or from any general user book on Windows XP.

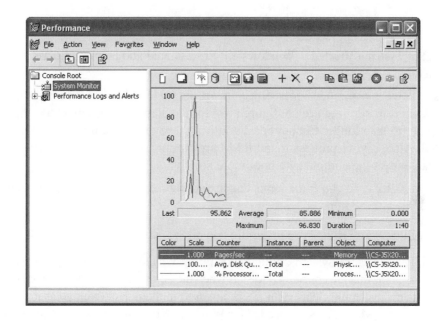

The Truth About Virtual Memory

Maybe you have a computer friend who has said something like, "Hey dude, I pump up my computer's virtual memory settings and make things run a lot faster—with less RAM!" Sound right? Wrong! Here's what virtual memory does. Let's say you have three applications open, named 1, 2, and 3. That's a lot of data for Windows XP to have to keep in RAM. If you are using application 3, Windows XP may write the memory data for applications 1 and 2 onto your computer's hard disk until it is needed in order to free up more RAM. When you need application 1 or 2 again, it will read that data from the hard disk back into memory. So, Windows XP has to do a lot of reading and writing to the disk when a lot of virtual memory is required—which is slower than real RAM. Simply put, virtual memory is a way that Windows XP helps RAM, but it is in no way a replacement for physical RAM. You will not see performance gains by boosting the amount of virtual memory that is used.

My computer boots very slowly.

Operating Systems Affected   Windows XP Professional and Home Editions are affected.

Cause   If your computer boots slowly, the problem may be that a number of applications or services are configured to begin at startup. This can cause the computer to take longer to boot because all of these extra features have to be loaded. Also, if your processor and RAM are barely meeting the requirements, you can expect the computer to boot more slowly.

The Pain Killer   To check the items that are configured to start when the computer boots, follow these steps:

1. Click Start | Run. Type **msconfig** and click OK.

2. This opens the System Configuration utility. On the Services tab, you see a list of items that are configured to start when the computer starts. You can take out items by simply clearing the check box next to them. However, you should be careful. Many items are needed for Windows XP to run properly. A good way to use this is to look in the Manufacturer column. Look for manufacturers other than Microsoft, and you might see a number of programs that you really do not use or even need. Check your computer documentation for details, and don't hesitate to contact technical support for help.

> NOTE
>
> *Make sure you know what you are doing before removing any of the startup programs—some of them may be needed by software or hardware on your system.*

Service	Essential	Manufacturer	Status
Alerter		Microsoft Corporation	Stopped
Application Layer Gatew...		Microsoft Corporation	Running
Application Management		Microsoft Corporation	Stopped
Windows Audio		Microsoft Corporation	Running
Background Intelligent T...		Microsoft Corporation	Stopped
Computer Browser		Microsoft Corporation	Running
Indexing Service		Microsoft Corporation	Stopped
ClipBook		Microsoft Corporation	Stopped
COM+ System Application		Microsoft Corporation	Running
Cryptographic Services		Microsoft Corporation	Running
DHCP Client		Microsoft Corporation	Running
Logical Disk Manager Ad...		Microsoft Corp., Veritas Software	Stopped

System Configuration Utility — General, SYSTEM.INI, WIN.INI, BOOT.INI, Services, Startup tabs. Hide All Microsoft Services. Enable All, Disable All. OK, Cancel, Apply, Help.

TIP
> *You can click the Hide All Microsoft Services check box at the bottom of the window so that you can more easily view the third-party listings.*

Another way that you can help speed up the boot process is to disable the Recent Documents History feature. Windows XP includes a feature that keeps track of all of the recent documents you have opened or used. The idea is that you can click Start | Recent Documents History and quickly re-open any document you have used recently. The bad thing about Recent Documents History is that Windows XP has to calculate what should be put there each time you boot Windows, which can slow things down. So, if you never use the Recent Documents History, it's a good idea to disable it. Here's how:

1. Open the Registry Editor by clicking Start | Run. Type **regedit** and click OK.

2. Navigate to HKEY_CURRENT_USER\Software\Microsoft\Windows\ CurrentVersion\Policies\Explorer.

3. Create a NoRecentDocsHistory D_WORD key. Double-click the value to open it once it is created.

4. Set the Data Value to **1** to enable the restriction.

5. Click OK and close the Registry Editor. You'll need to restart the computer for the change to take effect.

TIP
> *As we are talking about boot speed, make sure all of your device drivers are up to date. While Windows XP can use older device drivers, they tend to slow the boot process down. So, keep up to date!*

Application Performance Problems

Applications that you run on Windows XP can certainly cause you problems. This is due to a number of factors, but is usually based on the system resources your computer has free, and the compatibility of the application with Windows XP. In fact, most application performance problems come down to those two items.

 ## An application makes my computer run very slowly.

Operating Systems Affected   Windows XP Professional and Home Editions are affected.

Cause   If an application causes the computer system to run very slowly, your computer does not have enough CPU or memory power to manage the application or the multiple applications that you might have open at the moment.

The Pain Killer   Check the minimum requirements for the application and make sure your computer meets (or exceeds!) them. Some applications, especially graphics applications, are very resource intensive and your computer must have enough power to keep up. Also, when you run the particular application, make sure all other programs are closed. This will give your computer more resources with which to run the application.

My computer cannot run multiple applications at the same time.

Operating Systems Affected   Windows XP Professional and Home Editions are affected.

Cause   If your computer cannot run multiple applications at the same time, there are two possible explanations. First, there is a conflict with one or more of the applications that causes the applications to stop running. Or, your computer's memory and/or processor cannot keep up with the task of running all of the programs (usually memory).

The Pain Killer   The only real cure is to increase the RAM on the computer or not open all of the applications at one time.

I have an application that locks up.

Operating Systems Affected   Windows XP Professional and Home Editions are affected.

Cause   If an application locks up (stops responding), something has happened in the software code that has made it quit working or something has happened when the application is trying to work with Windows XP. If this is a one-time occurrence, it is usually not a big deal.

The Pain Killer   To end the application, press CTRL+ALT+DEL to open Task Manager and click the Applications tab. Select the process that is not responding and click End Task, as you can see in Figure 16-1. You can then normally restart the application.

Windows Task Manager

File Options View Windows Shut Down Help

Applications | Processes | Performance | Networking

Task	Status
46116w - Microsoft Word	Running
CH 8 - Microsoft Word	Running
XP Headaches CH 16	Running
Control Panel	Running
Windows Messenger	Running

End Task   Switch To   New Task...

Processes: 28   CPU Usage: 11%   Commit Charge: 217092K / 6329(

FIGURE 16-1   Applications tab

> **NOTE** *When you use the Applications tab to end a task, any unsaved data in the application will be lost. Of course, if the application has locked up, there's not much you can do about that anyway.*

I have an application that locks up repeatedly.

Operating Systems Affected   Windows XP Professional and Home Editions are affected.

Cause   If you are having problems with the same application locking up time and time again, the problem is usually compatibility with Windows XP.

The Pain Killer   The only solution is to either purchase an upgraded version of the software that is designed for Windows XP, or you can try to use the Program Compatibility Wizard to get the program to work. See Chapter 4 for more information.

Windows XP and Lockups

If you used Windows 9x or Me, you were probably used to holding your breath, waiting for something to lock up. You probably also learned to save your data frequently because you never knew when things would go wrong. For the most part, you can relax. Windows XP is built on a completely different operating system model and is rock solid. Although applications may sometimes fail for a number of reasons (including poorly written software), you are not as likely to lose control of Windows XP as you were in earlier versions of Windows.

Aggravations with Printing Performance

You can find out more about printing Headaches in Chapter 8, but I do want to mention a few printing performance issues here. First and foremost, if you are having printing problems, always refer to the printer manufacturer's web site and product documentation for information. Many times, there are "known issues" with the printer's behavior and simple fixes you can use. So, always start there. For other Headaches, read on…

Printing slows my computer's responsiveness down.

Operating Systems Affected   Windows XP Professional and Home Editions are affected.

Cause   When you print a document, the print file is sent to a location on your hard disk called the spool until it is sent to the printer. In order to take care of all of this and return control of the operating system back to you, RAM is used. If your computer doesn't have quite enough RAM, you will experience sluggishness or possibly even a big slowdown until the print job is finished.

The Pain Killer   There is no workaround for this problem except to add more RAM to your computer.

I lose control of my computer until printing is finished.

Operating Systems Affected   Windows XP Professional and Home Editions are affected.

Cause   If you lose control of your computer when you print, the computer is configured to print directly to the printer instead of using the printer spool. This causes the system to use all of its resources on the print job, which may cause you to lose control of the desktop and applications.

The Pain Killer   To make sure your printer is using the print spool, follow these steps:

1. Click Start | Control Panel | Printers and Faxes.

2. Right-click the Printer icon and click Properties.

3. Click the Advanced tab. Make sure the Spool Print Documents So Program Finishes Printing Faster radio button is selected. Under this setting, make sure the Start Printing Immediately radio button is also selected. Click OK.

My printer's output does not look good.

Operating Systems Affected   Windows XP Professional and Home Editions are affected.

Cause   If your printer output does not look good, there are a few possible explanations. First, you may not be using the correct printer driver. An incorrect driver can cause you a number of problems, so see Chapter 8 to learn more about this issue. Also, the printer cartridges may need replacing or the printer heads may need cleaning.

The Pain Killer   Refer to the manufacturer's web site or printer documentation for more detailed information about the printer output problems.

Performance Issues with Laptops

Laptop computers are very handy and work well with Windows XP, but there are a few specific performance issues that may cause you some problems. As with a desktop PC, you need to make sure that your laptop meets the minimum hardware requirements for running Windows XP—and preferably, exceeds those requirements. In most cases, this is not a problem, especially if you have purchased a new laptop.

Battery power runs down quickly.

Operating Systems Affected   Windows XP Professional and Home Editions are affected.

Cause   If your battery power runs down quickly, there are a few things you can do that will help.

The Pain Killer   Follow these steps:

1. First, check your laptop's documentation about the battery. You may simply need a new battery to solve your problems.

2. Use Power Options System Standby features and Hibernation in order to conserve power when you are not using the computer. See Chapter 1 for details.

3. If you have multiple PC cards, consider creating a hardware profile that disables everything that you are not using when you are mobile. These resources consume valuable battery power, even when you are not directly using them. See Chapter 5 for more information about hardware profiles.

Don't leave CDs in the CD drive when you are running on batteries. The spinning CD burns battery power!

Colors are difficult to see on the LCD screen.

Operating Systems Affected   Windows XP Professional and Home Editions are affected.

Cause   The Windows XP theme may cause you some visual problems with LCD screens, due to the vivid colors and fonts used in the XP theme.

The Pain Killer   Try some different theme settings and check your display settings as well. See Chapter 1 to learn more.

Chapter 17

Windows XP *Migraine* Headaches

In this chapter, you'll cure...

- ■ Problems with installation

- ■ Pains with system crashes and boot failures

- ■ Problems with activation

Ah, those migraine headaches. If you have ever suffered a real migraine headache, as I have, you know how painful it can be and how much you desperately need relief. I've titled this chapter "Windows XP *Migraine* Headaches" because this chapter explores installation problems and other nasty behaviors, such as crashes and lockups. The Headaches in this chapter completely stop your computer from working and can just about drive you crazy. Unfortunately, these problems are difficult to cure and often require advanced help, usually from a support person who can troubleshoot your system over the phone. In some cases, you may even have to take your computer to a professional for some serious help. So, in this chapter, I'll help you understand and cure the headaches I can, and if I can't solve a headache for you in these pages, I'll direct you to the proper resource.

Problems with Installation

If you bought your computer with Windows XP preloaded, you have not had to worry about installation. For others, who have upgraded or tried to install Windows XP on a computer with no operating system, there are some installation problems you may have run into. As a general rule, Windows XP installation works well and is usually problem free. In fact, the installation can often detect incompatibilities and stop itself before it is too late. However, the main problems you are likely to have during installation are hardware incompatibilities.

My computer stops responding during installation.

Operating Systems Affected   Windows XP Professional and Home Editions are affected.

Cause   During the hardware detection phase of installation, Windows XP may stop responding due to hardware conflicts or problems. This does not mean that you will not be able to install Windows XP; it just means that a conflict has occurred, most likely during an upgrade from Windows 98 or Windows Me.

The Pain Killer   If the computer seems to have stopped responding during installation (that is, the computer seems frozen), do the following:

1. First, be calm. Your computer may look like it has stopped responding for periods during the installation when, in fact, it has not. If you think your computer has stopped responding, look at the clock and give the computer another 30 minutes before doing anything. Nothing bad is going to happen, so be patient and give Setup time to work.

2. If after 30 minutes nothing has happened, turn the computer's power off, wait 10 seconds, and turn it back on. Setup should continue where it left off. Wait to see if Setup hangs again in the same place; if it does not, allow it to continue. If Setup hangs up again in the same place, go to step 3.

3. Restart the computer and choose the option to Cancel Windows XP Setup. This will roll back the installation to Windows 98 or Windows Me. Then, uninstall any antivirus or disk management programs, remove all USB devices and other external devices, and start Setup again.

4. If there is no option to Cancel Windows XP Setup or if Setup hangs again, there is some kind of hardware incompatibility on your computer that is causing Setup to fail. At this point, you will need some help from technical support. Refer to your Windows XP installation Compact Disc (CD) for support information.

My computer gives me a file copy error message during installation.

Operating Systems Affected   Windows XP Professional and Home Editions are affected.

Cause   File copy error messages often occur when there is a problem reading data from the CD. This glitch can often be skipped over by pressing the Continue button. If these errors continue to occur, you should abort Setup.

The Pain Killer   If you have to abort Setup, try copying the CD's I386 folder to your desktop, and then run Setup from there. This will hopefully solve the file copy problem. If not, you'll need to get help from technical support.

I receive a Stop message or an Error message during installation.

Operating Systems Affected   Windows XP Professional and Home Editions are affected.

Cause   Stop messages and Error messages usually occur because of system configuration problems or hardware problems. They can be difficult to troubleshoot, and they require advanced troubleshooting skills.

The Pain Killer   If you experience an error like this, you can try running Setup again. If you receive the same error a second time, you need to contact technical support for help.

I want to perform a clean installation.

Operating Systems Affected   Windows XP Professional and Home Editions are affected.

Cause   The Clean Installation option is available during an upgrade (when you run the installation CD). Essentially, the clean installation wipes away the old operating system, your applications, settings, and files. Normally, you should perform the Upgrade option instead of a clean installation, but if your older operating system (OS) has given you a lot of problems, the clean installation may help. However, Windows XP is more likely to have hardware problems with older hardware and peripherals during a clean installation than with an upgrade.

The Pain Killer   If you want to perform a clean installation, you should be aware of all of the issues at hand. Visit www.support.microsoft.com and search for "Windows XP installation" for more information. You should understand what you are doing and the risks completely before performing a clean installation. Also, visit the Hardware Compatibility List at www.microsoft.com/hcl to make sure all of the computer's hardware is compatible.

I upgraded to Windows XP from Windows 98/ Windows Me, but now my computer runs slowly.

Operating Systems Affected   Windows XP Professional and Home Editions are affected.

Cause   Windows XP has stricter hardware requirements than Windows 98 and Windows Me. For example, your 300 MHz processor with 64MB RAM may have worked fine under Windows 98 or Windows Me, but with Windows XP, this barely meets the hardware requirements. Windows XP will work slower on a same system with this hardware configuration.

The Pain Killer   The only solution is to upgrade your hardware so that it can meet the demands of Windows XP. However, be careful. Hardware upgrades can be expensive, and in many cases, it doesn't cost much more to buy a new computer. In addition, the upgrade itself can make XP run slower than with a clean install!

Don't Dig Your Own Installation Grave

Pardon the expression, but I imagine you are familiar with the saying "getting in over your head." There's a lot of truth to that statement. A few years ago, I worked as a trainer in a Windows 98 support group. We had a lot of horrific installation calls, but one truth always came out: we could help users who called when they first started having problems faster than we could help those who tried to solve their own installation problems. The reason? If you are not a Windows expert, you can cause yourself more problems than you originally had. So, if installation fails and you are having problems as described in the Headaches in this section, get help. Do not randomly try this or that. If you don't know what to do, admit it and get help. After all, that's why technical support is available to you!

Problems with System Crashes and Boot Failures

In the days of Windows 9x and Windows Me, you were probably familiar with system lockup and other problems. In Windows XP, you are much less likely to have system lockups and related problems. However, there are occasions where your system will crash (that is, completely stop working, even on a reboot), or you can't boot Windows XP at all without getting some error message. What do you do? The following Headaches provide some common remedies.

My computer has stopped responding.

Operating Systems Affected   Windows XP Professional and Home Editions are affected.

Cause   Windows XP may stop responding due to a hardware or software conflict.

The Pain Killer   To solve the problem, press CTRL+ALT+DEL, which opens Task Manager. Look on the Applications tab, select the application that is Not Responding, and then click the End Task button. (See Chapter 16 for more details.) If that doesn't work, press CTRL+ALT+DEL two times in a row to restart your computer. If that doesn't work either, hold down the computer's power button for five to ten seconds until the computer restarts. If that also does not work, unplug your computer, wait ten seconds, and then plug it back in and restart it.

 Never unplug your computer from the power source to turn it off unless you already have tried everything else. Then, make sure you wait ten seconds before plugging in the system again; this gives the hard drive time enough to stop spinning before you turn it back on.

My system has crashed; and upon reboot, it gives me an error message.

Operating Systems Affected   Windows XP Professional and Home Editions are affected.

Cause   If some problem or conflict causes Windows XP to crash (or crash again and again) or if the computer will not restart, you need to use the System Restore feature to restore the settings on your computer so that it will work.

System Restore must be enabled on your computer for the feature to work. See Chapter 16 for more information about System Restore setup.

The Pain Killer   If you can boot Windows, follow these steps to run System Restore:

1. Click Start | All Programs | Accessories | System Tools | System Restore.

2. Click the Restore My Computer to an Earlier Time radio button, as shown in the illustration, and then click Next.

System Restore

Welcome to System Restore

You can use System Restore to undo harmful changes to your computer and restore its settings and performance. System Restore returns your computer to an earlier time (called a restore point) without causing you to lose recent work, such as saved documents, e-mail, or history and favorites lists.

Any changes that System Restore makes to your computer are completely reversible.

Your computer automatically creates restore points (called system checkpoints), but you can also use System Restore to create your own restore points. This is useful if you are about to make a major change to your system, such as installing a new program or changing your registry.

System Restore Settings

To begin, select the task that you want to perform:

○ Restore my computer to an earlier time

○ Create a restore point

○ Undo my last restoration

To continue, select an option, and then click Next.

[Next >]   [Cancel]

3. A calendar and selection list is presented to you. You can select different days to find a desired restore point. If you did not create a restore point, you should choose to use the latest one available. The latest one will be listed first in the current or previous day window. Select a restore point and click the Next button.

System Restore

Select a Restore Point

The following calendar displays in bold all of the dates that have restore points available. The list displays the restore points that are available for the selected date.

Possible types of restore points are: system checkpoints (scheduled restore points created by your computer), manual restore points (restore points created by you), and installation restore points (automatic restore points created when certain programs are installed).

1. On this calendar, click a bold date.   2. On this list, click a restore point.

<	February, 2002					>
Sun	Mon	Tue	Wed	Thu	Fri	Sat
27	28	29	30	31	1	2
3	4	5	6	7	8	9
10	11	12	13	14	15	16
17	18	19	20	21	22	23
24	25	26	27	28	1	2
3	4	5	6	7	8	9

< Monday, February 18, 2002 >

There are no restore points created yet for this day. To restore immediately, pick another day and restore point, and then try again.

[< Back]   [Next >]   [Cancel]

4. A message appears, telling you to save all files and close all open applications. Do so at this time, and then click the Next button.

5. Restoration now takes place on your computer, and your computer automatically reboots once the restoration is complete. The restoration process may take several minutes, so be patient. Click OK to the restoration message that appears after booting has taken place.

If you cannot boot Windows, follow these steps to run System Restore:

1. Turn on your computer and press the CTRL or the F8 key until you see the Startup menu options.

2. Choose Safe Mode, and then press ENTER.

3. Once Windows boots, the Help screen that appears gives you the option to restore your computer. Click the System Restore link.

4. Click the Restore My Computer to an Earlier Time radio button, and then click Next.

5. A calendar and selection list is presented to you. You can select different days to find a desired restore point. If you did not create a restore point, you should choose to use the latest one available. The latest one will be listed first in the current or previous day window. Select a restore point and click the Next button.

6. A message appears, telling you to save all files and close all open applications. Do so at this time, and then click the Next button.

7. Restoration now takes place on your computer, and your computer automatically reboots once the restoration is complete. Click OK to the restoration message that appears after booting has taken place.

> **TIP**   *Current documents, files, e-mail, and so on are not affected during a restoration. However, if you installed an application after the last restore point was made, you will need to reinstall that application.*

I have tried to use System Restore, but now the system does not work well or I receive error messages.

Operating Systems Affected   Windows XP Professional and Home Editions are affected.

Cause   In some cases, System Restore might cause more problems than you are trying to solve. If this happens, you can undo the restoration.

The Pain Killer   To undo your last restoration, follow these steps:

1. Click Start | More Programs | Accessories | System Tools | System Restore.

2. In the System Restore window, click the Undo My Last Restoration radio button, and then click Next.

NOTE   *The Undo My Last Restoration option does not appear unless you have previously run a restoration.*

3. Close any open files or applications, click OK, and then click Next.

4. The previous restoration is removed, and your computer reboots. Click OK to the restoration message that appears after booting has taken place.

I have tried to use System Restore, but now my computer will not boot.

Operating Systems Affected   Windows XP Professional and Home Editions are affected.

Cause   If System Restore fails and your computer will not boot, you will need to undo the installation using Safe mode.

The Pain Killer   To undo your last restoration if you cannot boot, follow these steps:

1. Turn on your computer and press the CTRL or the F8 key until you see the Startup menu options.

2. Choose Safe Mode, and then press ENTER.

3. Once Windows boots, the Help screen that appears gives you the option to restore your computer. Click the System Restore link.

4. Click the Undo My Last Restoration radio button, and then click Next.

5. A message appears telling you to save all files and close all open applications. Do so at this time, and then click the Next button.

6. The previous restoration is removed, and your computer reboots. Click OK to the restoration message that appears after booting has taken place.

> NOTE
>
> *Before making any major configuration changes on your computer, always create a restore point so that you can use System Restore if things do not go well. See the Windows XP Help and Support Center to learn more about creating a restore point.*

I installed a new device driver, and now the computer will not boot.

Operating Systems Affected   Windows XP Professional and Home Editions are affected.

Cause   If you install a new device driver and the computer will not boot, you can use a Safe mode option called Last Known Good Configuration. This option uses a backup of the computer's registry to replace the bad driver with the one that worked previously.

The Pain Killer   To use the Last Known Good Configuration option, follow these steps:

1. Turn on your computer and press the CTRL or the F8 key until you see the Startup menu options.

2. Use the arrow keys to select Last Known Good Configuration, and then press ENTER.

My computer fails during bootup.

Operating Systems Affected   Windows XP Professional and Home Editions are affected.

Cause   As a general rule, if the system fails during bootup, there is usually some hardware conflict or problem with the Windows XP Help and Support Center.

The Pain Killer   You can boot using Safe mode, and then use System Restore if necessary:

1. Turn on your computer and press the CTRL or the F8 key until you see the Startup menu options.

2. Use the arrow keys to select Safe Mode, and then press ENTER.

When I try to boot my computer, a message appears that says "Invalid System Disk."

Operating Systems Affected   Windows XP Professional and Home Editions are affected.

Cause   Most computers try to boot from the floppy drive first, and then from the hard disk. If you have accidentally left a floppy disk in your disk drive when you restart the computer, the "Invalid System Disk" message will appear.

The Pain Killer   Just remove the floppy disk from the disk drive and press CTRL+ALT+DEL twice to restart the computer. If there is no floppy in the disk drive, the hard drive has crashed. In this case, you'll need to get help from technical support, which usually involves taking your computer to a repair center.

One of my applications keeps crashing.

Operating Systems Affected   Windows XP Professional and Home Editions are affected.

Cause   Applications must be compatible with Windows XP in order to function properly.

The Pain Killer   If an application keeps crashing the computer, you can try to use the Program Compatibility Wizard to fix the problem, or you may simply need to upgrade the application so that it is compatible with Windows XP. See the application manufacturer's web site for details.

Problems with Activation

Depending on your computer, you may need to activate Windows XP. Windows XP includes a new feature not found in previous versions of Windows called *activation*. Microsoft uses this feature to protect the licensing of software. Activation prevents someone from installing a bunch of computers using the same software CD. Essentially, activation is just a new step in the setup key and licensing agreement portion of Setup.

Once you install Windows XP, you have 30 days to activate the operating system with Microsoft. The activation doesn't require you to supply any information; so don't worry, this isn't like "big brother" or anything. The activation process records a serial number from your computer's hardware and couples it with your CD installation code. That way, if someone tries to install a bunch of computers with a single CD, activation will recognize that the key has already been used and will not allow the activation to continue. Once the 30-day period expires, Windows XP will cease to function.

I am having trouble connecting to the Internet for activation.

Operating Systems Affected   Windows XP Professional and Home Editions are affected.

Cause   The only activation headache you might experience is not being able to access the Internet. You may have problems dialing the access number or connecting, and this sometimes happens when you boot Windows XP for the first time.

The Pain Killer   If you cannot connect to the Internet, you can activate Windows XP by calling the Activation Support Center and activating your computer with the help of an operator. Click Start | All Programs | Activate Windows.

NOTE   *If you do not see the Activate Windows option under Start | All Programs, it means Windows XP has already been activated. If you did not activate Windows during final installation, it may have been activated by the computer manufacturer. At any rate, if the option is not available in All Programs, you have nothing to worry about.*

Appendix A

Curt's Top 20 Windows XP Headaches

All right, now it is time to take a look at my top 20 Headache picks. These are the Headaches that have annoyed me and plenty of other users, according to the newsgroups and Internet searches I've seen. You may or may not agree with my list, depending on what experience you have had, but one thing is for sure: you are bound to find some solutions here that will make your life with Windows XP a little easier. So, here are my picks, starting with Headache 20 and ending with the most common Headache as number 1.

20: My printer/scanner used to work fine, but now that I've upgraded to Windows XP, it does not work or does not work well.

Operating Systems Affected   Windows XP Professional and Home Editions are affected.

Cause   When you upgrade to a new operating system, the drivers that used to run your computer hardware are kept, and Windows XP tries to use them. The problem is that some drivers simply do not work with Windows XP—especially those written for Windows 98 or Windows Me. In this case, your printer, scanner, or other device may not work or may not work well once the upgrade is complete.

The Pain Killer   The only solution is to locate a new driver that is compatible with Windows XP and install it. You can find an updated driver (if there is one) by visiting the printer or scanner manufacturer's web site and downloading the driver. You can then install the driver on your computer. See Chapter 5 to learn more about device driver installation and management.

19: I want to use the New Technology File System (NTFS) because Windows XP is optimized for it, but my hard disk is a FAT32 drive.

Operating Systems Affected   Windows XP Professional and Home Editions are affected.

Cause   Windows XP works best with NTFS, but it is completely compatible with FAT32. If your drive is currently formatted with FAT32, you can convert it to NTFS without any problems. However, you should make certain you really need to. NTFS drives provide you with compression capabilities and security features, but depending on your use of Windows XP, you may not need any of these features. See the Windows XP Help and Support Center for comparisons and more information about using NTFS and FAT32.

The Pain Killer   If you decide you want to use NTFS, you can convert your FAT32 drive easily and without any loss of data by following these steps:

1. Log on with an administrator account.

2. Back up your data, just to be safe.

3. Click Start | Run. Type **command**, and then click OK.

4. At the command prompt, type **convert** *driveletter*: **/FS:NTFS**, where *driveletter* is the letter of the drive you want to convert. For example, if I wanted to convert my C drive, the command would be **convert C: /FS:NTFS**, as you can see in the illustration.

```
C:\WINDOWS\System32\command.com                                    _ □ ×

Microsoft(R) Windows DOS
(C)Copyright Microsoft Corp 1990-2001.

C:\DOCUME~1\CURT>convert c: /FS:NTFS_
```

5. Press ENTER. The conversion process may take several minutes to complete.

18: Windows Update keeps trying to connect to the Web and download stuff without my permission.

Operating Systems Affected   Windows XP Professional and Home Editions are affected.

Cause   Windows Update is a feature that allows Windows XP to check for operating system updates and automatically download them so you can install them. This feature works wonderfully, especially if you are on a broadband connection; but if you are not, it can be a real pain because it will try to dial your connection. You can disable this feature, however, if you don't want to use it.

The Pain Killer   To turn off the Windows Update feature, follow these steps:

1. Log on with an administrator account.

2. Click Start | Control Panel. In Control Panel's Classic view, click System.

3. Click the Automatic Updates tab. Choose the Turn Off Automatic Updating option, and then click OK.

17: Windows XP keeps turning itself off when I leave it idle.

Operating Systems Affected   Windows XP Professional and Home Editions are affected.

Cause   If your computer hardware supports it, Windows XP provides a hibernation feature. After a period of inactivity, Windows XP can save all of the data held in random access memory (RAM) to the hard disk, and then shut itself down. Then, when you reboot, the data is read off the hard disk and back into RAM so that your computer is in the same state it was in when you left it. No data is lost on any open applications using hibernation. However, if the feature gets on your nerves, you don't have to use it.

The Pain Killer   To turn off hibernation, follow these steps:

1. Click Start | Control Panel. In Control Panel's Classic view, click Display.

2. Click the Screen Saver tab, and then click the Power button.

3. On the Power Schemes tab, change the System Hibernates option to Never. Click OK.

NOTE   *If you do not see the System Hibernates option, then your computer hardware does not support the feature.*

16: I don't like the appearance of Windows XP, or I am having difficulty managing the Start menu.

Operating Systems Affected   Windows XP Professional and Home Editions are affected.

Cause   Windows XP provides a lot of new interface features that, theoretically, make using Windows XP easier. However, you may not like some of the settings or the behavior of the Windows XP interface. No problem, though, you can change it.

The Pain Killer   To change the features of the Windows XP desktop, you can use two different options in Control Panel:

■ To change display properties, click Start | Control Panel. In Control Panel's Classic view, click Display.

■ To change taskbar and Start menu properties, click Start | Control Panel. In Control Panel's Classic view, click Taskbar and Start Menu.

For specific interface problems and solutions, see Chapter 1.

15: Folder views use large icons that require me to scroll around a lot.

Operating Systems Affected   Windows XP Professional and Home Editions are affected.

Cause   Windows XP provides new folder viewing options, such as Details, List, Icons, Tiles, and Thumbnails. You can easily switch to a view that works best for you.

The Pain Killer   To change the folder view, open a folder, click the View menu, and choose a view option other than the one currently selected. On the View menu, you can also select the Arrange Icons By option for additional organizational options.

> NOTE   *Click the Folder Options icon, in Control Panel's Classic view, to make additional changes to folder configuration.*

14: I can't find the encryption or Remote Desktop features in Windows XP Home Edition.

Operating Systems Affected   Windows XP Home Edition is affected.

Cause   Windows XP Home Edition does not contain all of the features of Windows XP Professional. For example, it does not include encryption, Remote Desktop, or certain other features, such as NTFS permissions and Backup.

The Pain Killer   There is no workaround for this problem except to upgrade to Windows XP Professional.

13: My network does not work.

Operating Systems Affected   Windows XP Professional and Home Editions are affected.

Cause   With Windows XP, you can set up a home network based on a number of networking technologies, including Ethernet, HomePNA, or even wireless. If you are having problems with your network, there can be many different reasons and solutions.

The Pain Killer   To troubleshoot specific problems on your network, see Chapter 12.

12: On my ICS network, network users can control the Internet connection.

Operating Systems Affected   Windows XP Professional and Home Editions are affected.

Cause   In Windows XP, your Internet Connection Sharing (ICS) clients can control the Internet connection, if allowed to do so from the ICS host. This feature is new in Windows XP and can be useful in a number of scenarios. When the option is turned on, users can connect, disconnect, and even reconfigure the connection. If you do not want users to be able to manage the Internet connection, however, you can disable this feature.

The Pain Killer   To stop ICS clients from managing the Internet connection, follow these steps:

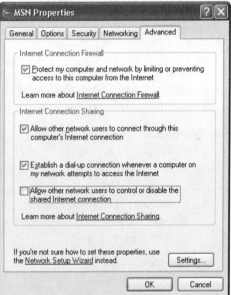

1. On the ICS host computer, click Start | Network Connections | Show All Connections.

2. Right-click the Internet connection, and then click Properties.

3. Click the Advanced tab. Clear the Allow Other Network Users to Control or Disable the Shared Internet Connection check box, and then click OK.

11: On my network, I can access all other computers, but none can access mine.

Operating Systems Affected   Windows XP Professional and Home Editions are affected.

Cause   The odds are good that Windows Firewall is turned on for the network adapter. WF protects your Internet connection by preventing all unsolicited network traffic. However, if you enable the firewall on the network adapter, client computers will not be able to access shares on your computer.

The Pain Killer   To turn off WF on the network adapter, follow these steps:

1. On the ICS host computer, click Start | Network Connections | Show All Connections.

2. Right-click the local area connection, and then click Properties.

3. Click the Advanced tab and click Settings. On the Settings window, choose the Off button and click Close.

10: Internet Explorer will not let me view certain sites due to "security settings."

Operating Systems Affected   Windows XP Professional and Home Editions are affected.

Cause   Internet Explorer 6 has a number of beefed up security settings, including privacy settings that protect the use of cookies on the Internet. However, if the security settings are too tight, your surfing will be hindered.

The Pain Killer   To adjust the security settings of Internet Explorer, follow these steps:

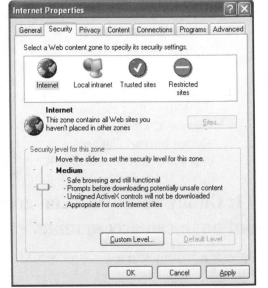

1. Click Start | Control Panel. In Control Panel's Classic view, click Internet Options.

2. On the Security tab, select the Internet zone and adjust the security setting as desired using the slider bar.

> **NOTE**   *See Chapter 10 to learn more about Internet Explorer options and settings.*

9: My modem keeps hanging up when there is idle time.

Operating Systems Affected   Windows XP Professional and Home Editions are affected.

Cause   Both modem and dial-up account configuration can hang up an Internet connection if a certain period of idle time goes by. However, you can stop this behavior.

The Pain Killer   To stop the automatic disconnection feature, follow these steps:

1. Click Start | Control Panel. In Control Panel's Classic view, click Phone and Modem Options.

2. Click the Modems tab. Select your modem in the list, and then click Properties.

3. Click the Advanced tab, and then click the Change Default Preferences button.

4. On the General tab, clear the Disconnect a Call If Idle for More Than check box, or change the value if desired. Click OK, and then click OK again.

5. To check the connection properties, click Start | Network Connections | Show All Connections.

6. Right-click the Internet connection, and then click properties.

7. In the Properties window, change the Idle Time Before Hanging Up to Never, as shown in the illustration. Click OK.

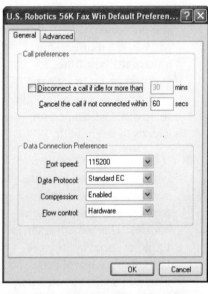

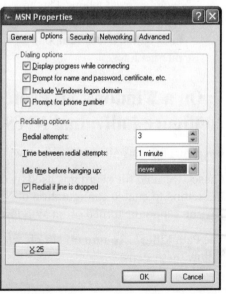

8: The Internet is too slow.

Operating Systems Affected   Windows XP Professional and Home Editions are affected.

Cause   The speed of your Internet connection depends on a number of different factors, many of which are out of your control.

The Pain Killer Take note of these issues:

- The speed of your connection often depends on your Internet service provider (ISP). If you believe you should have better speeds than what you are getting, you can talk with your ISP's technical support staff; they may have some suggestions.

- Keep in mind that the Internet will be slower during peak usage times. Web servers are busy, and often this causes a lot of congestion. Late at night and early in the morning are always the best times to surf—even for broadband connections, which provide relatively fast connection speeds to begin with.

- If Internet Explorer seems to have slowed down over time, you can dump all of the temporary Internet files and cookies. This sometimes helps Explorer speed up its work. Click Start | Control Panel. In Control Panel's Classic view, click Internet Options. On the General tab, click the Delete Files button under Temporary Internet Files.

7: On a Windows XP Professional computer, I cannot configure individual NTFS permissions for a share.

Operating Systems Affected Windows XP Professional Edition is affected.

Cause Simple file sharing is used by default on Windows XP, but you can change the setting to enable configuration of NTFS permissions. Note that simple file sharing cannot be turned off in Windows XP Home Edition.

The Pain Killer To turn off simple file sharing in Windows XP Professional, follow these steps:

1. Click Start | Control Panel. In Control Panel's Classic view, click Folder Options.

2. Click the View tab, shown in the illustration to the right. Scroll to the bottom of the window and clear the User Simple File Sharing check box. Click OK.

Folder Options

General | **View** | File Types | Offline Files

Folder views

You can apply the view (such as Details or Tiles) that you are using for this folder to all folders.

[Apply to All Folders]   [Reset All Folders]

Advanced settings:

☐ Launch folder windows in a separate process
📁 Managing pairs of Web pages and folders
  ⦿ Show and manage the pair as a single file
  ○ Show both parts and manage them individually
  ○ Show both parts but manage as a single file
☑ Remember each folder's view settings
☐ Restore previous folder windows at logon
☐ Show Control Panel in My Computer
☑ Show encrypted or compressed NTFS files in color
☑ Show pop-up description for folder and desktop items
☐ Use simple file sharing (Recommended)

[Restore Defaults]

[OK]   [Cancel]   [Apply]

6: My wireless network does not work.

Operating Systems Affected   Windows XP Professional and Home Editions are affected.

Cause   Wireless networks can certainly cause you some Headaches. Of course, there is no one solution, since many different issues can cause connectivity problems. However, see the Pain Killer to get moving in the right direction.

The Pain Killer   If you are having connectivity problems on your wireless network...

- Read through your wireless hardware documentation. Often, you'll find the solution in print. Also, make sure the physical setup and connections are accurate.

- Check the security settings. All of your wireless PCs must use the same security key. See your documentation for details.

- Check the channel. All wireless PCs must use the same channel. You may also try switching to a different channel. Again, see your documentation for details and don't hesitate to call technical support.

5: Certain applications do not work on Windows XP.

Operating Systems Affected   Windows XP Professional and Home Editions are affected.

Cause   All software, including applications and games, must be compatible with Windows XP in order to work.

The Pain Killer   If you are having problems with older applications or problems getting games to work with Windows XP, you can try using the Program Compatibility Wizard to configure a compatibility mode. See Chapter 4 for more information. If this does not work, your only option is to upgrade the software to a version that supports Windows XP.

> **NOTE**   *You should never use antivirus programs or disk management programs that are not explicitly written for Windows XP. If you upgraded from a previous version of Windows, you should upgrade these programs as well. Check the program manufacturer's web sites for details.*

4: Windows XP performs tasks slowly.

Operating Systems Affected   Windows XP Professional and Home Editions are affected.

Cause   Windows XP requires a processor and enough RAM to meet the needs of the operating system. If you upgraded from a previous version of Windows that barely supported Windows 98 or Windows Me, you are likely to have performance problems.

The Pain Killer   In order to resolve the performance problems, consider upgrading the hardware or even purchasing a new computer. If this is not practical, you can optimize the Windows XP interface for performance. This will reduce the graphical appearance of Windows XP, but may give you a little more power. To adjust the setting, follow these steps:

1. Click Start | Control Panel. In Control Panel's Classic view, click System.

2. Click the Advanced tab, and then click the Settings button under Performance.

3. Choose the Adjust for Best Performance radio button, as shown in the illustration, and then click OK.

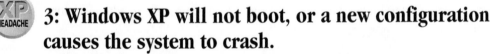

TIP *The best solution, of course, is to have more RAM installed!*

3: Windows XP will not boot, or a new configuration causes the system to crash.

Operating Systems Affected   Windows XP Professional and Home Editions are affected.

Cause   Windows XP crashes and boot failures are typically caused by problems within the operating system files or by hardware incompatibilities.

The Pain Killer   You may need to get help from technical support to solve the problem, but you can also try using System Restore and Safe mode. See Chapter 17 for specific instructions on these features.

2: A hardware device will not work with Windows XP.

Operating Systems Affected   Windows XP Professional and Home Editions are affected.

Cause   Windows XP can automatically detect and install most Plug and Play devices. However, in some cases, a device may not be compatible with Windows XP or the driver may not work with Windows XP.

The Pain Killer   To manually install the hardware, you can use the Add Hardware Wizard, and you can use Device Manager to configure and install the driver. You should check the manufacturer's web site for updates and details specific to Windows XP. See Chapter 5 for more information about hardware Headaches.

1: Windows XP keeps giving me a permissions message instead of letting me perform certain actions.

Operating Systems Affected   Windows XP Professional and Home Editions are affected.

Cause   Windows XP does not have an open door policy, as did Windows 98 and Windows Me. You cannot make most significant changes unless you are logged on with an administrator account. A typical account allows only basic configuration changes and does not allow system-wide changes, hardware installations, or hardware removal. This feature prevents unauthorized users from making unwanted changes on the system.

The Pain Killer   If you are getting the permissions error when you try to configure the system, you need to log off Windows XP and log on again with an administrator account.

Appendix B

Four Signs You Need Help from Technical Support

Unfortunately, not all Headaches can be solved easily. In those cases, you should try to get technical support over the telephone or via the Web from your computer manufacturer or Microsoft. See your computer's documentation for details, and check out these five important signs that you need help from technical support.

Your Computer Often Locks Up/Acts Strangely

If you are having a lot of problems with lockups and crashes, see Chapters 16 and 17. If none of the solutions in those chapters helps you, or you can't seem to pin down what is causing the problem, you need to call technical support. There may be a problem with the operating system or software, but there could also be a problem with your processor, power supply, or display.

NOTE   *If lockups always occur when you try to use a certain application, then there is a problem with the application. Uninstall it and see if there is an updated version. If you reinstall the program and the same thing happens, contact the application manufacturer for support, because Windows XP technical support will not help you solve problems with a third-party application.*

You Get the Blue Screen of Death

The "blue screen of death" is a blue screen telling you that some horrendous error has occurred. These errors are coded, so you'll have no idea what happened. Reboot the computer. If the problem continues to happen, see if you can note when it happens; or if the problem is random, call technical support for help. Always try to write down what you doing before the blue screen occurred. Technical support will ask you this question as they troubleshoot the problem.

Windows XP Makes No Attempt to Boot/Fails to Boot

If you cannot boot Windows XP, see Chapter 17 for help. If the suggestions and solutions in that chapter do not get Windows XP back up and running, take note of any changes that have been made and call technical support for help.

If your computer tries to boot but fails during the process, see Chapter 17 for help. Try using Safe mode to boot and then try running System Restore. If the problem continues, call technical support.

A Hardware Device Will Not Work

If you have a hardware device that will not work with Windows XP, see Chapter 5. You need to make sure the device is compatible with Windows XP and that you are using the correct driver. If you have exhausted all of the troubleshooting operations in Chapter 5, call the device manufacturer's support line (not Windows XP technical support) for help.

Appendix C

Five Things Computer Users Do That Cause Headaches!

Okay, now the blame is on you! Well, maybe not on *you* directly, but there are five big problems that computer users often do that create headaches. Having worked as a technical support person in the past, believe me, I know this to be true. The good news is that I am sharing them with you, and now you can avoid them!

Use the Internet Without Antivirus Software

Never, never, *never* use the Internet or e-mail without antivirus software! It's that plain and simple. Thousands of users are infected with computer viruses every day, and the problems can be mild to catastrophic. Good antivirus software will only set you back about $40, and it is worth every penny. Don't cause yourself a bunch of headaches—use antivirus software! See www.symantec.com and www.mcafee.com for details and make sure you keep your antivirus software updated regularly.

Change Settings Randomly

Believe it or not, computer users often create a lot of problems by changing items in dialog boxes and properties pages without noting the change or being aware of what they are doing. Then, when things go wrong, they can't remember how to solve the problem. If you want to try a new configuration setting, write down what you do and where the setting is located, and then try modifying only one setting at a time. That way, you can back out of the problem if necessary.

TIP   *If you get in over your head or your kid decides to change a bunch of settings, you can usually undo them easily using the System Restore tool. See Chapter 17 for details.*

Fail to Read Device Instructions

If you purchase a new device, such as a USB device or a scanner, printer, or camera, invest a little time getting familiar with the product and how it works with Windows XP. You can usually prevent a great many problems by just reading the instructions. (I hate to read instructions, too, but it *does* help!)

Use Incompatible Software

For software to work as it is supposed to, it has to be compatible with Windows XP. In other words, applications written for Windows 3.*x* probably are not going to work. In fact, you may have a number of problems, even with applications written for systems as late as Windows Me. The best solution is to spend a little money and upgrade your applications. If you can't do that, then learn about and use the Program Compatibility Wizard; see Chapter 4 to learn more about it.

Upgrade to Windows XP Without Doing Your Homework

You can upgrade to Windows XP, but you might have problems. Your computer must be able to handle the Windows XP operating system. This means it must have enough processor power and random access memory (RAM). Before upgrading to any operating system, make sure you have done your homework and that your computer is capable of handling the new system. One more thing… always make backup copies of your data!

Upgrade to Windows XP Without Doing Your Homework

Appendix D

Service Pack 2 Headaches

In August 2004, Microsoft released the long-awaited update to Windows XP called Service Pack 2. If you have installed Service Pack 2 (SP2), you may or may not be impressed by the updates and changes, and that's okay. After all, SP2 is primarily a security update, regardless of what else you may have heard. Sure, you get the new Security Center and some changes to Windows Firewall and Internet Explorer, which we have examined in this book, but most of the changes are "under the hood." You don't work directly with the security patches and updates, but SP2 is designed to make your system work better.

Across the board, SP2 is an easy install, and you are not likely to experience any particular problems with installation. Just turn on Automatic Updates and SP2 will be downloaded and automatically installed to your computer (although the download will take some time if you are using a dial-up connection). If you would prefer to order SP2 on CD, visit www.microsoft.com/windowsxp. However, what if you install SP2 and run into some problems? Again, you're not likely to experience any, but I have found a few issues that can come your way, and I'll explore those few issues in this appendix.

Some of my programs do not work now that SP2 is installed.

Operating Systems Affected Windows XP Professional and Home Editions are affected.

Cause SP2 causes problems with some programs, typically because of the way those programs are designed to operate. In other words, the security fixes applied in SP2 can cause some problems.

The Pain Killer Typically, you'll need to download an updated patch or software version from the software manufacturer to fix the problem. Also, Microsoft maintains a list of programs that have problems with SP2; look for it at http://support.microsoft.com/default.aspx?kbid=842242. In some cases, such as multiuser games and FTP clients, you'll need to configure Windows Firewall to allow these programs to function. See the next Headache for details.

Windows Firewall does not allow some programs to work.

Operating Systems Affected Windows XP Professional and Home Editions are affected.

Cause   The new Windows Firewall is turned on by default and may block some programs that access the Internet. Although pre-SP2 XP computers have a firewall, it is not turned on by default. This is a normal part of the firewall's functionality, although a pain. No worries, though, you can easily fix the problem.

The Pain Killer   To solve this problem, you'll need to create an exception in the Windows Firewall so that the program will work with the firewall. This task is quick and easy.

1. Click the Windows Security Center in the Notification Area.

2. At the bottom of the Security Center under Manage Security Settings For, click the Windows Firewall icon.

3. In Windows Firewall properties, click the Exceptions tab.

4. On the Exceptions tab, click the Add Program button.

5. In the Add a Program window, select the desired program in the list (or click Browse if you don't see it) and click OK to bring up the dialog box shown here.

6. Click OK. The program is now added to the exceptions list. Click the check box next to the program to keep it from being blocked, as shown in this illustration, and click OK. Windows Firewall should now allow the program to work.

Windows Firewall

Add a Program

To allow communications with a program by adding it to the Exceptions list, select the program, or click Browse to search for one that is not listed.

- Acrobat Reader 5.1
- AVG 6.0 for Windows
- AVG Control Center
- AVG Virus Vault
- FreeCell
- Hearts
- Internet Backgammon
- Internet Checkers
- Internet Explorer
- Internet Hearts
- Internet Reversi

Path: C:\Program Files\MSN Gaming Zone\Window   [Browse...]

[Change scope...]   [OK]   [Cancel]

What are the risks of allowing exceptions?

[OK]   [Cancel]

Windows Firewall

General | Exceptions | Advanced

Windows Firewall is turned off. Your computer is at risk of attacks and intrusions from outside sources such as the Internet. We recommend that you click the General tab and select On.

Programs and Services:

Name
☑ File and Printer Sharing
☑ Internet Backgammon
☐ Internet Checkers
☑ Microsoft Broadband Networking Update Utility
☑ Microsoft Broadband Networking Utility
☑ Remote Assistance
☐ Remote Desktop
☐ UPnP framework

[Add Program...] [Add Port...] [Edit...] [Delete]

☑ Display a notification when Windows Firewall blocks a program

What are the risks of allowing exceptions?

[OK]   [Cancel]

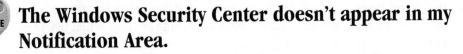

The Windows Security Center doesn't appear in my Notification Area.

Operating Systems Affected   Windows XP Professional and Home Editions are affected.

Cause   Windows Security Center appears on your desktop if you have a free-standing PC. What that means is you are not connected to a network where a network administrator manages your PC. If you connected to a business network with administrators, your PC is called a "managed desktop," and in this case, the Windows Security Center will not appear in the Notification Area. This behavior is normal.

The Pain Killer   Since the behavior is normal, there is nothing you need to fix. As a test, open Control Panel and locate the Security Center icon. Double-click it and a message should appear telling you that your computer is a managed desktop and the Security Center is unavailable.

I don't want the Security Center in my Notification Area.

Operating Systems Affected   Windows XP Professional and Home Editions are affected.

Cause   By default, the Security Center shows up in your Notification Area. If that gets on your nerves, you have to make sure it disappears. This doesn't change anything concerning the Security Center; it just removes it from the Notification Area.

The Pain Killer   Follow these steps:

1. Right-click the Taskbar and click Properties.

2. On the Taskbar and Start Menu Properties dialog box, click the Taskbar tab and click the Customize button under the Notification Area heading.

3. In Current Items, select Windows Security Alerts and click the drop-down menu shown here. You can choose the Always hide or Hide When Inactive options.

4. Make a selection and click OK and OK again.

My wireless network is giving me difficulties.

Operating Systems Affected   Windows XP Professional and Home Editions are affected.

Cause   There have been some reports of people having problems with wireless networks after installing SP2. I have two wireless networks, each using different hardware, and I haven't had any problems or found any specific solutions for problems with wireless networks. However, if you are having problems with your wireless network, see the Pain Killer for a few suggestions.

The Pain Killer

1. Open your wireless network interface card properties. You'll see the new wireless network interface, where you can connect to any detected

networks or disconnect from them. Notice that you can also access the
new Wireless Network Setup Wizard, which may help you regain network
connectivity.

2. Check out the wireless hardware vendor's web site for known issues,
   support, and possible upgrade downloads.

3. Try changing your security and channel settings. Once you get connectivity
   restored, you may be able to reconfigure the security settings.

4. Check out http://support.microsoft.com and search for wireless
   connectivity problems for any updates to known technical issues.

I'm having problems with some hardware.

Operating Systems Affected   Windows XP Professional and Home Editions are
affected.

Cause   Any time you make changes to an operating system, hardware problems
may arise. This is especially true if you were using older hardware to start with.

The Pain Killer   More than likely, you'll need a hardware upgrade. Consult your hardware vendor's web site to see if there are updated drivers that need to be downloaded and installed. This will probably fix the difficulty.

Index

A

Accessibility Options, 136
accounts, 63
    changing account icon feature, 63-65
    changing limited accounts to
      administrator accounts, 54-55
    configuring account restrictions, 66-68
    configuring for .NET Passport support,
      55-56
    creating user accounts, 50-53, 61
    deleting user accounts, 53, 61
    disabling, 65-66
    Fast User Switching, 56-57
    removing the Welcome screen, 57-58
ACPI. *See* Advanced Configuration Power
  Interface
activation, 341-342
ad hoc connections, 232
Ad-Aware, 84
Add a Printer Wizard, 147-149, 150-151
Add Hardware Wizard, 92-94
Add or Remove Programs
    installing programs, 72-74
    problems uninstalling, 75-76
    removing programs, 74-75
    shared files, 76
Add Printer Driver Wizard, 152
administrator accounts, 51
    changing limited accounts to, 54-55
    Group Policy, 66-68
    See also permissions
Advanced Configuration Power Interface, 26
adware, removing, 83-84
analog video, 287
    See also Movie Maker; video

antivirus software, 219
    using the Internet without, 360
APIPA. *See* Automatic Private IP Addressing
audio
    adjusting levels, 294
    checking volume controls, 296-297
    hearing while recording in Movie
      Maker, 289
    importing audio files in Movie
      Maker, 293
    recording narration, 293-294
    See also sound; video
AutoComplete, 197-198
auto-hiding the taskbar, 24
Automatic Private IP Addressing, 243
Automatic Updates
    stopping, 81-83
    See also Windows Update

B

Backup utility, 311-313
Balloon Tips, removing, 29
basic disks, 122-123
batteries
    creating a hardware profile to conserve
      battery power, 103-105
    power running down quickly, 330
    See also power management
blue screen of death, 358
booting
    boot failures, 355
    "Invalid System Disk" message, 341
    Last Known Good Configuration
      option, 340
    slowly, 324-325

System Restore, 336-340
using Safe Mode, 340
when to call tech support, 358
browsers, adding to the Start menu, 19
bus-powered USB hubs, 102-103

C

cameras, 158-159
installing, 159-160
updating drivers, 160
capture devices
conflicts with, 290
cost, 288
"device already in use" message, 289-290
Movie Maker doesn't recognize, 287-288
settings, 290
updating drivers, 289
See also Movie Maker; video
CD File System. *See* CDFS
CDFS, 109
CD-ROMs, stopping Windows Media Player
from opening, 127-128
CDs
adding to the Media Library, 278-279
CD player won't play music, 272-274
playback doesn't sound good, 274
See also Windows Media Player
Clean Installation option, 334
ClickLock, 139
color
desktop background, 11
difficult to see on LCD screen, 330
printing problems, 154
problems with screen color, 2-4
using in Outlook Express, 214-215,
218-219
compatibility
between capture devices and Movie
Maker, 290
drivers, 97
hardware, 90-91
with operating systems, 76-79
removing settings, 79-81
software, 153
compression
data connection preferences, 175-176
of files, 42, 126-127
of folders, 38-39
configuration settings, changing randomly, 360

connection speed, 351-352
Control Panel
changing Start menu link to a menu, 22
Classic view, 51
cookies, 203-205, 352
copy protection, 289
crashes, 355
application crashes, 341
computer stops responding, 336
"disk missing" messages, 117
System Restore, 336-340
when to call tech support, 358
CTRL+ALT+DEL, 336, 341
cursor, adjusting blink rate, 134-135
Cyber Sitter, 195

D

Date and Time tab, 299
date, changing, 299
daylight savings time, adjusting for, 300
defragmenting the hard disk, 115-117, 303,
304, 318
desktop
color background, 11
Customize Desktop feature, 11-12
Desktop Cleanup Wizard, 12-13
displaying Web pages on, 13-14
icons not appearing on, 11-12
wallpaper, 10-11
See also Remote Desktop
Device Manager, 95-96
and hardware profiles, 105
Roll Back Driver feature, 100
dial-up
alternative numbers, 168-170
changing IE's dialing behavior, 187-188
dialing rules, 177
redial attempts, 170
security settings, 171
slow ICS connections, 257
See also modems
digital certificates, 216
digital files, unsigned, 308-309
digital signatures, 216
File Signature Verification utility,
308-309
digital video, 286-287
See also Movie Maker; video
DirectX Diagnostic tool, 309

disabilities, support for users with, 135-136
disabling hardware, 102
Disconnect If Idle feature, 174-175
Disk Cleanup, 47, 112-113
    automatically running, 300-301
disk defragmenting, 115-117, 303, 304, 318
Disk Management console
    checking the status of the hard disk, 117-119
    converting basic disks to dynamic disks, 122-123
    creating new partitions, 119-122
display, 2
    changing properties, 347
    color background desktop, 11
    Desktop Cleanup Wizard, 12-13
    displaying a Web page on your desktop, 13-14
    distortion, 5-6
    drivers, 2-4
    font size, 6-7
    icon size, 4-5
    icons not appearing on desktop, 11-12
    logon screen, 8
    My Pictures screen saver, 9-10
    problems with screen color, 2-4
    screen savers, 7-8, 9-10
    wallpaper, 10-11
DNS, 186
documents, pinning to the Start menu, 20-21
Domain Name System, 186
downloading
    enabling Internet Explorer to download drivers, 100-101
    launching downloads, 82
    skins, 269
    slow downloads, 176
    stopping automatic downloads, 81-83
DPI settings, 4-5
dragging and dropping
    ClickLock, 139
    to the Start menu, 21-22
drivers, 88-89, 96-97
    Add Printer Driver Wizard, 152
    cameras, 160
    capture devices, 289
    compatibility, 97
    display, 2-4

    enabling Internet Explorer to download, 100-101
    hardware, 95
    installing, 97-99
    printer, 329-330
    Roll Back Driver feature, 100
    scanners, 160
    self-installing, 97-98
    sound problems, 298
    updating after Windows XP upgrade, 149, 344
DVDs
    black screen, 129
    decoder problems, 277-278
    regions, 129-130
    sound, 128
    See also Windows Media Player
dynamic disks, 122-123

E

e-mail
    not working with ICS, 257
    See also Outlook Express
encryption, 348
    of files, 42
    of folders, 39
    using in Outlook Express, 215-216
End Process option, 322
error messages
    file copy, 333
    during Windows XP installation, 334
error-checking the hard disk, 113-114, 303-304
Ethernet networks, 232
Event Viewer, 117
Everyone group, removing, 250-251
extensions
    renaming files with valid extensions, 41
    showing file extensions, 38

F

Fast User Switching, 56-57
    and offline files, 43
FAT16, 109
FAT32, 109
    compression and encryption, 39
    converting to NTFS, 109-110, 344-345
    and floppy disks, 125

file copy error messages, 333
file formats, readable by Movie Maker, 288, 294
file sharing
    configuring NTFS permissions for,
        249-250, 352-353
    and Windows Firewall, 251-252
File Signature Verification utility, 308-309
file systems, 108-109
    See also CDFS; FAT16; FAT32; NTFS
files, 40
    choosing a program to open files, 40-41
    compression and encryption, 42
    deleting immediately, 46
    moving from one computer to your XP
        computer, 304-308
    renaming with valid file extensions, 41
    showing file extensions, 38
    temporary, 47-48, 193
    See also offline files
Files and Settings Transfer Wizard, 305-308
FilterKeys, 136
firewalls, 177-178
    disallowing exceptions, 180-181
    and file sharing, 251-252
    programs not working with Windows
        Firewall, 364-366
    turning off Windows Firewall on network
        adapter, 349-350
    turning on Windows Firewall, 178-179
    viewing the log file, 179-180
FireWire, ports, 90
floppy disks, 123-124
    compressing files for, 126-127
    opening, 124
    problems opening, 125
    using on NTFS systems, 125
flow control, 175-176
folders, 32-33
    changing the appearance of, 36-38
    compressing, 38-39
    creating, 33
    customizing toolbars, 35-36
    encrypting, 39
    PreFetch, 48
    private, 248
    putting pictures on, 37
    restoring defaults, 38
    showing details, 34-35
    showing file extensions, 38
    Temp folder, 47-48
    views, 33-34, 36-38, 348
fonts
    printing problems, 154
    size of, 6-7
    using in Outlook Express, 214-215,
        218-219
Forgotten Password Wizard, 62
fragmented disk, 115-117, 303, 304, 318

G

garbled text, 152
graphic equalizer, 274, 275
Group Policy, 66-68
    See also administrator accounts

H

hang-ups, 170
hard disks, 108-109
    Audio CD status, 118
    basic, 122-123
    cleaning up to gain space, 110-113
    compressing to save space, 111
    converting basic to dynamic, 122-123
    converting to NTFS, 109-110, 344-345
    crashes, 117
    creating new partitions, 119-122
    defragmenting, 115-117, 303, 304, 318
    disabling indexing feature, 111
    Disk Management console, 117-119
    "disk missing" messages, 117
    dynamic, 122-123
    error-checking, 113-114, 303-304
    Foreign status, 118-119
    multiple, 117-119
    New Partition Wizard, 120-122
    No Media status, 119
    noise, 115
    Not Initialized status, 119
    reading and writing slowly, 115-117
    Unreadable status, 119
hardware
    Add Hardware Wizard, 92-94
    compatibility, 90-91
    computer stops responding during
        installation, 332-333

defined, 88
Device Manager, 95-96
disabling, 102
draining battery power, 103-105
drivers, 88-89, 95, 96-101
installing, 88-90
installing internal devices, 90
installing manually, 91-94
managing, 101-102
for networking, 230-231
ports, 89-90
profiles, 103-105, 330
uninstalling manually, 95-96
using older hardware with Windows XP,
   94-95
using with USB hubs, 102-103
Windows XP not detecting new device,
   91-94
hardware acceleration, 6
Hardware Compatibility List, 91
hardware conflicts
   computer stops responding, 336
   with SP2, 369-370
   when to call tech support, 358
   with Windows XP, 355-356
   and Windows XP upgrades, 334-335
Hardware Update Wizard, 98-99
HCL. *See* Hardware Compatibility List
headaches, top 20, 344-356
hibernation, 26-27, 330, 346-347
   See also power management
HomePNA, 232
hubs, USB, 102-103

I

icons
   account icons, 63-65
   hiding inactive icons on taskbar, 24
   not appearing on desktop, 11-12
   size of, 4-5
ICS. *See* Internet Connection Sharing
IEEE 1394. *See* FireWire
incompatible software, 360-361
indexing, disabling, 111
infrared ports, 90, 143
installing cameras, 159-160
installing drivers, 97-99

installing hardware, 88-90
   compatibility, 90-91
   computer stops responding during
      installation, 332-333
   internal devices, 90
   manually, 91-94
   See also drivers
installing programs, 72-74
installing scanners, 159-160
installing Windows XP
   Clean Installation option, 334
   computer stops responding during
      installation, 332-333
   file copy error messages, 333
   stop messages or error messages, 334
instructions, reading, 360
internal devices, installing, 90
Internet connection
   Cannot Find Server message, 185-186
   changing IE's dialing behavior, 187-188
   changing the default connection,
      171-172, 187
   configuring alternative dial-up numbers,
      168-170
   connecting IE through a proxy server or
      broadband hardware, 189-191
   connecting to activate Windows XP, 342
   creating an Internet connection, 163-167
   IE providing pages intermittently, 186
   IE's Always Dial My Default Connection
      option, 189
   Internet Explorer problems, 184-191
   ISPs, 163
   making your connection private, 167-168
   New Connection Wizard, 164-167
   reconfiguring redial and hang-up
      options, 170
   requirements for connection, 162-163
   security settings for dial-up, 171
   speed, 351-352
   See also modems; Windows Firewall
Internet Connection Sharing, 252-253
   clients can't use ICS computer, 258
   clients controlling the connection, 349
   configuring after the network is
      configured, 253-254
   dialing a connection when needed,
      256-257

IP address conflict message, 255-256
saving user name and password for all
  users, 254-255
slow dial-up connections, 257
stopping users from controlling
  connection, 256
Internet Connection Wizard, 209-211
Internet Explorer
  Always Dial My Default Connection
    option, 189
  Approved Sites tab, 196
  AutoComplete, 197-198
  blocking sites, 202-203
  Cannot Find Server message, 185-186
  changing default programs to open,
    198-199
  changing the default connection, 187
  changing the dialing behavior, 187-188
  configuration problems, 191-200
  configuring the Privacy policy, 203-205
  connecting through a proxy server or
    broadband hardware, 189-191
  connection problems, 184-191
  default home page, 192
  enabling to download drivers, 100-101
  filtering content, 194-197
  history, 194
  pop-up windows, 205-206
  printing background colors and images,
    199-200
  providing pages intermittently, 186
  security settings, 350
  temporary Internet file settings, 193
  toolbar, 191
  zone security settings, 200-202
Internet Service Providers. *See* ISPs
IP addressing
  Automatic Private IP Addressing, 243
  and ICS, 258
  manually configuring, 244
ISPs, 163
  Disconnect If Idle feature, 175

K

keyboards
  adjusting speed, 133-134
  FilterKeys, 136

not working, 132-133
one-touch buttons, 135
ports, 89, 133
StickyKeys, 136
support for users with disabilities,
  135-136
ToggleKeys, 136
wireless, 143

L

Last Known Good Configuration option, 340
limited accounts, changing to administrator
  accounts, 54-55
Local Users and Groups console, 61
locking the taskbar, 25
lockouts, configuring, 66-68
lockups
  application, 326-327
  when to call tech support, 358
  Windows XP and, 328
logon screen, 8

M

mail. *See* Outlook Express
managed desktop, 367
Media Library
  adding CDs to, 278-279
  creating a playlist, 280-281
Media Player
  adding CDs to the Media Library,
    278-279
  adjusting graphic equalizer settings,
    274, 275
  anchor window, 271-272
  creating a playlist, 280-281
  DVD decoder problems, 277-278
  exporting playlists, 281
  importing playlists, 281
  interface, 266, 267
  More Skins option, 268-269
  Rip feature default options, 282
  ripping takes too long or too much disk
    space, 284
  showing menu bar, 266-267
  Skin Chooser, 269
  stopping from opening when a CD is
    inserted, 127-128

streaming media problems, 276-277
switching between skin mode and full mode, 267-268
video playback quality is poor, 274-276
View Album Info feature, 283
visualizations, 270-271
See also CDs; DVDs
memory
  RAM, 316-317, 318-320
  virtual, 320, 323
microphones
  adding microphone volume to Volume Control window, 298-299
  adjusting volume configuration, 297-298
modem, hanging up when idle, 350-351
modems
  checking port speed and settings, 173-174
  connection noise volume, 172-173
  data connection preferences, 175-176
  dialing rules, 177
  Disconnect If Idle feature, 174-175
  initialization commands, 177
  sending data slowly, 173-174
  slow downloads, 176
  working sporadically or disconnecting randomly, 176-177
monitor, turning off when idle, 25-26
mouse
  changing button configuration, 137-138
  changing the mouse pointer, 138-141
  ClickLock, 139
  double-click speed, 138
  pointer disappearing, 141-142
  ports, 89
  scrolling, 142
  sticking, 136-137
  trail effect, 141
  wheel, 142
  wireless, 143
Movie Maker, 286
  adding clips to storyboard/timeline, 291
  adjusting audio levels, 294
  combining clips, 292
  conflicts with capture devices, 290
  copying commercial movies, 289
  creating transitions, 292
  creating trim points, 290-291

"device already in use" message, 289-290
  doesn't recognize capture device, 287-288
  file formats, 288, 294
  hearing the audio while recording, 289
  importing audio files, 293
  importing movie files, 288
  minimum requirements, 288
  recording narration, 293-294
  saving files, 294
  setting beginning and end of trim points, 291
  splitting clips, 291-292
  works slowly, 288
  See also audio; video
msconfig, 85, 324
music
  burning and syncing, 284
  ripping, 282-284
  See also audio; CDs
My Pictures, screen saver, 9-10

N

Net Nanny, 195
.NET Passport, configuring accounts for, 55-56
Net View command, 246
NetKeys Internet Security, 195
Netscape, adding to the Start menu, 19
Network Connections folder, 231
network redirector, 126
network shares
  configuring NTFS permissions for file sharing, 249-250, 352-353
  private folders, 248
  removing the Everyone group, 250-251
  sharing resources, 247-248
  viewing available resources, 245-247
  and Windows Firewall, 251-252
networks, 348
  "access denied" message, 245
  accessing NTFS drives over, 126
  Automatic Private IP Addressing (APIPA), 243
  configuring IE to connect through a proxy server, 189-191
  connecting to a network printer, 150-151
  Ethernet, 232

HomePNA, 232
ICS networks, 349
and Linux or Macintosh computers,
   238-239
network adapter card, 230-231,
   239-241, 252
Network Setup Wizard, 233-234,
   236-237
setting up client computers, 236-237
setting up down-level (non-XP)
   clients, 238
TCP/IP configuration, 239, 242-243
what kind to use, 232
and Windows Firewall, 349-350
See also Internet Connection Sharing;
   wireless networks
New Connection Wizard, 164-167
New Partition Wizard, 120-122
New Technology File System. *See* NTFS
Norton Internet Security, Family Edition, 195
Notification Area, 23, 27
changing behavior of, 28
removing Balloon Tips, 29
removing old items from, 28-29
removing Windows Security Center
   from, 367-368
Windows Security Center not appearing
   in, 367
See also taskbar
NTFS, 109
"access denied" message, 245
accessing over a network, 126
compression and encryption, 39, 42
configuring permissions for file sharing,
   249-250, 352-353
converting from FAT32 to, 109-110,
   344-345
and floppy disks, 125

O

offline files, 42
and Fast User Switching, 43
synchronization of, 43-44
turning on and configuring, 42-43
one-touch keyboard buttons, 135
operating systems, compatibility with software,
  76-79
optimizing XP, 354-355

Outlook Express, 208
attachments, 219-220
avoiding junk mail, 224
blocking senders, 223
changing accounts, 211-212
colors, 214-215, 218-219
creating mail or news rules, 225-227
digitally signed messages, 215-216
disconnecting after mail is sent or
   received, 221-222
editing blocked senders list, 223-225
e-mail not working with ICS, 257
enabling BCC field, 214
encoding, 216
encrypted messages, 215-216
fonts, 214-215, 218-219
interface, 216-218
news messages, 220-221
preview pane, 216-218
reading or sending messages in another
   language, 216
remembering passwords, 212
rich text, 214-215
setting up mail accounts, 209-211
stationery, 214-215
timeouts, 213
viruses, 219-220

P

parallel ports, 89
partitions, creating, 119-122
passwords, 58
case sensitivity, 59
configuring, 58-59
creating a good password, 63
creating a password reset disk, 62
enforcing restrictions, 59-61
resetting without a password reset disk,
   61-62
using a password reset disk, 62
See also security
PC cards
draining battery power, 103-105
multiple, 330
performance
application causes computer to slow
   down, 325-326
battery power running down quickly, 330

booting slowly, 324-325
computer runs too slowly, 316-317
disabling Recent Documents History, 325
losing control of computer while printing, 328-329
Performance tool, 322-323
printing output doesn't look good, 329-330
printing slows down computer, 328
removing startup programs, 324
running multiple applications, 326
slow to open and close files, 318
streaming media problems, 276-277
Windows Task Manager, 321-323, 326-327
See also RAM
peripherals
adjusting cursor blink rate, 134-135
draining battery power, 103-105
keyboards, 132-134, 135-136, 143
mouse, 136-143
permissions, 51-52
"access denied" message, 245
configuring NTFS permissions for file sharing, 249-250, 352-353
errors, 356
See also administrator accounts
pinning items to the Start menu, 20-21
pointers
changing, 138-141
disappearing, 141-142
trail effect, 141
pop-up windows, 205-206
ports
checking modem port speed and settings, 173-174
types of, 89-90
power management, 25
adjusting power options, 25-26
battery power running down quickly, 330
creating a hardware profile to conserve battery power, 103-105
hibernation, 26-27, 330, 346-347
See also batteries
PreFetch folder, cleaning, 48
printer setup, 146
Add a Printer Wizard, 147-149, 150-151
Add Printer Driver Wizard, 152

changing IE print settings, 199-200
configuring printer restrictions, 157-158
connecting to a network printer, 150-151
older printer not working with Windows XP, 149
print orientation, 156-157
sharing printers, 157
spool settings, 155-156
updating drivers, 149, 344
USB cables, 146
USB printers, 150
Windows XP not detecting printer, 147-149
printing problems
certain files will not print, 153
changing to portrait orientation, 156-157
cleaning printer heads, 329
color or font problems, 154
flushing out print queue, 153-154
losing control of computer while printing, 328-329
output doesn't look good, 329-330
printer prints garbled text, 152
printer working slowly, 155
replacing printer cartridges, 329
slowing down computer, 328
spooling, 155-156, 328-329
stopping a document from printing, 154
processor speed, 316-317
profiles, hardware, 103-105, 330
Program Compatibility Wizard, 76-79, 327, 341
programs
application causes computer to slow down, 325-326
application locks up, 326-327
compatibility with operating systems, 76-79
installing, 72-74
removing, 74-75
removing compatibility settings, 79-81
removing spyware and adware, 83-84
removing using Safe Mode, 75-76
running multiple applications, 326
shared files, 76
startup, 84-85, 324
programs not working
after SP2 install, 364
with Windows Firewall, 364-366

on Windows XP, 353-354
See also software
protocols, 175-176
PS/2 ports, 89

Q

Quick Launch, showing in taskbar, 24

R

RAM, 316-317
conserving, 318-320
See also virtual memory
Recent Documents History, disabling, 325
Recycle Bin, 44
deleting files immediately, 46
managing storage space used for, 45
recovering emptied files, 44-45
retrieving files from, 44
stopping confirmation message, 46
redial attempts, 170
regions, DVD, 129-130
Remote Assistance, 262
creating an invitation, 263
stopping remote control, 264
Remote Desktop, 258, 348
configuring, 259-260
configuring clients to access, 261
configuring Windows Firewall to
allow, 260
slow performance, 261-262
oving programs, 74-75
shared files, 76
using Safe Mode, 75-76
ion, 4
er 2000, 45
t, 214-215
ack Driver feature, 100

lode
booting using, 340
Last Known Good Configuration
option, 340
removing programs using, 75-76
rf, 195
r and Camera Installation Wizard,
160

scanners, 158-159
installing, 159-160
updating drivers, 160, 344
Scheduled Tasks, 300-301
not running, 301-303
screen resolution, 4
screen savers, 7-8
My Pictures Slideshow, 9-10
See also display
security
blocking sites in IE, 202-203
Cyber Sitter, 195
encrypting folders, 39
Internet Explorer, 200-206
Internet Explorer's content feature, 195
Internet Explorer's Privacy policy,
203-205
logon screen, 8
Net Nanny, 195
NetKeys Internet Security, 195
Norton Internet Security, Family
Edition, 195
pop-up windows, 205-206
Safe Surf, 195
zone security settings in IE, 200-202
See also passwords
Security Center, 367
removing from Notification Area,
367-368
turning on Windows Firewall, 178-179
self-powered USB hubs, 102-103
serial ports, 89
Service Pack 2
and hardware conflicts, 369-370
installing, 364
programs not working after SP2
install, 364
and Windows Firewall, 364-366
and Windows Security Center, 367-368
and wireless networks, 368-369
settings, changing randomly, 360
shared files, 76
shares
configuring NTFS permissions for file
sharing, 249-250, 352-353
private folders, 248
removing the Everyone group, 250-251
sharing resources, 247-248

viewing available resources, 245-247
and Windows Firewall, 251-252
Sharing tab, 248
slow performance, 354-355
software
   antivirus, 360
   application causes computer to slow
      down, 325-326
   application locks up, 326-327
   compatibility, 70, 153
   compatibility with operating systems,
      76-79
   incompatible, 360-361
   installing programs, 72-74
   for networking, 231
   removing compatibility settings, 79-81
   removing programs, 74-75
   removing programs using Safe Mode,
      75-76
   removing spyware and adware, 83-84
   running multiple applications, 326
   shared files, 76
   startup programs, 84-85, 324
   system requirements, 70-71
   See also programs; programs not working
sound
   adjusting microphone volume, 297-298
   checking volume controls, 296-297
   and DVDs, 128
   plays erratically or computer locks up, 298
   See also audio
sound cards, conflicts with, 298
SP2. *See* Service Pack 2
spooling, 155-156, 328-329
Spybot, 84
spyware, removing, 83-84
standby feature, 330
Start menu, 16
   adding programs to, 20
   changing Control Panel link to a menu, 22
   changing properties, 347
   changing to Classic style, 16-17
   customizing, 17-19
   dragging and dropping items onto, 21-22
   items on, 17
   making Netscape appear on, 19
   pinning items to, 20-21
   removing items from, 16
   See also taskbar

startup programs, 324
   controlling, 84-85
stationery, 214-215
StickyKeys, 136
streaming, 274
   performance, 276-277
synchronization, of offline files, 43-44
System Configuration Utility, 85
System Properties, 70-71
System Restore, 336-338
   turning on, 310-311
   undoing, 338-339
   undoing if you cannot boot, 339-340

T

Task Manager, 321-323, 326-327
taskbar, 23
   auto-hiding, 24
   changing properties, 347
   changing settings, 23-24
   hiding inactive icons, 24
   locking, 25
   moving, 25
   showing Quick Launch, 24
   See also Notification Area; Start menu
tasks
   not running as scheduled, 301-303
   scheduling, 300-301
TCP/IP configuration, 239, 242-243
technical support
   four signs you need help from, 358
   when to call, 335
Temp folder, cleaning, 47-48
temporary Internet files, 47, 352
   changing settings in Internet Explorer, 193
text, garbled, 152
themes, 14
   Modified listing, 14
   returning to the default, 15
   viewing colors on LCD screen, 330
time
   adjusting for daylight savings time, 300
   changing, 299
ToggleKeys, 136
toolbars
   customizing, 35-36
   Internet Explorer, 191

trim points
     creating, 290-291
     setting beginning and end of, 291

U

Undelete utilities, 45
uninstalling hardware, 95-96
uninstalling programs, 74-75
     shared files, 76
     using Safe Mode, 75-76
Universal Serial Bus. *See* USB
unsigned digital files, 308-309
updates
     drivers, 344
     stopping automatic downloads, 81-83
     See also Windows Update
upgrading to Windows XP
     and hardware conflicts, 334-335
     without doing your homework, 361
USB
     hubs, 102-103
     ports, 89
     printer cables, 146
     printer setup, 150
users
     changing account icon feature, 63-65
     changing limited accounts to
         administrator accounts, 54-55
     configuring account restrictions, 66-68
     configuring accounts for .NET Passport
         support, 55-56
     creating user accounts, 50-53, 61
     deleting user accounts, 53, 61
     disabling user accounts, 65-66
     Fast User Switching, 56-57
     Local Users and Groups console, 61
     removing the Welcome screen, 57-58
utilities, automatically running, 300-301

V

video, 286-287
     adding clips to storyboard/timeline, 291
     checking video stream settings, 277
     combining clips, 292
     copying commercial movies, 289
     creating transitions, 292
     creating trim points, 290-291

file formats, 294
importing movie files, 288
Movie Maker doesn't recognize capture
     device, 287-288
playback quality is poor, 274-276
saving files, 294
setting beginning and end of trim
     points, 291
splitting clips, 291-292
See also audio
video overlay, 129
views, folders, 33-34, 348
virtual memory, 320, 323
     See also RAM
viruses
     avoiding in Outlook Express, 219-220
     using the Internet without antivirus
         software, 360
volume
     adding microphone volume to Volume
         Control window, 298-299
     adjusting microphone volume, 297-298
     checking controls, 296-297

W

wallpaper, 10-11
Web addresses, 186
Web pages, displaying on your desktop, 13-14
Welcome screen, removing, 57-58
WF. *See* Windows Firewall
Windows Firewall, 177-178
     configuring to allow Remote Desktop, 260
     creating an exception in, 364-366
     disallowing exceptions, 180-181
     and file sharing, 251-252
     and networks, 349-350
     turning off on the network adapter
         card, 252
     turning on, 178-179
     viewing the log file, 179-180
Windows Media Player
     adding CDs to the Media Library,
         278-279
     adjusting graphic equalizer settings,
         274, 275
     anchor window, 271-272
     creating a playlist, 280-281

DVD decoder problems, 277-278
exporting playlists, 281
importing playlists, 281
interface, 266, 267
More Skins option, 268-269
Rip feature default options, 282
ripping takes too long or too much disk
   space, 284
showing menu bar, 266-267
Skin Chooser, 269
stopping from opening when a CD is
   inserted, 127-128
streaming media problems, 276-277
switching between skin mode and full
   mode, 267-268
video playback quality is poor, 274-276
View Album Info feature, 283
visualizations, 270-271
See also CDs; DVDs
Windows Security Center, 367
   removing from Notification Area, 367-368
Windows spooler, 155-156
Windows Task Manager, 321-323, 326-327
Windows Update
   disabling, 345-346
   stopping automatic downloads, 81-83
Windows XP activation, 341-342
Windows XP installation
   Clean Installation option, 334
   computer stops responding during,
     332-333
   file copy error messages, 333
   stop messages or error messages, 334
Windows XP, slow performance, 354-355
Windows XP upgrade
   and capture devices, 289

and hardware conflicts, 334-335
WinZip, 39, 127
   See also compression
wireless networks, 232
   connectivity problems, 353
   problems after SP2 install, 368-369
   setup, 235-236
   using wireless keyboard and mouse, 143
   See also networks
Wireless Network Setup Wizard, 369
wizards
   Add a Printer Wizard, 147-149, 150-151
   Add Hardware Wizard, 92-94
   Add Printer Driver Wizard, 152
   Desktop Cleanup Wizard, 12-13
   Files and Settings Transfer Wizard,
     305-308
   Forgotten Password Wizard, 62
   Hardware Update Wizard, 98-99
   Internet Connection Wizard, 209-211
   .NET Passport Wizard, 55-56
   Network Setup Wizard, 233-234,
     236-237
   New Connection Wizard, 164-167
   New Partition Wizard, 120-122
   Program Compatibility Wizard, 76-79,
     327, 341
   Scanner and Camera Installation Wizard,
     159-160
   Wireless Network Setup Wizard, 369

Z

zipped folders, 39
   See also compression

INTERNATIONAL CONTACT INFORMATION

AUSTRALIA
McGraw-Hill Book Company
Australia Pty. Ltd.
TEL +61-2-9900-1800
FAX +61-2-9878-8881
http://www.mcgraw-hill.com.au
books-it_sydney@mcgraw-hill.com

CANADA
McGraw-Hill Ryerson Ltd.
TEL +905-430-5000
FAX +905-430-5020
http://www.mcgraw-hill.ca

**GREECE, MIDDLE EAST, & AFRICA
(Excluding South Africa)**
McGraw-Hill Hellas
TEL +30-210-6560-990
TEL +30-210-6560-993
TEL +30-210-6560-994
FAX +30-210-6545-525

MEXICO (Also serving Latin America)
McGraw-Hill Interamericana Editores
S.A. de C.V.
TEL +525-1500-5108
FAX +525-117-1589
http://www.mcgraw-hill.com.mx
carlos_ruiz@mcgraw-hill.com

SINGAPORE (Serving Asia)
McGraw-Hill Book Company
TEL +65-6863-1580
FAX +65-6862-3354
http://www.mcgraw-hill.com.sg
mghasia@mcgraw-hill.com

SOUTH AFRICA
McGraw-Hill South Africa
TEL +27-11-622-7512
FAX +27-11-622-9045
robyn_swanepoel@mcgraw-hill.com

SPAIN
McGraw-Hill/
Interamericana de España, S.A.U.
TEL +34-91-180-3000
FAX +34-91-372-8513
http://www.mcgraw-hill.es
professional@mcgraw-hill.es

**UNITED KINGDOM, NORTHERN,
EASTERN, & CENTRAL EUROPE**
McGraw-Hill Education Europe
TEL +44-1-628-502500
FAX +44-1-628-770224
http://www.mcgraw-hill.co.uk
emea_queries@mcgraw-hill.com

ALL OTHER INQUIRIES Contact:
McGraw-Hill/Osborne
TEL +1-510-420-7700
FAX +1-510-420-7703
http://www.osborne.com
omg_international@mcgraw-hill.com